THE ETERNAL SUMMER

THE
ETERNAL
SUMMER

PALMER, NICKLAUS, AND HOGAN
IN 1960, GOLF'S GOLDEN YEAR

CURT SAMPSON

FOREWORD BY DAN JENKINS

Taylor Publishing Company
Dallas, Texas

Published by Taylor Publishing Company
    1550 West Mockingbird Lane
    Dallas, Texas 75235

Library of Congress Cataloging-in-Publication Data

Sampson, Curt.
 The eternal summer : Palmer, Nicklaus, and Hogan in 1960, golf's
golden year / Curt Sampson : foreword by Dan Jenkins.
  p. cm.
 ISBN 0-87833-788-1 : $19.95
 1. Golf—United States—History—20th century. 2. Palmer,
Arnold, 1929– . 3. Nicklaus, Jack. 4. Hogan, Ben,
1912– . I. Title.
GV981.S26 1992
796.352'-09—dc20   91–43043
                      CIP

Printed in the United States of America

10 9 8 7 6 5 4 3 2 1

To the men of the senior tour,
the heroes of my youth

Contents

Sixteen pages of photographs follow page 120

Foreword

The older a golf writer gets, the more he lives in the past. This may be true of real people, too. I can only speak for golf writers. Youth is in the past, for one thing, and golf writing may have been a hobby as much as a profession, based on the salaries most of us made.

There have been many splendid, important, landmark years in golf, and 1960 goes in there with four other years that come to mind immediately. There was 1913, when Francis Ouimet did that thing to Harry Vardon and Ted Ray. There was 1930, when Bobby Jones did that thing with the Grand Slam. There was 1945, when Byron Nelson did that thing with eleven in a row. And there was 1953, when Ben Hogan did that thing with the Triple Crown.

A lot of things put 1960 in there, things that Curt Sampson will tell you about in more detail, but mainly I will always remember it as the year Arnold Palmer became the Arnie of "Whoo, ha, go get 'em, Arnie!"

It was the year that Palmer, sweating, chain-smoking, driving balls through tree trunks, shirttail flying, took golf to the masses.

It was the year Arnie's Army was born, a horde of happy street rabble that would later encourage enlistments into Nicklaus's Navy, Lee's Fleas, Ben's Wrens (as in Crenshaw), and Greg's Groupies.

It started happening at the Masters in '60, when Arnie birdied the last two holes to win, and then he was truly ordained as America's golfing darling at the U.S. Open in June.

Thanks to the expense account departments at the *Fort Worth Press*, the *Dallas Times Herald*, *Sports Illustrated*, and *Golf Digest*, in order of their appearance in my life, I'm quite sure I've covered more majors than any golf writer, living or dead. Something like forty-three years of them to date. And I'm certain I've never seen a more thrilling tournament than the '60 U.S. Open at Cherry Hills in Denver.

Three eras came together on the final day, or "Open Saturday," as it was known. The day embraced the last hurrah of Hogan, the confirmation of Palmer, and the preview of a burly Ohio State undergraduate with terrifying length and frightening powers of concentration—Jack W. Nicklaus.

It's a pleasure to recall that I was an up-close witness to all of the drama that day, but 1960 had other remarkable theater, subplots, undercurrents, and characters that would help change the game as we know it.

History is only as interesting as the historian makes it, and here I must congratulate Curt Sampson on his passion for the game as well as his skill with a pen. And, while I may not agree with every characterization or interpretation in *The Eternal Summer*, at least the author comes by his prejudices honestly.

Sampson was the golf course equivalent of a gym rat as a kid—caddie, shop assistant, greens mower, and gofer. He played hooky regularly to watch the CBS Golf Classic, which was taped at Firestone Country Club every fall in the late sixties. Inspired by all this proximity to golf pros, he became a minor league touring professional himself, though his name was hard to find among the money winners.

He then sold widgets for ten years before returning to golf as a writer, and made the unhappy discovery that widget salesmen play more golf than golf writers do.

The Eternal Summer will make you feel like you are there at Augusta, Cherry Hills, St. Andrews, and many other places.

I know. I was there. In some ways, I'm still there.

DAN JENKINS

Thy eternal summer shall not fade . . .

SHAKESPEARE

Florence Zupnik and the Proettes

The leader of the Free World was a golf nut.

Dwight David Eisenhower, war hero, Supreme Allied Commander in Europe in World War II and the president of the United States from 1953 to 1961, played golf about eight hundred times during his two terms as president. That's almost twice a week. Pretty good considering he had a heart attack in 1955, abdominal surgery in 1956, and a stroke in 1957. The First Golfer had a practice green installed on the White House lawn, a driving range built in the basement, and a putting green placed next to his farm house in Gettysburg, Pennsylvania. He was also a compulsive carpet putter in the Oval Office. He became a member at Augusta National, home of the Masters, one of the four major golf championships. The members built for their important new associate a lovely, three-story white frame house—or, as they called it, a "cabin" or "cottage"—by the tenth tee. Ike visited Augusta twenty-nine times while he was president, and usually stayed a week or two. He liked to play a round with the new Masters champion the day after the tournament concluded. "I love to play the game, no matter how badly I may play," he said, which may have been true, but, like many golfers, Ike got mad as hell when he didn't play well.

His scores were a closely guarded secret. Democrats and other critics said Eisenhower feared voters would think he was playing too much golf if every result was recorded—particularly if his scores were good. Writer Lewis Grizzard recalled what it was like when the newspaper arrived at his house in 1953: "The adults [w]ould read of Ike and then spend the rest of the day cursing him because he was at Augusta National playing golf when, in the words of my grandfather, his butt ought to be in Washington running the country." No, no, that's not it at all, replied the legions who felt kindly toward the Old General. He doesn't tell us what he shot because he knows so many people are pulling for him and he doesn't want to disappoint them with a bad score. Besides, his supporters said, the doctor says it's good for his health. As in most things, the truth lay somewhere in the middle. Ike did play a lot of golf. And he played very well on occasion, too: a 77 at Cherry Hills in Denver in 1954, 79's at Augusta National, Burning Tree (Washington, D.C.) Gettysburg Country Club and 84 once at beautiful, difficult Cypress Point, in Monterey, California (normally a 90-shooter, the President's big weakness was the short irons; he didn't seem to possess a half-swing—he could duck-hook a wedge). But Eisenhower was one of America's best-loved presidents and most people did not begrudge him his hobby, even if they didn't understand the attraction of hitting a rubber ball in a pasture with metal sticks.

The lure of the game was exposed—if not explained—during the Eisenhower years. When Ike took a "working vacation" at the Newport (Rhode Island) Country Club in 1957, he brought 282 newsmen and photographers with him. Pictures of his bad follow-through—he hung back on his right side too much—were standard on newspaper front pages. All this media attention had an effect on the popularity of the sport. Golf was not a game for the masses when Ike took office, but it was when he left. Coincident with his presidency was an unprecedented increase in the number of American golfers, from about 3.25 million in 1952 to about 4.4 million in 1960.

The golf boom of the fifties started in Washington, D.C. Trend-following bureaucrats all over town found clubs in their attics or bought new ones. Among those who followed the boss's lead in recreation was Vice President Richard M. Nixon. Round-shouldered and unathletic, Nixon was less of a golfer than Eisenhower. He cut a less-than-dashing figure in golf clothes; he favored a "high pockets" look, with his pants worn practically up to his chest and a tightly buttoned sports shirt. But he became infatuated with the game.

From the October, 30, 1959 issue of *Golf World* magazine:

> Evangelist Billy Graham was taking a shower at the Burning Tree Club, outside Washington, after losing a close match with Vice President Nixon.
> President Eisenhower entered the locker room after playing and told Mr. Nixon he would like to talk to the evangelist. Mr. Nixon told Mr. Graham in the shower. The evangelist wrapped a towel around himself and became what he thinks is the first clergyman to talk with the president under such circumstances.

Nixon played frequently in the fifties, though less often than Ike. He was the first member at a new golf club in Yorba Linda, near his home in Los Angeles. He played business golf on occasion, such as the time in March 1960 when he had a match with George Smathers at Key Colony, near Miami, and did not allow the senior senator from Florida to win a hole. In January of 1960, Nixon was the featured speaker at the National Golf Award Dinner at the Plaza Hotel in New York, where among those honored were the winner of the 1959 National Amateur, "Jackie" Nicklaus, and Bobby Jones, the venerated golf champion who founded Augusta National. The vice president tried a joke: "Jones is the only man I know who went to Georgia Tech and Harvard and is a Republican."

Nixon was campaigning for president when he gave that speech and told that joke, which reminds us that 1960 was a watershed year in politics as well as in golf, and for some of the same reasons. For one thing, the population grew more in the fifties—18 percent, from 151.3 million to 179.3 million—than in any other ten-year period in American history. Practically all the growth occurred in the suburbs, where two thirds of the twenty-eight million new citizens lived; cities and rural America lost population. Some time during the fifties, for the first time ever in the United States, white-collar workers (professional, managerial) outnumbered blue-collar workers (productive, operative). More people with more time and money meant more golfers.

The new voter, the new golfer—suburban, middle class, white collar—was personified by Ward Cleaver, the fictional father on "Leave it to Beaver," a television show of the late fifties. Mr. Cleaver, an engineer, played golf on Saturday mornings. "How was your golf game, dear?" June Cleaver, in long dress and pearls, would ask her husband. Invariably, Ward would place his clubs—he always carried them backwards—in the hall closet, say something rueful about what Fred Rutherford had done on the golf course that Saturday morning, then ask: "Where's Wally and the Beaver?"

Ward Cleaver, the new American (television) Everyman, would have been wearing something close to the latest in golf fashion, which *Sports Illustrated* defined in its "Spring [1960] Quarterly Sporting Look" as "a golf jacket of Kodel-and-Topel blend ($15) by Robert Lewis, 'Ban-Lon' golf shirt by Puritan and checked golf slacks ($15) of Dacron-cotton blend with hidden bellows pockets and tuck-away towel loop in back, by Hickok." Perhaps Mr. Cleaver had selected a shirt made by Munsingwear that day; he knew from advertisements that Don January had won the Tucson Open in a Munsingwear shirt, and Dow Finsterwald had worn the shirt with the penguin logo to win at Los

Angeles. It was, after all, as the ad said, "the shirt with the exclusive UNDERARM FEATURE."

Ward Cleaver, Beaver's father, wasn't really a golfer making the difficult choice between wrinkleproof Ban-Lon and armpit comfort. But reality-blurring television could make it seem so. Television. Hardly anyone had one in 1950; by 1960, the tube was absolutely pivotal in entertainment, politics, and in the growth of golf and other sports. Only 8 percent of U.S. families had a TV in 1950. By the end of the decade, 88 percent—or forty million of the forty-four million families in the country—owned at least one set. Television allowed the nation to choose its next president in 1960. The two major candidates, Vice President Nixon and Senator John F. Kennedy of Massachusetts, squared off in a series of three televised debates, the first ever. Nixon looked bad on television, especially in the first debate. He was tired and had been ill—he had spent eleven days in the hospital with a staph infection of his knee two weeks before the first television encounter with Kennedy in Chicago. There was a problem with his makeup, and the TV lights made him perspire heavily and accentuated his five o'clock shadow. "The harshness of the television eye and the electronic cruelty of the camera to his countenance" caused Nixon to "lose" the debates, wrote Theodore White, in *The Making of the President 1960*. Kennedy won the election. He looked better on television. "In 1960," wrote White, "television won the nation away from sound to images."

The flickering images on American television in 1960 were of game shows ("What's My Line?", "The Price is Right," "I've Got a Secret," "To Tell the Truth"), news (Walter Cronkite on CBS, Huntley and Brinkley on NBC), westerns ("Maverick," "Gunsmoke," "Bonanza," "Bronco"), cop shows ("Dragnet," "Highway Patrol"), situation comedies ("Love That Bob!", "Make Room For Daddy," "My Little Margie," "I Love Lucy," "The Real McCoys"), and old movies. A nervous gentleman named Jack Paar hosted a late-night variety program called "The Tonight Show." It was the first modern TV talk show. Paar had an opening monologue, sat in a chair behind a desk, bantered with his sidekick, Charley Weaver, and traded witticisms with Zsa Zsa or Sammie or Jayne or Dean, who sat on a couch to his right. Fidel Castro and his cigar were his guests soon after they had overthrown Cuban dictator Fulgencio Batista. One night in February 1960 the neurotic Paar, looking like a man who couldn't find the restroom, simply walked off the stage during the show. NBC broadcast an image of his empty chair for a long minute.

Like television throughout its history, most of it was drivel. Program notes from old TV Guide magazines provide the evidence: "The Joey Bishop Show"—"Joey's laundresses, both ex-vaudevillians, come up with an ultimatum—either they appear on Joey's TV show or they will starch his pajamas." "Make Room For Daddy"—"Linda is punished for not cleaning her room." "Bonanza"—"Gunslinger Duke Miller is the impatient type. When he goes to get a haircut and finds Carlos Rodriguez in the barber's chair—he shoots him dead." Movie—*Here Come the Co-eds* (1945)—"Two zany caretakers set things jumping at a school for young gentlewomen. Bud Abbott, Lou Costello."

And, of course, there were sports on television. It had occurred to people early on that the tube and games were made for each other. Indeed, the first telecast of a sports event took place in the medium's pioneer days: on April 13, 1939, a single camera "covered" the Columbia-Princeton baseball game at Colonel Baker Field in Manhattan (Princeton won, 2–1 in ten innings, to clinch fourth place in the Ivy League). Golf made its national debut on American televsion on August 23, 1953. ABC stationed one camera with a wide angle lens behind the eighteenth green at the Tam O'Shanter World Championship in Chicago; about 646,000 televisions were tuned in. They got a great show. Lew Worsham holed a long wedge shot from the fairway—"The Shot Heard 'Round the World"—and won by one shot the biggest first prize in golf, twenty-five thousand dollars. Jimmy Demaret, the golfer/announcer, lost his composure for a minute. "The son of a bitch went in!" he shouted on the air.

ABC's experiment was a success. George S. May, the organizer of the World Championship, paid the network thirty-two thousand dollars to televise that first tournament. The next year, ABC broadcast the event for free. And by 1960, televison was *paying* $150,000 a year for the rights to broadcast a handful of tournaments. Money could be made, the TV boys had discovered—that is, advertising could be sold—by televising golf. The three most important golf tournaments in the United States were televised by the end of the decade. The U.S. Open debuted on the tube in 1954, as did The Masters in 1955 and the PGA Championship in 1958.

Chris Schenkel broadcast that first Masters for CBS. Schenkel, from Bippus, Indiana, a slight, polite man with a soothing bass voice, says that golf—and television—"were much more relaxed then. I worked with Byron Nelson a lot and he had such a wonderful attitude. Nothing bothered him. We'd do a lot of cheap things for fun. I remember once during a rain delay at the Colonial tournament in Fort Worth, Don January and I went up with Arnold [Palmer] in his airplane. We drank beer while Arnie flew us around. . . . Great times.

"The players weren't playing for that much money back then. They felt they were so lucky to have us televise their sport. Not like now."

Schenkel theorizes that golf and television grew up together because golf on TV "was an emotional buy by the account executives, most of whom played golf." In other words, ad agencies chose to spend their client's dollars—and to show the commercials the agencies produced for those clients—on golf telecasts. People with something to sell—tires, cigarettes, cars, insurance—started to perceive golf to be a conduit to the Ward Cleavers of America. As Sylvester Pat Weaver, once the president of NBC, said, "We are first of all in the advertising business, because that is where our money comes from."

At any rate, golf on TV did not succeed because it was so visually appealing: the fairways were not a beautiful emerald green nor the skies robin's-egg blue—because the broadcasts and the televisions were black and white only. Even with color, golf is the hardest sport to televise. The ball in flight is usually too small to see. There is no time clock to add urgency. The playing field is not standardized, as it is in almost every other major sport, so finding the right vantage points for the bulky cameras was a problem. No one runs, punches, jumps, or gets tackled in golf, activities that show up well on the tube. "The cameras were so heavy and immobile," recalls Schenkel. "We'd have ten of them at the most to cover four holes." Scoring was another problem. Schenkel and his "color" commentators—former touring pros like Horton Smith, Vic Ghezzi, Claude Harmon, Cary Middlecoff, and Nelson, his favorite—could rarely tell the viewer with confidence who was in first place and by how much, because walkie-talkies were not yet in use to keep tabs on the seventy or so players on the 150-or-so-acre playing field. "But they beat that problem at Augusta National," says Schenkel. "Cliff Roberts [the tournament chairman] put some men from the Fort Gordon army base in Augusta in charge of scoring. They used their army wire telephones. They were accurate as hell."

Few tournaments that were not the Masters or the Open were televised in 1960. One event that made the tube was the Bing Crosby Pro-Am. The print announcement of the telecast seems to hint that ABC thought golf alone would not attract viewers: "Blonde Miss Maury Orr, handicap 4, will direct the ABC telecast of the climax of Bing Crosby's annual tournament, Sunday, January 24, 5:30–7 P.M. eastern time. She is associate director of ABC-TV's western division. . . . Among the celebrities lined up (to play in the tournament) are George Gobel, Tennessee Ernie Ford, Jim Garner, Desi Arnaz, Bob Hope, Jack Lemmon, Bud Wilkinson, Ed Sullivan, Johnny Weissmuller, Phil Harris, Ray Milland, Gordon MacRae, Randolph Scott. . . ." Demaret signed on to work as a roving assistant to Crosby, the chief commentator. The final three holes were covered.

ABC also showed a made-for-television series of golf matches called All-Star Golf, "presented to you by Reynolds

Aluminum and by Miller High Life, the champagne of bottle beer." The program, which first aired in 1957, was filmed—not taped; this was before the advent of videotape—in the spring and summer for broadcast in the fall and winter, on Saturdays between 5:00 and 6:00 P.M. "Greatest Sport Show on TV," said its ads. "One full hour of exciting golf thrills!" Actually, it was fifty-one minutes of exciting golf thrills and nine minutes of station identifications, network promos, and commercials. Total prize money was $88,500 for the twenty-six-week series, which featured, according to *Golf Digest*, "bulky" Bill Casper, "rangy" Cary Middlecoff, Jack Burke ("the curly haired Texan"), Jimmy Demaret ("the genial Texan"), Billy Maxwell ("the squat Texan") "mustachioed" Lloyd Mangrum, "slim, spectacled" Eric Monti, Gene Littler ("the quiet Californian"), Tommy Bolt, Bob Rosburg, Sam Snead, Doug Sanders, and Paul Harney ("the thin Holy Cross graduate"). Demaret narrated the matches he didn't play in, wearing an unwieldy contraption that suspended a giant microphone from his sternum. No headsets in 1960.

An All-Star Golf match took two six-hour days to film. Five cameramen would set up by the first tee, record the tee shots, then scramble down the right side of the fairway with their cameras in cars, carts, and trucks. The process was repeated as the players hit their second shots. At the green, two additional cameras would join the other five, and all seven loudly whirring cameras would be on. "We found that if we stopped one of the cameras," said art director/unit manager Don Hill, "the players could tell the difference in the noise, so the cameras keep rolling even if one or more of them runs out of film. And when a player takes quite a bit of time to get his chip or putt off, we can use an awful lot of film!"

If you wanted to watch the *women* pros on television on some summer Sunday in 1960, you couldn't. They weren't on— which meant, to the thousands of new, casual golf fans, that the women's tour didn't exist. Yet the Ladies Professional Golf Association (LPGA) had been in business since 1950 and now had three of the greatest women golfers in history—Louise Suggs, Betsy Rawls, and Mickey Wright—in a fierce, weekly rivalry. Suggs, Rawls, and Wright won fourteen of the twenty-five LPGA tournaments in 1960. But who knew?

Lack of media attention was one symptom of the LPGA's malaise that could be called the Post-Babe Blues. Babe Didrikson Zaharias, one of the founders of the LPGA and the most popular, colorful woman golfer ever, died in 1956. "How do I hit it so far? I just loosen my girdle and let 'er rip," the Babe would announce in a loud voice, and her large, adoring gallery would laugh out loud. She had been an Olympic champion and world record holder in the high jump, high hurdles, and javelin, the top female basketball player in the country, and an unbeatable amateur golfer. She played the harmonica on "The Ed Sullivan Show"; for a brief time before she got serious about golf, she had a vaudeville act. She was boisterous, uninhibited, magnetic, a genuine national heroine, and played the press like a maestro. The LPGA didn't even have a commissioner, someone to oversee publicity and promotion of the tour; when the Babe was alive, the crowds just showed up. When she died (of colon cancer) a lot of people stopped following women's golf.

Not all of her peers missed her. "The Babe was *not* a good sport," explains her good friend Betty Dodd, who also played the women's tour and definitely does miss her old pal. "She *had* to win. You didn't want to be around her when she lost." Louise Suggs, who disliked Babe intensely, could not have been happy when she would open a newspaper the day after winning a tournament and read the headline: BABE LOSES. Zaharias was also a braggart, in the funny, flamboyant style of Muhammad Ali. "Which one of you girls is going to finish second this week?" she would ask so everyone could hear.

As first among equals, Babe dictated that the LPGA tourists would play their tournaments from the men's tees, instead of the shorter, easier ladies' tees. This gave Babe, an extraordinarily long hitter, an advantage, but it also made the scores high. Casual golf fans like low scores and birdies. Even after Babe's death, the LPGA stayed on the back tees. Today, the women pros play mainly from the ladies' tees and there is an unwritten rule that most of the par-five holes must be reachable in two by most of the field. Nancy Lopez, the best woman golfer in 1985, averaged 70.73 strokes per round; Mickey Wright had the best stroke average in 1960, 73.25, two and a half shots higher. Yet Wright was as good as or better than Lopez. Touring pros Kathy Whitworth, Jo Ann Prentice, Bonnie Randolph, and Lesbia Lobo averaged above 77 in 1960. Nobody scores that high today and lasts on the tour.

No one got rich. "A living wage was all you hoped for," says Whitworth. Only five players made more than ten thousand dollars in 1960: Suggs (the leading money winner with $16,892.12), Wright, Rawls, Joyce Ziske, and Fay Crocker. For prize money and media attention to increase, the women's tour needed more pizzazz, more color. It wasn't getting it from its top players. Suggs had a wonderfully workmanlike swing and golf game, but no particular flair. Rawls, a Phi Beta Kappa physics graduate of the University of Texas, was charming and personable, but "she couldn't hit the ball as well as the other top players," says Dodd. Rawls had an exceptional short game, which purists appreciate, but less serious golf fans like to watch home run balls. They liked Wright, who could hit the big tee ball and had, according to many, the best swing ever. But she was shy, sometimes painfully so, and endured, rather than enjoyed, crowds, interviews and autograph hounds.

When *Sports Illustrated* ran an instructional series for women golfers, one John A. Hastings of Portland, Oregon, wrote in to complain. He did not like to see women encouraged to play: "Visions of ten minute delays and magpie chatterings in the middle of my backswing caused a violent shudder," he wrote in the May 16, 1960 issue. "I almost dropped your magazine in disgust."

The LPGA had a problem and knew it. Prize money had declined for the first time in the tour's history, from $202,500 in 1959 to $186,700 in 1960. "Our organization was terrible," says

Dodd. "We did our own pairings, dispersed our own checks and we didn't have a commissioner. We couldn't afford one." Barbara Romack, a former U.S. Women's Amateur champion and one of the better LPGA players, had a plan to make at least professional golf more popular. Will Grimsley of the Associated Press recorded her thoughts; his story appeared in *Golf World* under the headline PROETTES DOLL UP:

> "We're tired of being referred to as a bunch of dowdy old bags," the pert former National Amateur champion from Sacramento, Calif., said. "If it's glamor people want, we figure we can give them some, too."
>
> Barbara has noticed some radical changes since she joined the pro circuit in November, 1958.
>
> "Instead of pouring [sic] over Ben Hogan's *Power Golf* the girls are reading glamor or fashion magazines.
>
> "At night, they put their hair in curlers, polish their fingernails and fret over their wardrobe. They've learned that fans expect more than a good golf shot. They want a little sex appeal also. . . ."
>
> The fetching Miss Romack said the girl golfers had their pride stung when Maria Bueno, a Brazilian tennis player, beat out Betsy Rawls, leading money winner among the links ladies, as the Associated Press' woman athlete of the year (1959).
>
> "This Bueno girl won a couple of tournaments, Betsy won 10," complained Barbara. "We all felt it was because tennis had got so much publicity from Gussie Moran's lace panties and Karol Fagero's gold underwear.
>
> "We admit we've been the poorest dressed athletes in sports, but we're perking up. We're going more for colorful Bermuda shorts, tight fitting sweaters and skirts and fancy hair-dos. We have some girls who can hold their own in this league. . . ."

In an era when professional athletes could be called "proettes," *Golf Digest*, the oldest and most respected golf publication in the United States, annually elected a Most Beautiful Golfer. The Most Beautiful Golfer of 1960 was Florence Zupnik.

"My father [Joseph Zupnik] sent in my picture," she recalls.

"He was my inspiration. My older brother wasn't interested in golf, but I was, so Dad taught me how to play." Miss Zupnik was thirteen when she started to learn the game at Woodmont Country Club in Rockville, Maryland; by age seventeen she was the women's club champion. *Golf Digest* described her as "a pert, dark-haired University of Maryland sophomore . . . her 112 pounds are prettily distributed in a 32–21–31 pattern." Two black-and-white photographs accompanying the article captured a smiling Miss Zupnik looking . . . pert.

Richard Aultman was then associate editor of the magazine. "No, we never got letters complaining about our [Most Beautiful Golfer] contest," he recalls. "We stopped doing it in the early seventies, I think, about when the women's movement started. We heard complaints about it more from the secretaries in the office than from letters from our subscribers. . . . The two things that got us the most mail were stories on how to rate your own golf course and how to knit your own club covers."

Despite the frivolity implicit in ranking and measuring the beauty of woman golfers, *Golf Digest* was a magazine for serious players. "We thought of our audience mostly as men who shot in the mid- to high-eighties," says Aultman. "Hard core golf nuts, interested in getting better." *Golf Digest* was small, "digest"-sized, only five inches wide and eight inches high, with about eighty pages. It was published in Evanston, Illinois, eleven times a year and had about 140,000 readers. Other features in the October 1960 issue that proclaimed Florence Zupnik America's Most Beautiful Golfer were titled "Ben Hogan, Golfer of the Decade;" "Jack Nicklaus, Best Bet for the Sixties"; and "Pro Purses Doubled Since 1950." Some of the writing is dated, of course—seemingly everyone had a one word adjective attached to his name, like *pudgy* Jack Nicklaus, *slim* Art Wall and *colorful* Jimmy Demaret—but there is a timeless quality to the articles in *Golf Digest* and the other influential golf magazine of the day, *Golf World*. Replace the names in features like HOW I PUTT by Arnold Palmer and THIS CAN BE VENTURI'S BIG YEAR and you'd have a typical piece from a current magazine.

What has changed is advertising. The same things were sold then as now—balls, clubs, clothes, gloves. But what equipment ads had in 1960 that you don't see as much anymore were LOTS OF WORDS IN ALL CAPITAL LETTERS, hyphenated, mock-scientific names for almost any product feature and exclamation points. Hundreds, thousands of exclamation points. For instance, First Flight sold a ball that was "guaranteed to lower your score! [It's] patented steel power center helps on every shot!" Worthington's ball, the Sweetshot, gave you "THE *LONG* BALL, CONSISTENTLY!" The new 1960 Haig Ultra irons were "alone in their greatness!" The champion in frantic ad copy was Spalding, whose "amazing new DISTANCE DOT looks like new after 18 holes and even more!" One thirteen-sentence ad for the Dot ball had eight exclamation points and concluded "We're still trying to meet the demand! Play the new DISTANCE DOT yourself!" MacGregor's "Eye-O-Matic" woods had "Pro-Pel" shafts; it's DX ball had "the exclusive Power-Pak liquid center" and a cover called "Permolec" with a "Resilicote" finish. Hillerich and Bradsby PowerBilt clubs had "Tru-Arc Balancing." Wilson's "Dyna-Powered" irons had "non-oxidizing Pro-Tack grips." U.S. Royal's ball was whiter than others, "thanks to the new 'U.S.' Ultra-White paint." And the Maxfli ball, manufactured by Dunlop, featured the "unique Energy-Bank liquid center."

Just as they do now, pro golfers endorsed various products or companies. Cary Middlecoff appeared in ads for the Golf-master Battery Charger, as did Gene Sarazen for Teacher's Scotch, as did Billy Casper and Arnold Palmer for Wilson clubs and balls, as did Jimmy Demaret for First Flight. The smiling face of Ken Venturi (sometimes with Bill Collins) graced U.S. Royal advertisements. Pictures of Don January, Ernie Vossler and J. C. Goosie accompanied ads for Buccaneer slacks, which cost $10.95 at Pro Shops and better men's stores everywhere, and had "Velva-Grips" inside the waistband to keep the wearer's shirttail in. One ad featuring Sam Snead seemed a bit of a reach and enhanced his take-the-money-and-run reputation:

"To Anyone Who Wants to Stop SMOKING, by Sam Snead. 'I am confident that Bantron can help you stop or cut down smoking pleasantly, quickly and easily. . . .' "

Several minor controversies played themselves out in the magazines. Hard-bitten pro Lloyd Mangrum said in a point/counterpoint feature in *Sports Illustrated* that amateurs should not be allowed to compete in tournaments with professional golfers. Wrong, responded 1959 U.S. Amateur champion Jack Nicklaus. Deane Beman, the 1959 British Amateur champion, felt strongly both ways. "He is both right and wrong," said Beman, presaging a career in diplomacy or politics. Sam Snead caused two other tempests in the golf teapot. He admitted he intentionally lost a television match with Mason Rudolph when he dicovered he had more than the legal fourteen clubs in his bag. Rather than call a penalty on himself, he tanked the match. A number of golf fans felt cheated by Snead's charade and wrote letters to editors. Rudolph, a tour rookie in 1960, told *Golf World* that his feelings were hurt, too. "The way I feel about Snead now," he said, "is that he would have some excuse ready if I beat him again. Before I'd get on a course with that guy for a match again he would have to sign some sort of statement that there wouldn't be any kind of alibi." Snead also had a running verbal battle with the owner of Starmount Forest Country Club in Greensboro, North Carolina. The course hosted the Greensboro Open, which Snead won for the seventh time in 1960, but Sam wasn't happy. Your course is in lousy shape, sniped Snead. Then don't come back, the course owner said. Ever.

Two more important items caused little notice. First was the USGA's decision to change the penalty for hitting a ball out of bounds. In 1960 you could hit your tee shot into someone's backyard, play another ball from the tee, then be lying two. Up to then, a player would be deemed to have played *three* under those circumstances. A second development that was widely ignored was the announcement that a new Cleveland company, National Sports Management was offering the services of some of the top American golf professionals—Palmer, Finsterwald, Casper, Wall, and others—for clinics and exhibitions.

The real controversy for golfers in 1960, the thing that made voices rise and fists clench, what they talked about and thought about even more than Hogan, Palmer, and Nicklaus, was. . . golf carts. There were traditionalists on one side of the argument, modernists on the other, and club professionals on another. The issue was brought to a head by George S. May, the crotchety owner/operator of the Tam O'Shanter Golf Club in Chicago. Early in the year, he fired all his caddies—and bought power carts to replace them. May had the rough on his course clipped short so that his caddieless members could find their golf balls. Preposterous, ridiculous, fumed the traditionalists. "Almost degenerate," said Richard S. Tufts, a past president of the USGA. Horton Smith, twice the Masters champion and a member of the Hall of Fame, told a group of Minnesota club pros, "for the sake of golf, I hope the live caddie will never be obsolete . . . the day they stop using caddies something will have gone out of golf." His audience was probably not so sure; they could make a buck by renting carts, while caddies brought the pro no income. But carts already had a good toehold at American golf courses; May's showy action merely demonstrated that carts had a brighter future than caddies. Still, something about such a wholesale injection of modernity into such a tradition-loving sport didn't ring true; it was like Mickey Mantle taking a motorcycle to first base. A visiting Japanese newspaper publisher named Kuniya Kozaki told *Golf World* that he found Americans stange in many ways, particularly when they played *gorufu*. "I always thought a golf course was for walking exercise," he said. "But in this country many golfers ride about the course on small vehicles. They play the game, but miss the exercise."

Some people applauded May's move at Tam O'Shanter. Some people, like this editorial writer at the Charlotte *Observer*, just didn't like caddies:

The modern caddie is little more than a warm body with a chronic contempt for the game and a low regard for the players.

He carries your clubs as an unwanted burden, eyes the flight of your ball with drowsy disinterest, yawns when you sink a long putt, sneers when you miss.

He couldn't find a ball in the rough if he used bifocals, but he's always trying to sell you balls he "found" in your own bag.

His interest in your welfare begins and ends in the size of the tip you're able to offer or the personal "loan" you're willing to make.

He is, in short, shiftless and shameless—a human wart on the social conscience.

So we can't get much aroused over the Tam O'Shanter edict which is, we suspect, a portent of things-to-come elsewhere. We're prepared, when the blow falls, to bid farewell to our caddies and climb on the cart. Call it progress.

There were other things to worry about, of course. Kennedy won the West Viginia primary in March after spending thirty-four thousand dollars on television advertisements, a huge sum. Could an election simply be bought in the new era of television? Senator Hubert H. Humphrey (D-Minn) withdrew from the race. Nixon finished third in the New Hampshire primary. On May 1 the Soviet Union shot down an American U-2 spy plane that had crossed its border. Soviet Premier Krushchev told his congress and the world all about it on May 5. A summit conference in Paris then collapsed in bickering. There was rioting in Turkey and Korea and black sit-ins in the American South. The disaffection of young, white Americans was reflected by folk singers Phil Ochs and Pete Seeger. Seeger popularized a song written by Malvina Reynolds called "Little Boxes," which decried suburban conformity: "And they all play on the golf course/and they drink their martinis dry/and they all live in boxes, little boxes/and they all look just the same . . ." In June, Castro loudly embraced Russia and expropriated American businesses in Cuba. Clark Gable died. The Democrats opened their convention in Los Angeles on July 11 and nominated Kennedy for president and Lyndon Baines Johnson for vice president. The Republicans convened in Chicago on July 27 to nominate Nixon and his running mate, Henry Cabot Lodge. Fear—widespread, persistent, palpable—put a sharper edge on all this turbulence. What were Americans afraid of? Communism. And the Bomb.

Against this backdrop, fun and games like golf appear now to have had no significance, except as diversion. Yet golf began to *seem* important. President Eisenhower played it, cared about it, passionately. And it was on TV. The "greenhouse effect," television newscaster Daniel Schorr once called it: "things observed by the cameras tend to grow abnormally fast and large." Moreover, golf at its highest level—the pro tour in the United States—was a damn good show. In fact, 1960 was arguably one of the two or three most exciting years in golf's history. The past, present, and future of the game collided. In 1960, golf's Big Question was answered:

Who would succeed Hogan?

▼

CHAPTER ONE

William Ben

B *en Hogan points wordlessly at a spot on the ground.*

His caddie, a tall, thin youth of fifteen, unzips the dark blue and white leather shag bag and out tumble 250 new golf balls. He arranges them in a rough pyramid, the balls clicking together softly. Hogan watches silently, his eyes narrowed, a burning cigarette in the center of his mouth.

"Unh." Hogan is pointing again, to another spot fifty yards away. The caddie, with empty shag bag, sprints to it. The Hogan practice ritual is a ceremony for two, with no words and no wasted motion. The golfer hits golf balls and smokes cigarettes, sometimes simultaneously; he waves the shagger left, right, back, and finally, in. The shagger's part is to respond to the semaphore, catch the balls, and put them in the bag. One story, probably apocryphal, has the super-accurate Hogan, from 230 yards, beaning his caddie with a full one-iron shot, knocking him unconscious. Before he can get up, Hogan allegedly hits him twice more. Another story, probably true: Hogan could hit his short irons with so much backspin that, after catching, say, a

pitching-wedge shot on one bounce, the golf ball would seem to ex-plode out of the caddie's hands.

Today's practice session, the first of the year, takes place in the se-cluded few acres in the center of Shady Oaks Country Club in Fort Worth, Texas. Hogan doesn't use the driving range here at his home course. He doesn't want to chat, or be interrupted—or watched. More-over, he wants to be able to hit either into the wind—which accentuates the spin on a golf ball—or with a right-to-left breeze, which mitigates the slight left-to-right curve of his standard shot; on the range, of course, you always have to hit in the same direction. So he takes cad-die, clubs, and balls to one of the protected hollows on the lightly used nine-hole par-three course that Shady Oaks members call the Little Nine.

This early February day in 1960 is seventy-two degrees and calm, unseasonably warm for north central Texas. Yet Hogan appears to be dressed for a much colder day. Even after ninety minutes of exertion, he hasn't shed either of his two sweaters. If it had been even a degree or two cooler, Hogan would not have even considered practicing today. He is a perpetually cold man.

The coolness of the Hogan personality is either congenital or was developed at an early age. His family was poor; his father was a suicide. Chester Hogan shot himself in 1922 with a .38 re-volver, leaving his wife, Clara, and children Royal, thirteen, Princess, eleven, and Ben, nine. At age eleven, "Bennie" began caddying at Glen Garden Country Club in Fort Worth, a seven-mile walk/run from his home. "Hogan's boyhood friends," wrote his biographer, Gene Gregston, "had the impression he was born with a chip on his shoulder, they recognized a keen combativeness in him, they learned he did not talk much and was a hard boy to get to know."

A caddie yard was a tough place, a fenced-in society of mostly young males, like a reform school. Even at the best coun-try clubs—Glen Garden was better than average—the caddie pen was a school for profanity, gambling—and cruelty. Big picked on little. Established picked on newcomer. And if the boy coming up the path was both small *and* green—as Bennie

Hogan was—he was fair game. The other caddies would throw Hogan's hat down the hill at the back of the caddie yard, then they'd throw *him* down. Once, they stuffed the skinny little new kid into a barrel and rolled it down the slope. Hogan finally won his place in this genteel community in the time-honored way: "For a new caddie to break in, he had to win a fist fight with one of the older, bigger caddies," Hogan recalled. "So they threw me in against one of those fellas and I got the better of him."

There were rewards. Caddies made good money—sixty-five cents for carrying a bagful of wooden-shafted clubs around eighteen holes; tips were a nickel, sometimes a dime. Some summer nights, Hogan slept in a sand bunker on the golf course so he could be first in line to pack a bag on Sunday morning. The money was a powerful motivator—it allowed him to not be a burden to his mother, something he was obsessed with— but soon, caddying was not such a hardship, not merely a job. Hogan found that he enjoyed walking over the beautiful green turf in the company of well-off men. He became intrigued by the etiquette and ritual of golf, by its polite but fierce competitiveness. He started to make a point of caddying for the better players, like Ed Stewart, even though Stewart, a man in his early twenties, was far from being the club's best tipper. Soon Hogan joined the other caddies on the Glen Garden practice range early on weekday mornings; they were allowed to hit old balls back and forth before the members arrived. "Closest to that tree for a nickel," someone would say. Hogan, trying to copy Ed Stewart's swing, didn't win many bets at first. He had an equipment problem. His only club, a third-hand, hickory-shafted, rib-faced mashie (equivalent to a modern five-iron), was left-handed. Hogan's early left-handed hacks gave rise to the myth that he is a lefty. He was, is, right-handed.

That Hogan developed from the caddie ranks into the greatest player of his day was not unique or even surprising; practically every top player in that era began by carrying someone else's bag. What *is* astounding, however, is that a tall, thin, moon-faced youth named Byron Nelson caddied at Glen Garden at the same time Hogan did. Nelson, six months older than Hogan, was the best player in the caddie yard in 1927 and the best player in the world from the late thirties to the mid forties. He was better, quicker than Hogan. In the thirties, Nelson won ten times on the pro golf tour, including the Masters and the U.S. Open; Hogan not only didn't win in that decade, he almost didn't survive. "Ben really had a lot of trouble at first with tournament golf," Nelson understates. Hogan turned pro and tried the golf tour at age nineteen, in 1932. He soon returned home, broke. Same thing in 1933. And 1934. He took a club professional job at the Cleburne (Texas) Country Club, and married Valerie Fox, the daughter of the projectionist at the local movie theater. He practiced constantly. The main flaw in his game then was a tendency to hit a big, uncontrolled hook—a severe right-to-left shot—at exactly the wrong time. It's a fatal flaw in a golfer, equivalent to a clergyman with an unpredictable but irresistible urge to laugh during funeral services.

The Hogans gave the tour another—final?—try in 1937. They loaded their 1934 Buick and joined the car caravan—no one flew in those days—from tournament to tournament. A year later, on a Sunday morning in Oakland, California, Hogan hit bottom. Ben and Valerie were down to eight dollars; the staple of their diet for weeks had been the "free" oranges that could be found growing near the golf courses in Southern California. Hogan walked out of the cheapest motel in town, to drive to the course and play in the final round of the Oakland Open . . . but someone had jacked up the Buick, put it on cinder blocks, and stolen the tires. Despair engulfed him. "Son of a bitch," he muttered, and pounded his fists against a wall. But he got a ride to the golf course, shot 69, and won $380, probably the greatest clutch round of his career.

The Hogans never ate another orange. Ben won another $3,770 in 1938, enough to get by; improved his play and his financial standing further in 1939; and in 1940, finally, he began to win. No more hooks for Hogan; now he played a gentle left-to-right shot, for, as Lee Trevino, another fader, would say years later, "You can talk to a fade, but a hook won't listen." Through determination and self-denial, Hogan had built himself into a master of the golf swing. He burned to *win*, to be rewarded, after so much effort and struggle, with the best the game had to offer. Just doing well wouldn't be enough. He had to win. Golf is a sport in which even the best players win very few tournaments compared to the number they play. Even fifty-odd years ago, a two- or three-win season was considered exceptional. Hogan won four times in 1940, five times in 1941 and six times in 1942. After World War II (he served two years in the Army Air Corps, stateside), Hogan succeeded Nelson as the best player in the game. He had thirteen wins in 1946, ten victories in 1948; between January 1945 and January 1949, he won thirty-seven tournaments, including three major titles, the PGA Championships of 1946 and 1948, and the 1948 U.S. Open. Then, disaster.

Ben and Valerie Hogan were en route from Phoenix to their new home in Fort Worth on February 2, 1949, for a brief break from the pro golf tour. At about 8:30 on that foggy morning, Hogan was slowly guiding his late-model black Cadillac across a two-lane bridge on Texas Highway 80 east of El Paso. Suddenly, terrifyingly, Hogan saw two sets of headlights coming at him out of the mist. There was no room to bail out; the low bridge was abutted with concrete. The impact of the twenty-thousand-pound Greyhound bus traveling forty-five miles per hour drove the car's steering column straight back through the front seat. Hogan was not impaled only because he threw himself protectively over his wife's body just before the collision. The steering wheel clipped his left shoulder; the Cadillac's big engine smashed into his left leg and stomach. His wife sustained only minor injuries.

Hogan survived the loss of blood, the trauma, and the broken bones—ribs, pelvis, ankle, and collarbone. Then, two weeks after the accident, he almost died again. Blood clots from his left leg threatened to obstruct his pulmonary artery, which carries blood from the heart to the lungs. So doctors ligated, or tied off, Hogan's inferior (lower) *vena cava*, the large vein that carries blood from the legs to the heart. Thus, Hogan would often feel uncomfortably cool for the rest of his days, simply because, as a result of this surgery, his blood does not circulate normally.

Ironically, the public perception of Hogan thawed after his near-fatal crash. The Scots called Hogan "The Wee Ice Mon" and the Americans knew him as "The Hawk"; the images are of *sang-froid* and fierceness. His recovery from the accident showed that he was not merely an invulnerable, somehow dull perfectionist; he was also a man of flesh and blood, and courage. He played much less after the crash and was appreciated much more. In 1946 through 1948 he played in eighty tournaments; from 1950 through 1960 he entered only five to seven events annually. In 1953 he teed it up in six tournaments—and won five of them, including the Masters and the U.S. and British Opens. Often he received standing ovations from the galleries at all eighteen greens. He was, endearingly, a small man succeeding against long odds. He limped.

What drove Hogan? "Three things," Hogan says. "I didn't want to be a burden to my mother. Two, I needed to put food on the table. Three, I needed a place to sleep." A typical Hogan answer: blunt, honest—and incomplete. He does not share his more intimate thoughts, so his true motivations remained something of a mystery. "I never thought Hogan was a puzzle," says Dan Jenkins, who, as the golf writer in the fifties for the *Fort Worth Press*, knew Hogan as well as any writer. "Ben was shy, embarrassed about his lack of education [he didn't finish high school] and was determined to make something of himself to prove a guy could come from something less than inherited wealth and be successful. . . . Much of the fire within him was lit by Byron Nelson, who came from the same town—the same caddie yard—and achieved fame and fortune several years ahead of Ben and who, as a kid, had always been popular and better-liked than Ben. No puzzle at all."

While Hogan gained greater public acceptance in the fifties—not love, just acceptance and appreciation—he hadn't really changed, even if the popular perception of him did. For Hogan was never a charismatic man. On the contrary, he thought it improper to emote at all. His pants and sweater were invariably gray, his shoes always black, his shirt and cloth cap perpetually white. Quite literally, Hogan wanted his golf to do his talking. He would clam up on the first tee and might not say a word all day to his playing partners. This silence came to be known as the Hogan Trance. There was an impenetrable, invisible force field around him. "Hogan was intimidating, just with his presence and the way he hit the ball," recalled Gene Littler, himself a very quiet man. "He sure didn't offer much help out there." The younger pros were at once slightly frightened of him and drawn to him, for this was Hogan, the ascetic who had made a science out of golf. Don January, then in just his fourth month as a touring pro—this was in 1956—summoned up the courage to approach the great man after their first tournament round together. "Mr. Hogan, excuse me, I'm new out here and I'd just like to know what you thought of my swing today," said January. Hogan froze him with a look and said nothing for a minute. "Something wrong with your elbow?" he said finally, then turned. Conversation over. January mumbled his thanks and dutifully went to work on the position of his left elbow. Maybe it was too high at address. Four years later he figured out that Hogan had been referring to his *right* elbow.

Other veteran touring pros tell stories similar to January's. Butch Baird remembers being paired with Hogan in 1960, his rookie year. He watched in awe as the Hawk maneuvered his ball around the course that day, a high hook here, a gentle fade there, high shots, low shots, in-between shots. Baird swallowed hard and approached Hogan on the eighteenth fairway. They hadn't exchanged a single word all day. Then Baird said, "Mr. Hogan, you never seem to hit a straight shot. Do you always hit it left-to-right or right-to-left?" Hogan fastened his bottomless blue eyes on Baird. Paused. "*Always,*" he said emphatically, and walked away. Another pro with another story is Bill Collins. Collins is a former auto worker and an ex-Marine, a big man with the deep metallic voice of Lee Marvin, not the kind of person to be intimidated by anyone. But, he says, "Hogan made you feel like you were holding the club upside down." Collins and Hogan were playing a practice round before a tournament and Collins, perhaps inspired by the great man's presence, was holding his own in his twenty-dollar bet with Hogan. "It took me a long time to ask, but finally I went up to him and said, 'What do you think I could do to work on my game?'" Collins recalls. "Hogan just looks at me for a minute, then he says, 'How do we stand?' How do we stand! He wasn't gonna help me if I was beating him!"

But on this day Hogan looks stiff, older than his forty-seven years. In his younger years he resembled handsome tough-guy actor George Raft. Now he is grim and gray; there are deep lines on either side of his mouth. Then he hits a golf ball. His swing is smooth, quick, compact, and powerful, as efficient as a carpenter driving nails. He hits short irons, medium irons, then long irons, the balls raining down with an almost eerie precision at the shagger's feet. The years disappear; this could be the Hogan of 1953—or 1940. Then fairway woods, the driver, and back down again, finishing with the short irons. Each shot is lined up; there are no careless or casual swings. Hogan, the most diligent practicer in golf history, is also the most precise ball-striker ever. Finally, he waves the shagger in, lights another cigarette, and trudges back to the clubhouse, alone.

Once Shelley Mayfield, the professional at Brook Hollow in Dallas, invited the course greenkeeper, Johnny Henry, to join him on the tenth tee at the club and stand with his back to the nearby practice range. Henry, curious, complied. "Just listen," said Mayfield. There were eight or ten men hitting practice shots. "You heard chink . . . chink . . . chink . . . *pow*!" recalled Henry. "It was the difference between a BB gun and a deer rifle." What on earth was *that*? he asked. "Hogan's here today," said Mayfield, simply. On another occasion, Henry noticed Hogan alone on the practice tee at River Crest Country Club in Fort Worth, drilling two-iron shots. It was 9:30 A.M. Henry attended his course superintendent's meeting; the group broke for lunch at noon. Henry peeked outside. And there was Hogan, still hitting balls—with the same club. "And lining every one up, too, like he needed it to win the U.S. Open."

Despite appearances, practice for Hogan was not self-flagellation; in a way, it was not even work. Golf "was a constant struggle of one kind or another," he told *Golf*'s George Peper, "but always a pleasant one. . . . You hear stories about my beating my brains out practicing, but the truth is, I was enjoying myself. I couldn't wait to get up in the morning so I could hit balls. I'd be at the practice tee at the crack of dawn, hit balls for a few hours, then take a break and get right back to it. And I still thoroughly enjoy it. When I'm hitting the ball where I want, hard and crisply—when anyone is—it's a joy that very few people experience."

Perhaps Hogan's joy at practice has been enhanced on this sunny day by his equipment. After all, *his* factory, just ten miles away, manufactured the balls he hit and the clubs he hit them with; it made his golf bag, his shag bag, even his shirt, his sweaters, and his trademark white cloth cap. The Ben Hogan Company, 2912 West Pafford Street, a relative newcomer to the growing golf equipment industry, was already a solid success.

Hogan started the business in 1953. He didn't like the looks of the first clubs off the assembly line, so he scrapped them, at a cost of tens of thousands of dollars. Some of the stockholders raised hell, but Hogan had absolute control of the company, from production to marketing to quality control. He clearly understood, years before the idea was given currency, that people do not merely buy products; they buy *image*. Thus Hogan equipment had to look perfect, because the Hogan image was a kind of sober perfectionism. Witness the sobriety of this copy from a 1960 ad for Hogan golf balls:

During my golfing career I have hit thousands of golf balls . . .
by studying those golf shots I discovered variations in their
flight patterns. The matter was so important that I became
deeply interested in golf ball manufacture and found that
there were manufacturing processes that could be controlled
to improve golf ball performance. I have tried to put my experience and the most advanced manufacturing techniques
into producing golf balls that will deliver the utmost in control and repeating performance.

The largest single stockholder (other investors were Pollard
Simons, George Coleman, and singer Bing Crosby) was Hogan's close friend and financial angel Marvin Leonard. The two
first met in 1927 at Glen Garden, where Leonard was a beginning golfer and new member. The wealthy, owlish gentleman
and the poor, quiet caddie hit it off. Leonard lent Bennie $225
in 1934 for one of his first, unsuccessful tries at the pro tour. Leonard used some of the fortune he had made as co-owner—with
his brother Obie—of the Leonard Brothers Department Store to
build two additional Fort Worth institutions, Colonial Country
Club in 1936 and Shady Oaks in 1956. He started the National
Invitation Tournament (NIT), a tour event at Colonial. Hogan
followed his patron to Colonial, then to Shady Oaks. He won
the first NIT in 1946, and four more including 1959. Possibly Hogan was the son Leonard never had; Leonard could have been
the father Hogan lost in his youth. They were best friends, golf,
gin rummy, and business partners. Business was very good.

Just how good business was had recently been made clear.
American Machine and Foundry Company (AMF), a firm best
known for the bowling balls it made, had offered to buy the company. The price AMF had put on the table was very attractive.
It would make Hogan rich, a condition he had never enjoyed.
In his best money year, 1946, he won thirteen tournaments and
was the leading money winner on the pro golf tour with
$42,556. But he'd had to travel at least thirty-two weeks to make
that princely sum; his net income was far less. Now, of course,
he was making an excellent living as a golf equipment manufac-

turer, but selling the business at a hefty profit was tempting.

After a short break, Hogan is practicing again. He stands on the upper level of the long, two-tiered practice green, with a handful of golf balls and two putters. Other February golfers are milling around. As at many golf courses, the Shady Oaks putting green is near the pro shop, the driving range, and the first and tenth tees. But no one greets or approaches Hogan. He drops the balls and one of the clubs and begins to putt at a hole twenty feet away. His putter has a flat lie, like a hockey stick, and a round, very thick, built-up grip. It's apparent that something is wrong. Hogan looks uncomfortable, tentative; he can't seem to get his feet set. His stroke looks merely adequate. It's not the miniature version of his elegant, assured full swing you might expect . . . if you didn't know the awful truth. Hogan can't putt anymore.

"I am embarrassed to get before people and putt," he once told a reporter. "Hell, I'm even embarrassed to putt when I'm alone, but the only way to beat this thing is to play. I hear children and ladies saying, 'For God's sake, why doesn't he hit it faster?' So I say to myself, 'You idiot. You heard them. Why don't you hit it faster?'"

Hogan's putting problems were so vivid, so incongruous, because his full shots were so good. Exactly why older players lose their ability to execute golf's simplest stroke is a mystery. Hogan himself puzzled over this. Even at forty-seven, he could get the ball from the tee to the green better than anyone. Then he putted worse than everyone. LPGA pro Marilynn Smith was paired with Hogan in an eighteen-hole event in Dallas in about 1958; she shot 72, the same as her hero. "That was probably my biggest thrill in golf," says Smith, who won twenty-two women's tour events. But, she admits, "Hogan missed five putts from two feet or less." Long putts were no problem but on short putts, he froze. It was embarrassing, almost agonizing to watch. Hogan just couldn't. Start. The clubhead. Back. People sent him putting tips.

The air turns sharply colder as the afternoon wears on. Hogan sees that his clubs and balls are put away, pays his shag boy, changes shoes, and retreats into the Men's Grille for a drink— vodka and tonic, lime. He sits at his table by the windows over- looking the ninth and eighteenth greens, where the clubhouse juts out like the prow of a ship. "Hogan's watching you," Shady Oaks members sometimes whisper to their opponents as they prepare to stroke a crucial putt. From either green you can make out Hogan's solitary, unmoving figure; you also notice that no one sits at the tables near him.

What is he thinking about? Perhaps, since he's been practic- ing, Hogan is mulling over his tournament schedule for 1960. He will play in five, maybe six events. Certainly at Colonial, where he is the defending champion; the Masters and the United States Open, of course; the Seminole Pro-Am, a minor tournament on a course he loves, as a warm-up for the Masters; and possibly at Memphis, two weeks before the Open.

The Open. Hogan had won golf's ultimate tournament four times. Winning the one competition of the year with the best players on the most difficult golf course under the most pres- sure, was, for Hogan, sweet, complete vindication for his ded- ication to the game. And while he burned to become the first-ever five-time Open champion, the previous four hours had proven both that it was possible, given the way he could still hit the ball, and highly unlikely, because his putting was awful.

Who, Hogan may have wondered, would be the man to beat at Cherry Hills in Denver in June, at the sixty-fourth U.S. Open? Probably someone like Venturi, Finsterwald, Littler, or Wall. Maybe a great putter, like Rosburg or Casper. Hogan fin- ishes his drink, signs his check with his member number, H-8, and walks out the front door to his car, a black Cadillac, for the short ride home.

Perhaps someone else. Perhaps Palmer. Wasn't he leading in Palm Springs?

CHAPTER TWO

Arnold Daniel

While Hogan practiced alone in North Texas, Arnold Palmer, amid palm trees, celebrities, and galleries, tried to win a golf tournament. But Johnny Palmer (no relation) was at that moment leading Arnold by one shot after the fourth round of the inaugural, five-round Palm Springs Desert Classic. Johnny, from El Dorado, North Carolina, and Arnie, from Latrobe, Pennsylvania, both shot 66 that day. But it was Arnold, not Johnny, that Hogan thought about.

In some ways, Palmer was Hogan flipped. The differences were obvious in terms of age—Palmer was a robust thirty; health—Palmer had not endured the battering of a near-fatal automobile accident, as Hogan had; and outlook. Palmer was cheerful, gregarious. Autographs? No problem. He might even have a drink with the boys from the press after a round. Hogan, on the other hand, was utterly standoffish to fans and other players on the golf course and careful off it. Palmer had the putting touch of a god; Hogan's putting skill had deserted him. The two diverged most sharply, however, in the way they swung at a golf ball.

Hogan was a scientist. It helped him to think of his swing in terms of *supination* and *pronation,* words from kinesiology, the science of human muscular movement. He dissected and examined every move and position in the golf swing in his *Five Lessons: The Modern Fundamentals of Golf* (1957) instruction book. Even the "waggle," the little movement of hands and club many players have *before* the swing begins, was grist for the Hogan mill: "The left hand is the controlling hand. . . . EACH TIME YOU WAGGLE THE CLUB BACK, THE RIGHT ELBOW SHOULD HIT THE FRONT PART OF THE RIGHT HIP, JUST ABOUT WHERE YOUR WATCH POCKET IS. WHEN THIS TAKES PLACE, THE LEFT ELBOW, AS IT MUST, COMES OUT SLIGHTLY, THE LOWER PART OF THE ARM FROM THE ELBOW DOWN ROTATES A LITTLE, AND THE LEFT HAND MOVES THREE INCHES OR SO PAST THE BALL. . . ."

Palmer, as revealed by *his* instruction book (*My Game and Yours,* 1963), believed that such analysis leads to paralysis. On the weight shift during the swing, Palmer wrote, "If you will just trust your instincts. . . . you will be all right." On swing plane, that is, whether you should swing the golf club from shoulder to shoulder, up around your ears, or somewhere in between: "I don't think you should worry about it. . . . . Do what comes naturally and let the other fellas worry about theory." Palmer seemed to be talking directly to Hogan and his followers. What about the wrist break in the backswing? "If you asked me at what point in the backswing my own wrists begin to break, I'd have to tell you that I don't know. I can't think of any single piece of knowledge that would help me less, or be more likely to confuse me." Hogan, of course, went into exacting detail on both these matters in his book. Palmer dismisses them. His game was built on the simplest foundations: a good grip, a steady head during the stroke—and desire. "The whole thing about the golf swing," Palmer writes, "is that it is a whole lot easier and a lot more natural than has been advertised." "*If he ever stopped to think / How he did it he would sink*" British writer

Hilaire Belloc once wrote about a waterbug, but the sentiment could apply to Palmer's golf game.

While Hogan and Palmer were day and night in terms of personality and philosophy, in some respects they were nearly identical. The midforties to midfifties had been The Age of Hogan; by 1960 he was sort of Top Dog Emeritus. Palmer was one of the handful of heirs apparent who looked to be as competitive, as *passionate* about winning as The Hawk. Both were uncommonly strong men. Palmer, who stood five feet ten inches, had the arms and shoulders of a stevedore; Hogan, five feet nine inches, looked like a retired welterweight boxer. Both men were superb athletes; both swung at the ball *hard*. One writer compared Hogan to a mechanic and Palmer to an artist, a useful analogy in that Hogan was precise and Palmer was emotional, but that was too simple. Hogan's golf was built on subtlety and finesse with power, not mere mechanics. And if Palmer seemed to rely on bursts of artistic inspiration, at least he'd been practicing his art since he was four.

Arnold Daniel Palmer was the oldest of the four children of Milfred Jerome (he was called "Deacon" by most people, "Pap" by his son) and Doris Palmer of Latrobe, Pennsylvania, a small town thirty miles east of Pittsburgh. In 1921 "Deac" took the greenkeeper job at the new nine-hole Latrobe Country Club, which was built and owned by the Latrobe Steel Corporation. A few years later, in a Depression-era economy move, the company asked him to also serve "temporarily"—but, as it turned out, permanently—as golf professional, in effect a second full-time job. Arnold, born in 1929, was soon running around the golf course, building castles in the sand traps and riding in his father's lap as he drove the club's tractor. Soon the greenkeeper's son was around the club almost full-time. When he first piloted the tractor, he had to stand up to steer. And, naturally, he played golf. In the company of his sister, Lois Jean, he broke 100 for eighteen holes for the first time at age seven. His parents didn't believe him, remembers Arnold, "and I was putting them all out that day, too." He became a denizen of the driving range. "Hey Pap, watch this! Pap! Watch! Pap!" little Arnie would yell ("You'd get so sick of him you'd feel like hitting him a lick," Deacon recalled.) Then he'd thrash at the ball with all his might. "I swung so hard I'd lose my balance on every drive, and sometimes both feet would come off the ground," Palmer remembers. The purists at the club winced. Why do you let your son swing like that, Deac? What about balance? What about form? "He'll balance himself better when he gets older and he'll hit the ball hard, too," replied Deacon.

Palmer kept the hard swing he grew up with, the swing Deacon liked. "Every time I try to hit a cute shot of some kind, he'll really scoff," Palmer would say years later. "He doesn't think I'm playing well unless I beat the ball to death. He has never thought I hit the ball hard enough. My overriding philosophy of the game, to hit it hard, comes from him. But I have never hit it hard enough to suit him."

Arnie did practically everything at Latrobe Country Club— he mowed fairways, cut greens, changed holes, raked bunkers, repaired clubs, caddied, served as caddiemaster for a short time (Deacon fired him; he was constantly AWOL, with his golf clubs), and, of course, played and practiced every day he could get away with it. He did *practically* everything. Latrobe Country Club was private, and Deacon Palmer and his son were not members, they were employees. Deacon ate his meals at home or in the kitchen at the club. Young Arnold was not allowed to play golf with the members' children, and although he won the caddie's tournament four times, he remembers that his father would not let him accept the winner's prize; he wasn't really a caddie *or* a member. "I couldn't have or use or do all the things many of the kids I was going to school with could, because their parents were members of the club," recalls Palmer. "I could beat them all in golf, but I couldn't swim in the club pool, for instance. I had to go down to the stream. So, I was raised in a country club atmosphere but was never able to touch it. It was like looking at a piece of cake and knowing how good it was, but not being able to take a bite. It was sort of a frustrating thing for me . . . [it was] a part of the society I was looking at but couldn't touch."

Palmer played in his first national tournament, the USGA Junior, in Los Angeles in 1947. He was then seventeen, soon to start his senior year in high school, and a self-described "hell-raiser." He liked, for instance, to break up the school day by playing pool at lunchtime. He played a little football for the La-trobe High Wildcats, and was good—tackle on defense, half-back on offense—but he gave it up. He was an indifferent student, but on two points he was far ahead of the other schol-ars at Latrobe High: he was the best young golfer anyone had ever seen, and he had decided on his goal in life. He would be a golf professional. Yet both the objective and the path to his goal were unclear. Would he be a club pro, like his father? No, he would not work at a club. He'd seen a club pro's life up close. That was second-class citizenship. He would have to become good enough as a player to join the pro tour. But how to get good enough, experienced enough, to compete and win against the best players in the world?

That week Palmer found an answer. It was given to him by Marvin ("Buddy") Worsham, another seventeen-year-old con-testant in the tournament, who was, like Palmer, related to a golf pro (Lew Worsham, Buddy's brother, won the first televised tournament on the PGA Tour, the 1953 World Championship, as well as the 1947 U.S Open). Buddy told his new pal Arnie that he was being recruited by a small school in North Carolina called Wake Forest College. Wake Forest is upgrading its golf team from just being a club sport, Worsham explained. They'll have a coach, and play in tournaments. Why don't we both go? The two teenagers entered Wake Forest fourteen months later with the Class of 1951.

Palmer's college days were some of the happiest of his life. He and Worsham became extremely close and were the best players on a very good team. Palmer won the Southern Confer-ence championship in 1948 and 1949 and was NCAA Championship medalist in 1949 and 1950. Dow Finsterwald, who would often serve as Palmer's foil in the years to come, was also a college golfer then. "The first time I met Arnie," he recalls, "it was about 1949. Ohio University against Wake Forest at Carolina Country Club. I had to play Palmer." Finsterwald said how do you do, took two of his smooth, metronomic practice strokes, teed his ball up, and shot a very competent, even par 35 on the first nine holes. Meanwhile, his opponent, with a desperate-looking slash of a golf swing, shot 29. Palmer flattened Finsterwald and the Demon Deacons demolished the Bobcats. "Man, they had a good team. Buddy Worsham was darn good, too," Finsterwald says. Golden times for Palmer: he had friends, dates, parties, his first national success and recognition, not *too* much academic pressure, and the opportunity to play lots and lots of golf. But it all ended abruptly in 1950.

There was a dance one night at nearby Duke University. Buddy wanted to go, Arnie didn't. So Worsham went alone, wrecked his car, and was killed. Palmer was shattered. The fun was suddenly over. Nothing felt the same anymore: college, the social whirl, even golf seemed suddenly trivial. "I thought I'd go crazy," he recalled. "I was always looking around for Buddy." He had been so sure about what he wanted from life and now nothing was clear. Confused and extremely depressed, Palmer quit school. Without a student deferment, he was eligible for the draft and, perhaps, service in the Korean War—he knew he didn't want *that*—so he enlisted in the Coast Guard.

After completing boot camp in November 1951 at Cape May, New Jersey, Palmer waited to find out where in Florida his permanent assignment would be. He got Cleveland instead. Cleveland! Palmer didn't know it at the time, but he could hardly have drawn a better posting, for Cleveland had everything (except weather) for an aspiring golfer. Ohio is a typically sports-mad midwestern state, with an atypical bias toward watching and playing golf. Only California and Florida had more golf courses; only New York and California had more golfers. Cleveland had amateur tournaments to play in as soon as there was even a hint of warm weather, that is, as soon as the snow began to melt. It had an abundance of good golfers and golf courses. Most important, the city had people with money and influence who were anxious to help Arnold Palmer.

"When I first went to Cleveland," Palmer recalled, "I worked with the Auxiliary. It was sort of a civilian thing. Later on, I was transferred to another office, and was in charge of the Coast Guard relations with various flotillas around the Great Lakes." One of Yeoman Third Class Palmer's first duties was to help build an indoor driving range for the district commander.

On a gusty March day the following spring, Palmer wandered out to a golf course he'd seen, Pine Ridge Country Club in Wickliffe, east of Cleveland. A member at the club, one Severino P. Severino, recalled seeing "this guy in a sailor suit up at the top of the hill by the first hole. I caught up with him and asked him if he'd like to play with me. He said, 'Sure.'" It was the beginning of a beautiful friendship. "We'd play three or four afternoons a week, all over the district," remembered "Sevy," who was the medical editor at the *Cleveland Press*. "He couldn't wait until he had a chance to get on the tour. He would talk about how anxious he was to get his hands on Ben Hogan and Sam Snead. . . . He was remarkable as a golfer even then. He was a great competitor and an amazing putter. He'd make ten- and twelve-footers as often as I'd make three-footers."

Sevy introduced Arnie to his friends. Helluva a nice kid, they all agreed. Helluva *player*. One of Sevy's pals was Art Brooks, the co-owner of Pine Ridge; Brooks "adopted" Palmer, made him a no-charge member at his golf course. Another of this fraternity was Ed Preisler, who owned Preisler Lumber and one of the best golf games in the state. As head of the Cleveland District Golf Association Rating Committee, he often took one or two foursomes to "rate" the golf courses in the area, and thus get Arnie on a different course, free. For money was always an issue with Palmer. His new friends had it and he did not. His Coast Guard pay was $140 a month.

"That was a real fun time," remembers Preisler. "We played

all over. Afterward, we'd go have a beer, or go and eat. Arnold came over to my house a lot for dinner. He's just a great guy to be with. . . . For example: I remember years later, Arnold made an eight or a nine on the last hole to lose the Los Angeles Open. I was there. If that happened to most guys, they'd be driving out of there with their spikes on. But there's Arnold, an hour and a half later, still signing autographs for kids.

"On the other hand . . . I was riding in an elevator in a hotel, I think it was during a U.S. Open [Preisler played in three Opens]. My son, who was about ten, was with me. Hogan and Demaret get on the elevator. I told my son that these men were very famous golfers, that he should ask for their autographs. Hogan says, 'I don't give autographs.' Demaret played it perfectly. 'Come on son, I can still write,' he says. I have no regard for Hogan as a person."

Palmer was discharged from the Coast Guard in January 1954. He returned to Wake Forest briefly, but left again, short of his degree in business administration. Soon he was back in Cleveland to play in the U.S. Open qualifying tournament. And he had a job interview, with a Mr. Heller, whose Cleveland-based company manufactured staplers. But the night before the interview, Heller dropped dead. Word spread. Arnie needs a job, we've got to help, his Ohio golf pals told each other. The next day, he had a job. He would be a paint salesman.

"Arnie was on my payroll the morning after the qualifier," recalls Bill Wehnes, who was another of the inner circle of Palmer's golf buddies. "I put $200 and a United Airlines ticket to the Open on my desk and I said, 'I'll pay you $300 a month and you work only half of each day.'" Wehnes (pronounced *way-nis*) is a live wire, a friendly, fast-talking, and very successful representative for maufacturers of paint and tapping compounds (tapping compounds are used when putting threads on metal, like screws). A two handicap, he had played in the British and French Amateur championships, and belonged to five golf clubs, including three of the best in the world: Riviera, in Los Angeles; Pine Valley, in New Jersey; and Canterbury, in Cleveland. And he was eager to help the finest young golfer he had ever seen. Wehnes offered to arrange for Palmer to represent a paint manufacturer, Cimonari, and to lay the groundwork for him to land a big customer, a company that made and painted the metal cabinets for Motorola and Zenith televisions. Palmer would probably have to play golf with the cabinet manufacturer once a month. With any luck, he could make as much as twenty-five thousand dollars a year and play all the golf he wanted. Well, what do you think, Arnie? asked Wehnes. Palmer held out his hand. "I'll take it," he said. It was an easy decision. His only other job prospect was with a Cleveland milk distributor, loading trucks.

Palmer did not go out and buy a briefcase and load it up with paint samples and business cards. His "job" that summer was playing golf. He played in tournaments, including his first U.S. Open; he played poorly and missed the cut. Occasionally, he teed it up with customers and potential customers of W. C. Wehnes Company. "I picked up all the tabs," says Wehnes. "Poor old Arnold, all he had were Foot-Joy shoes and golf balls." As an amateur, Palmer could accept no cash tournament prizes, just merchandise, like shoes and balls.

Late that summer Wehnes sent his new employee to the United States Amateur Championship at Oakland Hills Country Club, near Detroit. "I told him to get a suite at the Jefferson Hotel on Whittier Avenue—or was it the Whittier Hotel on Jefferson?—and that I'd join him during the week." Palmer was uptight, tense. This would be his most important tournament of the year. "Man, he just tossed and turned in bed. I don't think he got more than three hours of sleep a night," says Wehnes. To try to relax his charge, Wehnes insisted that he get a massage after his matches and that he have a drink. "Arnie drank Old Fitzgerald old fashioneds and I drank cognac." In the early rounds, Palmer beat several of the best amateurs in the country: Frank Strafaci, Don Cherry, Dick Whiting, and Frank Stranahan. In the semifinals, he faced a familiar foe, Ed Meister, from Cleveland. Meister had a reputation as an excellent player

and someone who would never be in the running for a sportsmanship trophy. Once, in a sudden-death playoff in a U.S. Amateur qualifier, Meister appeared deliberately to allow his
shadow to fall on his teenaged opponent's ball a half second before he hit it. The distracted youth's shot sailed into the woods;
Meister won the playoff.

Form held. It was against the rules in 1954 to clean your ball
during the play of a hole, even on the green. But Palmer observed his opponent gently scraping his dirty golf ball—deliberately?—with the coin he had used to mark it. Palmer, angry,
approached a Meister booster in the gallery. "Tell your buddy
if he knocks mud off his ball with his ball marker one more time,
I'm gonna punch him in the nose," he said. For the next several
holes, Meister made a great display of marking and replacing
his ball with exagerrated care, then holding it aloft with his fin-
gers extended, as though the ball were a Fabergé egg. Palmer
glared—and took the tense, contentious match in thirty-nine
holes. He won the next day in the finals against Bob Sweeny, a
forty-three-year-old banker. "Winning the National Amateur
Championship was one of the most exciting things that ever
happened to me," Palmer says. "I'll tell you this, it was the
toughest golf tournament I ever won."

Palmer's life as a public person had begun. The camera of
national scrutiny focused on its new amateur golf champion
and saw an expressive twenty-four-year-old with a fast, slightly
unorthodox swing, especially when compared to the beautiful,
rhythmic stroke of Gene Littler, the 1953 champion, and no
fashion sense. In front of the large gallery watching the final
round of the Amateur, Arnie had played most of the day with
his pants slipping down and his shirt tail falling out. He was
constantly pulling up his pants with the heels of his hands; he
did this so often it appeared to be involuntary, a twitch, a tic.
"The reason for this was, I was built like my father—big shoulders and no hips," Palmer explains. "My mother was always
saying, 'Arnie, put your shirt in.' I became very conscious of it.
Then, too, when I started playing golf, I sometimes didn't have

a pair of pants that fit me quite right; so they would be sliding off my hips, and I tugged them up. It was a way of life, a natural thing. It wasn't meant for show; it was meant to hold my pants up! Then people got onto it and thought it was funny."

On a Sunday evening several weeks after winning the Amateur, Palmer found himself in the front row of a theatre in New York City. On the stage was a man who, Palmer noticed, looked just as gaunt and lifeless and spoke just as haltingly in person as he did on television. "Ladies and gentlemen," said Ed Sullivan, "Would you welcome please, the lovely. Star of stage and screen. Gina Lollobrigida." The lovely star of stage and screen on Palmer's right rose and, smiling, acknowledged the applause. "Also in our audience tonight. Is our new, National Amateur. Champion golfer. Arnold Palmer. Arnie, would you please stand up." Sevy Severino had set up Palmer's debut on live national television; he knew Sullivan, a golfer himself, would go for it. Wehnes accompanied Arnie and remembers with a sigh that La Lollobrigida wore a black gown.

Things were happening fast for Palmer, professionally and personally. He fell in love at a tournament he had played in right after winning the Amateur. "You should have seen the girl Bill saw last night," Mrs. Wehnes told Arnie. "Gorgeous. Her name is Winnie Walzer." Palmer had taken out one of the club's waitresses in his patron's customized white Cadillac Fleetwood the night before and had missed the social function where the alert Wilferd Charles Wehnes had spotted a white lace dress filled with Winnie Walzer. John W. Roberts, like Wehnes a businessman/golfer, made the introductions at a cocktail party the next evening. Bells pealed, firecrackers exploded. Four days later, they were engaged.

But Arnie was still uncertain how he would support himself and his new bride. Naturally, he was thinking more and more about turning pro; Littler had done so immediately after winning the Amateur the year before. But the amateur golf establishment, as represented by United States Golf Association officals Joe Dey and Dick Tufts, wanted their appealing new

champion to stay in the fold. Talk to him for us, Bill, they said
to Wehnes. Remind him that he can play on our Walker Cup
team.(The Walker Cup is a prestigious bi-annual event between
the best American and English amateurs.) And while Palmer
was not particularly enamored of selling industrial paint and
tapping compounds, he also admits he wasn't too sure about
the tour. "I was a little frightened of the whole thing," he recalls.
"Not the golf end of it, not the playing, but the magnitude of going out and traveling and doing my own thing. I suppose that
was part of my father's influence, too, to be humble, to not go
out and try to be a big shot, to just take my time."

Arnie asked for advice from the folks at home. Deacon
wasn't sure his son was ready for the road; he also felt strongly
that if he did go ahead and turn pro, he must beware of making
long term finacial commitments with sponsors. Use your own
money to get started, Deacon counseled, and you won't have
to worry about anyone else. Then Arnie sought out Bob Drum
for another opinion. Drum was to Arnold Palmer what O. B.
Keeler was to Bobby Jones. Drum, a fierce Palmer partisan, a
funny, popular man known as The Drummer, chronicled the
exploits of the strong-armed kid from Latrobe for the *Pittsburgh
Press*. "I first met Arnie in what, 1946? at the only junior tournament he ever lost—the Western Pennsylvania Junior. Someone beat him in the first round," recalled Drum. "He cleaned up
in the other tournaments around Pittsburgh, then he won the
Pennsylvania Open. There was no doubt in anyone's mind that
he was going to be a top player." Actually, doubts *were* ex-
pressed about his future. Doc Giffin, another *Press* sportswriter
("I was the second string golf writer behind Drum"), remembered that Tom Burks, who wrote for the rival *Pittsburgh Sun-
Telegraph*, pointedly advised Palmer father and son against
Arnie turning pro. "But Burks was much older than us, he'd
been around since golf was invented," said Drum. "And remember, the tour was nothing like it is today. It was a ragamuffin bunch . . . not that you would call Demaret, Snead, and
Hogan 'ragamuffin.' But you had guys like Ed Furgol, who

talked to himself. And Moe Norman. God, Moe Norman! It was not the tour as we now know it. There wasn't much money or glamour back then." When Palmer sought out his friend from the *Press*—"Drummer, what should I do? Should I turn pro?"—they were standing on the steps in front of the magnificent Oakmont Country Club clubhouse. "Hell, yes," Drum replied.

Palmer took the advice of Drum and his father. He turned pro in November 1954 but made a point of not borrowing too much money at the start. An initial stake was provided by Wilson Sporting Goods. Arnie agreed to play Wilson clubs and balls; Wilson gave him four thousand dollars for the endorsement, a record amount for a new professional. Palmer also borrowed modest amounts from Wehnes, Preisler, and Brooks, and later, from his father and father-in-law. But the minimalist strategy almost backfired.

By the time he arrived at his first professional tournament, the McNaughton Pro-Am in Florida, Palmer was "really broke," he recalls. "The tournament started December 29, nine days after I got married, and I couldn't even take Winnie with me. I won $760, then flew to Panama to play in the Panama Open and finished tied for second with Roberto DeVicenzo. Tony Cerda beat us and I won fifteen hundred dollars. Now, in two weeks I've made $2,260. It was a lot of cash in those days. So I called Winnie and told her to meet me in Miami. Her mother drove down with her in my car [a '52 Ford], we sent her home on a plane, and Winnie and I drove to Brawley, California to play in a tournament."

Some of the pros, Palmer noticed, were towing trailers from town to town. He thought this was a dandy way to save expenses and bought his own home on wheels. He and another trailering pro, Dick Mayer, formed their own caravan. They'd help each other with mechanical problems, finding trailer parks, and setting up and taking down camps. Winnie cooked. Wehnes saw Palmer in Chicago and told him his lifestyle was holding him back. Too much togetherness, Wehnes said. "I don't take *my* wife to the office. You should send Winnie home."

Winnie went home. Two weeks later, with four spectacular rounds of 64, 67, 64, and 70, Palmer won his first tournament, the 1955 Canadian Open. With the twenty-four-hundred-dollar first-place check, he bought a new, bigger trailer.

His only anxious moment in the Canadian came in the final round. Palmer had a big lead and was playing with Tommy Bolt, who, like the guys in Cleveland, had "adopted" young Arnold. Palmer drove his ball into the woods late in the round. "Chip it out," whispered Bolt. Palmer pretended not to hear. "I was trying to move away from Tommy," he recalls. "Getting advice from anyone but your caddie is a two-stroke penalty and here is Tommy telling me how to play and all I can think of is how he is going to cost me the tournament." Bolt persisted. Just chip it out, dammit, don't do nothin' fancy, he said, louder this time. Then, Palmer remembers, "for a second I see that Tommy has his back turned [so] I grab an iron and real quick I hit the ball through the trees right at the green. I got there, too."

Palmer was off to the races. He won twice in 1956, four times in 1957, and three tournaments in both 1958 and 1959. After taking the 1958 Masters at Augusta National Golf Club, his first "major" win as a pro, Arnie was asked by one of the members of the club to stay in Augusta an extra day to play a round for fun. That member was The First Golfer, President Dwight Eisenhower, who, like everyone, liked the hell out of Arnie. Thus, by the late fifties, Palmer's position as a national figure was secure, his recognition growing.

Palmer's financial future looked rosy, too, as a result of a meeting he and his pal Finsterwald had in November 1958 with a bright, personable lawyer from Cleveland. Mark McCormack, an attorney with Arter, Hadden, Wykoff and Van Duzer, was thinking of forming a company to "represent" some of the top American golf pros, which then meant booking them for exhibitions at the best possible price. "Few of the pros had a representative of any kind. . . ." McCormack recalled. "Taylor [his partner, Dick] and I were confident that golf was going to get bigger and bigger and that the pros needed a representative."

They met at the Heart of Atlanta Motel. The meeting was friendly and McCormack and Taylor obviously knew their stuff, so Palmer and Finsterwald agreed to be represented for exhibitions by National Sports Management. McCormack got Arnold $350 to $500 per exhibition in 1959. Everyone was happy. Things went so well, in fact, that at the end of the year, Palmer asked his exhibition booker to expand his role, to represent him exclusively in all business matters, for he had no taste for business and no particular aptitude for evaluating the deals he was being offered with increasing frequency. McCormack obviously did. The decision was not clear-cut, McCormack says, because he also represented Art Wall, Bill Casper, and Finsterwald; "at that moment, they were all as big as Arnold." You picture a shaft of sunlight coming down from heaven, and the lawyer's hesitation ends. "I shook hands with Arnold Palmer. 'It's a deal,' I said. The handshake is the only contract we have ever had, or ever needed. It has bound us since."

Everything was in place for Palmer as 1959 became 1960. He had sold the trailer and was sleeping in hotel rooms when he traveled, he'd paid cash for a house overlooking the front nine of the Latrobe Country Club, he had no particular business worries, his wife loved him, and his golf game was in excellent shape. But something gnawed at him. Winning. He wanted to win more often. He absolutely craved the affirmation, the congratulations, and the intoxicating feelings of overcoming himself, the course, and the competition that come only with winning, never with merely playing well. But he was not the best in the game; perhaps there was no "best" then. Palmer had a disturbing tendency to finish weakly in the most important events. For instance, he missed a two-foot putt on the seventeenth green and bogeyed two of the final three holes in his Masters win. Next year, 1959, same tournament, he shot a last-round 74—including a triple-bogey six on the twelfth— to lose by two to Art Wall. "In the fifties, all I thought about Arnold Palmer was that he dressed sloppily and had an ugly swing," recalls Dan Jenkins. "I thought Ken Venturi was the next great player. Arnold didn't become Arnold until 1960."

Now, in the Southern California desert, Palmer blasted a final round 65 to win the tour's first-ever five-round tournament. "That round was the beginning," he commented a year later. "It put me in orbit. It became the source, I think, that fed me through the rest of the year."

▼

CHAPTER THREE

Jack
William

He had blue eyes, a big butt, and huge thighs. His hair was short, slicked back, and blond, which made it appear that he had no hair at all. He stood a scant five feet ten, weighed about 210, and usually wore pressed slacks, a pullover sweater, and fashionably scuffed black-on-white or brown-on-white saddle shoes. The son of a pharmacist, he was a junior prepharmacy major at his father's alma mater, Ohio State University in Columbus, Ohio. He hadn't missed an Ohio State football home game since he was six years old. He got B's. He drank Blatz beer. He was a local kid, a "townie"; his parents lived ten minutes from the campus, in a pleasant, upper-middle-class suburb called Upper Arlington. The guys at the Phi Gamma Delta fraternity house nicknamed him, uncharitably, "Blob-o." His girlfriend, Barbara Bash, sometimes called him Fat Boy.

There was brawn beneath the blubber, however. He was a fierce, usually successful, and surprisingly graceful competitor in every intramural and intrafraternity sport that came along—

basketball, football, volleyball, fast pitch softball, tennis, and handball, not to mention fishing and water skiing—but he played no varsity sports at OSU. Jack Nicklaus appeared to be an unremarkable student.

But Jack/Blob-o/Fat Boy was not your usual undergraduate. For one thing, he was the most self-assured, most mature nineteen-almost-twenty-year-old on campus. For another, he was already well-known, if not famous. When he announced that he planned to marry Miss Bash that summer, *Golf World* ran a story on his plans for the year under the headline JACKIE NICKLAUS PLANS TO WED: "He said he will play in the Orange Brook four-ball with Deane Beman as his partner, the Masters, the Open, the intercollegiate and the amateur. 'I'm going to be married in July and I'll have to take some time from golf for a honeymoon,' he added." The managing editor of the *Columbus Dispatch* once called his sports editor, Paul Hornung (no relation to the football player of the same name), into his office. "Don't you think you're building this kid Nicklaus up too much?" he asked. "Maybe I am," Hornung replied, then returned to his desk to write another story about Columbus's own *wunderkind*. On January 26, 1960, five days after his twentieth birthday, "Jackie" flew to New York to be one of the guests of honor at the National Golf Awards Dinner. Richard Nixon would be there; so would the man young Jack idolized, Bobby Jones.

Jack William Nicklaus may not have looked like much in January 1960, but he was anything but typical.

He had won the Ohio Open at age sixteen. Shot 64 in the third round. He was eighteen when he played his first professional tour event, the 1958 Rubber City Open at Firestone Country Club in Akron, Ohio. After two rounds, he was one shot out of the lead. Shot 67-66-76-68. Finished twelfth. He was nineteen and a college sophomore when he won the United States Amateur in 1959. Jack Nicklaus was the best amateur golfer since his hero, Jones.

"The thing wasn't given to him. He worked hard at it," says Ivor Young, a Nicklaus friend since high school days. "He'd be at the course at 7:30, play eighteen, have lunch, play another eighteen. I remember walking out of the grill room at night and seeing Jack hitting balls out on the practice range. He'd pulled his father's car up and had its lights on."

You sit around Scioto Country Club, where Nicklaus played as a kid, or Muirfield Village Golf Club, or a restaurant by the Ohio State campus, and chat with the friends of his youth. Young, now a lawyer and land developer. Bob Hoag, retired from the insurance business. Pandel Savic, the All Big Ten quarterback and hero of the 1950 Rose Bowl for Ohio State. Putnam Pierman, the owner of a heavy construction business. Hornung, retired after twenty-three years in the newspaper business. Nicklaus was only ten or eleven years old when he met these men, but they've stayed close friends through the years. Suddenly you realize they're all older than Jack, significantly older: Pierman by four years, Young by seven, Hoag by ten, Savic and Hornung by twenty. Why? Nicklaus must have been precocious as both a person and as a golfer.

"But he was a normal kid," Young is saying, "other than his immense talent and his physical and mental maturity. He liked to date girls, play other sports besides golf. He could have been the first-string quarterback on our [high school] football team, if he wanted to."

Like Young, Bob Hoag has Upper Arlington High School, Ohio State University, and Scioto Country Club in common with Nicklaus. He enters the red brick Scioto clubhouse to a chorus of "Hi, Bob" and "Morning, Mr. Hoag." Handshakes and smiles all around. Hoag is vivid: sun-reddened face, gray hair, and dark blue windbreaker, all wrapped in a swirl of cigarette smoke. He recalls his first encounter with Nicklaus: "I was on the sixteenth fairway here. I'd won the club championship four times and could hit it a long way. So I hit my second shot—and then a ball rolls right between my legs. 'Who the hell hit *that*?' I say. 'Oh, that's little Jackie Nicklaus,' someone says. He was ten or eleven then. . . . He had his full growth when he was twelve or thirteen.

"Dow Finsterwald was a good friend of mine and I played with him and Arnold Palmer when Arnold was in Cleveland. I came back to Columbus and told the writers around here that Jack, who was sixteen, was as good as them *then*."

The strength of his game was strength. "Basically, I just hit the ball as far as possible off the tee, found it, hit it on the green, then hit it into the hole," Nicklaus says. "I was usually close enough to the green and/or strong enough to just bulldoze the ball out of anything I found myself in, short of a young forest." When Nicklaus at nineteen swung a driver, one was reminded of the line from "Casey at the Bat": "And now the air is shattered by the force of Casey's blow . . ." Of course, it wasn't that simple; distance without accuracy is almost worthless in golf. But wonder of wonders, young Jack also hit the ball *straight*. His power was unusual, but his coordination to use it was extraordinary.

Why was Nicklaus so good so young? Hoag believes it was a lucky combination of physical ability and an unusually dogged perfectionism. "Jack is the most tenacious perfectionist I've ever seen," he says. "As you know, he liked to hit the ball left to right. If he hit a ball right to left, he'd have a fit. Even on the practice tee, he'd have a fit." Perfectionism in golf is a dangerous thing; disappointment is built into a quest for the perfect golf swing. But Nicklaus could come close, because of what Young calls his "freaky" ability to focus on any task. Hoag illustrates: "I'm sitting with Jack in his home and his kids are raising hell, there's absolute bedlam around him. But he can't see or hear anything but the TV show he's concentrating on."

Putnam Pierman has another explanation for Jack's premature success—his competitiveness. "I didn't care for him at first," Pierman says. "He was a goddamn hot dog basketball player who shot all the time. But pretty soon I replaced that feeling with the recognition that he was the most intensely compet-

itive individual I ever met. In anything. Ping-Pong. Kicking a
football. I swear to God, when I had four children, he decided
to have five." Pierman, it turned out, was the same way; losing
at anything was abhorrent. As his relationship with Nicklaus
deepened, he quit golf. He couldn't bear losing to his young
friend. Pierman and Nicklaus had so much in common that for
a time they were inseparable, but later, like two magnets with
the same polarity, they repelled.

Hoag cautions you against digging too deep for the source
of his friend's mental strength. He didn't get it from his mother
Helen or his father Charlie, "it was from Jack himself. He was
his own man. The game itself, the challenge of the game and
Jack's perfectionism, that's what motivated him." But what
about those earliest days, inquiring minds want to know, what
made this child of privilege (relative to Hogan and Palmer) want
to work so hard at golf? Hoag considers. Perhaps there are a few
other things: the acclaim he received from his early successes at
golf may have kept him interested. "Plus this place. And Jack
Grout."

Not-so-little Jackie was ten when he started to hang out at
"this place," Scioto Country Club. His father had joined the
lush, private club two years before, and began playing golf for
the first time in thirteen years, since his senior year at Ohio
State. But he could hardly play because his right ankle hurt so
much. "The Famous Ankle Injury," Charlie Nicklaus would call
it years later. How did your son get started in golf? reporters
would ask. Nicklaus Senior would roll his eyes and recite the
story for the hundredth or thousandth time. He had chipped
his heel bone—the calcaneus, one of the seven bones that form
the ankle—in a volleyball game in 1944. The injury was undiag-
nosed for five years. It got worse; Charlie Nicklaus's ankles had
to support a lot of weight. In 1949 he had an operation to fuse
the ankle. His surgeon recommended that Charlie walk on soft
ground as much as possible when the cast came off. Sounds like
golf to me, he thought. "In the spring of 1950, after the operation, Dad discovered that he could play only a hole or two before

he had to sit down and rest the ankle," wrote Nicklaus in 1963 in *The Greatest Game of All.* "Since this ruled out his usual games with his friends at the club—golf carts were not in use yet—the thought occurred to him to have his ten-year-old son come along as his golfing companion. He got me a set of cut-down Hillerich and Bradsbys, and we started hacking around together. We would play a hole or two, and then while he took a breather, I'd practice chipping or putting or hitting sand shots."

The Nicklauses lived in a large Tudor-style house at 2480 Collingswood Street, a mile or so from Scioto's front entrance. But it was only a quarter mile or less from his front door to the fourth tee, as Jack discovered, if you took a short cut through a few backyards.

Scioto (pronounced *SI-oh-ta*) had other advantages for Jack besides proximity. The course itself was outstanding, one of the best in the state. It was designed in 1915 by the legendary Donald J. Ross of Scotland, and was opened for play the following year. Ross is to golf architecture what Stradivarius is to violins. His courses feature small, elevated greens and subtle contours; his masterpieces are Pinehurst #2, Oakland Hills, and Seminole. Scioto was a wonderful place to learn to play for another reason: it was historic. The 1926 United States Open had been held at Scioto; Bobby Jones, the gentleman golfer from Atlanta, won. Fifteen year-old Charlie Nicklaus idolized Jones and followed him all four rounds of the tournament. Charlie Nicklaus was hardly alone as a spectator or admirer, however. Robert Tyre Jones was an appealing, humble man with degrees in mechanical engineering, English literature, and law, an eloquent speaker, and a lucid writer, who also happened to be a golf champion. In 1930, after he won the then four major championships of golf—the Grand Slam—there was a ticker-tape parade for him in New York City. He was a national hero and an impeccable sportsman, the Amateur Who Could Beat the Pros. He retired from competition soon after winning the Slam, to practice law, build a golf course, and organize a tournament. He was twenty-eight.

Jones's influence on Charlie Nicklaus was profound. *If I ever have a son,* he must have thought. "Dad knew Jones's boyhood record by heart," Jack recalled, "and on some of those occasions when he thought I was a bit too complacent about my golf, he would reel off the things Jones had done: at thirteen, he had won the invitational tournament at Roebuck Springs, in Birmingham, plus won the club championships at East Lake and Druid Hills, in Atlanta. . . ." When he played with his father at Scioto, Charlie Nicklaus would say to his son, "Nice drive, Jack. But did you know Jones hit it way up *there* in the Open? And *his* clubs had wooden shafts."

In 1950, the year Jackie took up golf, the PGA Championship, another of golf's major tournaments, was held at Scioto. And there was Charlie Nicklaus's kid, absorbing everything, watching how the pros played and practiced, how they handled themselves. One day he stood expectantly outside the locker room, clutching an autograph book. CONTESTANTS ONLY said a sign on the door. On a whim, one of the players, Skip Alexander, led the awestruck boy inside and got him all the signatures he wanted. All that Jack remembered later was that Sam Snead seemed mad about his play that day and that Lloyd Mangrum, playing a game of chance, held his cards in one hand and a drink in the other, while a smoking cigarette dangled from his lips—"the complete riverboat gambler come to life." Chandler Harper won the championship, defeating Henry Williams, Jr., in the final. The host professional for the tournament was Scioto's new head pro, Jack Grout.

Grout was forty in 1950, wore rimless glasses, and, usually, a necktie. He had gotten his start as a golf instructor twenty years earlier from his older brother Dick, who was the professional at the Glen Garden Club in Fort Worth. Grout played frequently in those days with two nineteen-year-old former Glen Garden caddies who were allowed to play the course, Byron

Nelson and Ben Hogan. He was an above-average player, but when he couldn't keep up with these mere caddies, he decided his future was as a teacher of the golf swing. During his seven years in Texas, he often took educational trips to River Oaks Country Club in Houston to take lessons from and discuss swing theory with Jack Burke, Sr., the pro's pro.

"When these rich oil men wanted to hire my father [to be the first River Oaks pro in 1925], they asked him, 'What system do you teach?'" says his son, Jack Burke, Jr., the 1956 Masters and PGA champion. "'My only system is no system,' he said. 'Only a lazy person has a system.'

"Everybody took lessons from my father. Zaharias. Henry Picard [winner of the 1938 Masters and the 1939 PGA]. Demaret [a three-time Masters champion]. Grout. Me. . . ." Grout noticed that Burke had a unique method of teaching students how to release the hands as they hit the ball, the basic fundamental of hitting with power. He'd have his pupil take the club back, begin the downswing . . . then literally throw the club, hard, out onto the practice range. Jack, Jr., would run out and pick the clubs up.

Thus Burke begat Grout who begat Jack. Charlie's boy attended the new pro's Friday-morning group clinic for junior golfers and took private lessons every two or three weeks. Sometimes Grout's lack of dogma frustrated the analytical Nicklaus. "Should my left wrist be here or here when I'm trying to hit it low?" he would ask. Grout wouldn't answer. He had only three precepts. The first maxim—"keep your head still"— Jack learned for life at age eleven. Grout had his assistant, Larry Glosser, stand in front of his star pupil on the lesson tee and grab hold of his hair. Ok, Jack, swing, Grout would say. "Many times the pain this caused sent tears running down my face," recalled Nicklaus. "[But] this was the only way he could get me to stop bobbing my head, and in time I learned to hold it still no matter how hard I swung at the ball."

The second fundamental had to do with balance. To promote proper footwork, Grout insisted that his young students swing with both heels flat on the ground. "I must have played three or four years before Grout permitted me to raise my heels at all during the swing," Nicklaus remembered. Ironically, in later years Jack developed the highest possible left heel lift at the top of his backswing.

A final Grout commandment was vital. "Right from the start," Nicklaus recalled, "he encouraged us to hit the ball as hard and as far as we could" with the biggest swing (or, in instructorese, "the fullest arc") possible. Conventional wisdom had it that new golfers should learn control first. But both Jack and Arnold Palmer got basically the same nontraditional advice when they learned to play: whack the hell out of the ball. Worry about finding it later.

Grout asked Jack years later to write the foreword to his instruction book, *Let Me Teach You Golf As I Taught Jack Nicklaus*. "Too many golfers are too full of technical trivia ever to be able to make a decent pass at the ball," wrote Nicklaus, "and I think sometimes the fault lies in the sheer volume of needless information they pick up from overly detailed instruction. . . . One of the greatest favors Grout did was *not* answer many of the nitpicky questions I bombarded him with. . . ."

It all came together quickly for Nicklaus. With his first full-length clubs—a used set of Bobby Jones model woods and irons, with light-brown mock-wooden steel shafts, a gift from his father—he shot 81 at age eleven and 74 when he was twelve. As a five-foot ten-inch, 165-pound thirteen-year-old, he shot 69 at Scioto, his first sub-70 round. "I remember that afternoon as clearly as if it were yesterday," he recalled. "I was working at the drugstore that summer, and my dad and I went out to the club around four, as we often did. Par at Scioto was 36–36–72. I was out in 34." Nice nine, Jack, said Charlie. Let's go home and have dinner. " 'Dad, we can't do that,' I told him. 'I've got a chance to break 70.' " Charlie decided over Jack's objections that they would eat first, play later. They raced through dinner and raced back to the club for the second nine; Jack eagled the eighteenth hole in semidarkness for his 69—"the promised land."

Hornung recently looked up a number of Jack's high school and college pals for a story he wrote for a tournament program. In the article "The Columbus Years," Hornung quotes one of Jack's high school friends, Ron McHam, at length. "When I started messing around with him," says Ron McHam, "he was just a good, fun guy. I didn't even know he played golf. When he was a freshman and I was a freshman, he was dating the senior captain of the cheerleaders and that impressed me right there.

"Without question, Jack was the leader of the male side of our class. He didn't play football in high school and that was the reason three or four other guys didn't. If Nicklaus didn't do it, it wasn't good. He was a good student, with that amazing mind of his."

Another McHam recollection is one Nicklaus would just as soon forget. "Jack had just won the Ohio Open, the youngest ever to win it," he says. "Six or seven of us went to a Columbus Jets [minor league baseball] game. You had to be eighteen to buy beer, so we sent him because he was the only one who could have gotten it done. He was only sixteen, but he always looked older. . . . When he came down the aisle carrying two beers, we all stood up and said, 'There's Jack Nicklaus, the youngest Ohio Open champion in history at sixteen years of age.' We thought it was pretty funny. He didn't."

In 1955 Charlie and Jack met Bobby Jones. Jack was the youngest qualifier in the country for the United States Amateur, which was held at the James River course at the Country Club of Virginia, in Richmond. Jones accepted the USGA's invitation to attend the tournament and speak at the Players' Dinner, for the 1955 championship marked the twenty-fifth anniversary of his winning the 1930 Amateur at Merion, the last leg of his Grand Slam. On the day of the final practice round, Jones sat in a cart behind the eighteenth green and watched a few groups play into the 460-yard par-four hole. No one could hit the green in two. Finally, a stocky blond kid with a crew cut bombed his wood second shot onto the putting surface. *Who is that young man*, Jones wanted to know. *That's Jackie Nicklaus, from Colum-bus, Ohio*, a newspaperman told him. *He's only fifteen.* Jones asked to meet the boy. "My father and I went over together," Nicklaus remembered. "This session with Jones was a tremen-dous thrill for me, but I am sure it meant twice as much to my dad. Our chat lasted about twenty minutes—a good deal of it was about Scioto, naturally—and then Jones turned to me and said, 'Young man, I've heard that you're a very fine golfer. I'm coming out to watch you play a few holes tomorrow.'" Unfortu-nately, on the three holes that Jones watched the next day, Jack went bogey, double bogey, bogey; he lost his match to Bob Gardner, one up.

Despite all this—qualifying for the Amateur, meeting Jones, and winning tournaments, including, spectacularly, the Ohio Open when he was sixteen—Nicklaus did not consider himself to be just a golfer. In junior high school, he had been a football player (he was the quarterback and practiced diligently in his back yard to be a placekicker, "like Lou Groza of the Cleveland Browns"), baseball player (catcher) and track man (some years before he developed twenty-seven-inch thighs, he ran the hundred-yard dash in eleven seconds flat). He had to give up all these sports when he entered high school, though he was more than adequate in all three, because they interfered with the fall and spring golf schedules. But he did not give up his fa-vorite sport—basketball. He was good, too. He played guard and forward for the Upper Arlington Golden Bears and aver-aged eighteen points his senior year on a team that went seven-teen and four. He made All-Central Buckeye League his last two seasons and honorable mention all-state his senior year. He was an excellent free-throw shooter; he made twenty-six in a row at one point. Jack even expected to play basketball in college. But Ohio State had players named Bobby Knight, Larry Siegfried, Jerry Lucas, and John Havlicek, who would win the NCAA bas-ketball championship in 1960. The Buckeyes didn't seem to need a short, slow forward who weighed 190—and rising.

That Nicklaus would attend Ohio State—despite the fact

that his services as a basketball player would not be required—
was a foregone conclusion. "I had known since I was six," he
wrote. "As far as I was concerned, there was no other college."
Offers of financial aid from other institutions of higher learning
were declined; Jack would attend OSU without a scholarship
(he did, however, have a thousand-dollar grant from the Jay-
cees, as their national junior golf champion of 1957). Money, obviously, was not a big concern for the Nicklaus family. Charlie
had bought a drugstore on High Street, directly across from the
Ohio State campus, in 1942. Business was good. By 1960 he
owned four pharmacies in the Columbus area.

You try to picture seventeen-year-old Jack Nicklaus in September 1957, in his first week as a college student. The background music for this scene is "Carmen Ohio," the school song,
as performed by the Ohio State Marching Band (a very senti-
mental composition, it sounds a little bit like "My Old Kentucky
Home"; it is always performed at half-time of Ohio State football games). Perhaps Jack is wearing his Upper Arlington letter
sweater (a white pullover, size forty two, with a large gold "A"
on the front) to match his scuffed white bucks. The cars driving
by on nearby High Street have huge tail fins. The professors
walking among the hundreds of milling students wear narrow
ties. The weather has already cooled a bit from the summer's
heat; the wind blows through the huge elms and oaks, and a
few dry leaves, yellow and dusky red, skip over the green grass
and sidewalks. Greek letters might well be on Jack's mind as he
walks along. Beta Theta Pi, Sigma Chi, Phi Gamma Delta?
Which fraternity should he choose and which would choose
him? "It was crucial to make a fraternity," he recalled, "for the
undergraduate who didn't had no social life at all." Jack pauses
to chat with his girlfriend, a classmate at Upper Arlington who
is also a freshman at Ohio State. As they stand outside Men-
denhall Lab, a tall, slender, blue-eyed blonde who is passing by
recognizes Jack's girl and calls out to her. They reacquaint. *I'd
like you to meet Jack Nicklaus,* Jack's girl says. *Jack, this is Barbara
Bash.* The music swells . . . and cut.

It really happened that way. "She introduced us, then had to run off to class," remembers Barbara Bash Nicklaus. "I was working in the bacteriology department after classes to pay my way through college, so Jack walked me down to the bacteriology building. Then later that night he called me up and asked me for a date. We dated for three years and were married between our junior and senior years." Jack's version of the early stages of the Nicklaus/Bash Romance is a little more involved. A few weeks after meeting Barbara, Jack "called Barb and asked her to fix me up with someone attractive in her sorority. She fixed me up with someone who drank too much and got sick. I called Barb back one, to tell her off and two, to ask for a date. Playing it cool, I named a night three weeks away. She thought this was ridiculous, but she went out with me. We got along okay, so I asked her for a date the next night, which she agreed to, and then we began dating regularly."

Jack chose Barbara, then chose Phi Gamma Delta, "because I liked the kind of fellows they had . . . big guys and good athletes." He lived at home his freshman year (and passed Math 401, an algebra-trigonometry course, with tutoring from Barbara's father, Stanley Bash, a mathematics teacher at South High School), then, as a sophomore, learned the Phi Gam's secret handshake and moved into the fraternity house. Life in the frat house went like this: "On Monday nights we had our fraternity meeting, and every Saturday we had a party. Of course, during the football season everyone had lunch at the house with his date before going to the game—that was making the scene." The rest of the time, the Phi Gams played cards.

Was Jack a Big Man On Campus? Moreover, did he act it? "No," Bob Hoag says flatly. "He handled that real well. He was not *in the least* overwhelmed with himself. It's not in his makeup. He's too goddamned focused for that." Yet you do hear stories from his contemporaries about Jack losing a junior or a college match and allowing his displeasure to show. He acted, they say, like a spoiled rich kid. There is probably some truth in that, but he grew out of it. As Dan Jenkins says, "Jack is the most gracious loser in golf." Hornung concedes the point. "I think there was some natural resentment of Jack," he says. "We [Hornung and Kaye Kessler, the golf writer for the rival *Columbus Citizen-Journal*] made him a big thing around here. Sure, some people thought he was cocky. . . . He's so bright, he can be intimidating. I call to tell him something about Ohio State football and he disarms me, he already seems to know it, I don't know how. You've got to keep your wits about you with Jack to keep from looking foolish."

Nicklaus did not play golf for OSU his first year, since freshmen weren't eligible to compete in varsity sports. And he didn't play his sophomore season, either. In fact, he quit school in mid-May and flew to Scotland. He'd been named to play in the all-star game of amateur golf, the Walker Cup. "I felt like I had finally accomplished something," Jack said. Finally. He was nineteen. Deane Beman, a five-foot seven-inch University of Maryland student, whom the other players called "BB Eyes," also made the team. He would become one of Jack's closest friends. The captain of the squad, Charlie Coe, thirty-five, an oil man from Oklahoma, would be Jack's opponent in the finals of the United States Amateur several months later. The American side beat the British at Muirfield without incident, as they had every year since 1938, and Jack played superbly.

Upon returning to Columbus, Jack and Barbara were "pinned." That is, Jack gave Barbara his Phi Gamma Delta pin, which she was to wear at all times. Pinning, in fraternity/sorority ritual, means "We're not engaged, but almost. Keep your hands off." As tradition demanded, the brothers of Phi Gamma Delta marched en masse to Barbara's sorority house and serenaded her to celebrate the pinning. History does not record what songs were sung.

The thirty-six-hole U.S. Amateur final that summer at the Broadmoor in Colorado Springs between Coe, the wily veteran, and Nicklaus, the just-sort-of-engaged kid from Columbus, was exhausting and dramatic. Coe, wearing his lucky red University of Oklahoma baseball cap, won the first two holes with birdies and stayed at least one hole ahead for thirty holes. They went to the last hole even. Coe overclubbed his second shot to the par four, chipped back . . . and *almost* holed the shot. "Charley and I sort of smiled at each other," Jack recalls. Then, from eight feet below the cup, Nicklaus drained his putt. He was the youngest Amateur champion since 1910. A star was born.

Or was it? Nicklaus certainly was the best amateur of his day, but he dearly wanted to be the best *player*, as Jones had been. Could he do it? No one knew, of course. "I first played with Jack at the 1959 Open at Winged Foot," says Gene Littler, perhaps the best player in the game that year. He was impressed. "He was Fat Jack then. Geez, he hit the ball *so far*." Littler, a laconic man, looks off in the distance, a half smile on his face, and shakes his head. Dan Jenkins is less equivocal. "Nicklaus was awesome as an amateur, obviously the next great player. Golfers had been 'long' before Jack, but not as *straight* and long, and not even as long. His length, particularly with the long and mid irons . . . changed golf architecture. He was mature, even as a young man, and always a fascinating interview."

Was Jack at twenty as good as Bob Hoag and Jenkins thought he was? He would have two opportunities in 1960 to find out, to prove himself against the best in the world, at the Masters in April and in the U.S. Open in June. So in January, he began to prepare himself. In the shelter of a crude half of a quonset hut, Nicklaus hit balls on the practice range at Scioto, often with Grout watching. "When the snow wasn't too deep, I'd clear a patch of grass to hit from," he says. "When it was, I'd trample it down . . . when the snow was too deep to find [the balls], I'd leave them there until a thaw."

Occasionally, Jack acted his age. At the big National Golf Awards dinner at the Plaza Hotel, he was introduced to Vice President Nixon. Then, in his two-octaves-higher-than-you'd-expect voice, he chirped across the room to his father. "Hey, Dad, come here. I want you to meet Dick Nixon."

CHAPTER FOUR

▼

Ahno
Pomma

Q. Who won the Oklahoma City Open in 1960?

A. Gene Littler. He holed a twenty-foot birdie putt on the final hole to beat Art Wall by one shot and win the first prize of forty-three hundred dollars.

"I did?" asks Littler. He peers at a newspaper clipping. "Oh, yeah." Too bad you're not writing about 1959, he says, I remember that year better (Littler won five times in 1959). Other top players of the day are similarly vague about tournaments they won thirtysomething years ago. Dow Finsterwald, you won the first event on the the tour in 1960, the Los Angeles Open. What sticks in your mind about that week? The check for fifty-five hundred dollars? Finsterwald looks dubious. He examines a report of his three-shot victory over Bill Collins, Jay Hebert, and Dave Ragan. "Hmmm," he says. "Hmmm." Finster forgets. It's not that he is uncooperative or a bad historian; he can give you chapter and verse about the 1960 Masters or U.S. Open. It's just that, then as now, the "majors" mattered more. Even to most of the winners, the pro golf tour from January until the Masters in April was mere prologue.

But right over here are two gentlemen who can tell you all you want to know about *their* L.A. Open, and they took away exactly nothing in prize money. Allen Geiberger and Butch Baird remember L.A. the way other people recall their first date, first car, or first job; it was their first tournament on the pro tour. Geiberger was a tall, skinny twenty-two-year-old USC graduate from Santa Barbara with a unique golf technique. He stood so close to the ball when he swung that it looked like he might clip one of his extra-large feet instead of the ball. His walk was even more distinctive—short-strided and knock-kneed. He played in the pro-am preceding the tournament but felt strangely queasy. Was it stage fright? No: an infectious disease. Geiberger was one of several players who were affected by, as *Golf World* put it, "an epidemic of a mysterious flu which crippled industry, schools and courts in Los Angeles County." He withdrew without hitting a shot.

As a local player of some renown, Geiberger had been invited to play in the tournament; Baird had to qualify. (His father, a pathologist, had presided over the autopsy of Babe Didrikson Zaharias and had told his son that "she had the shoulder muscles of a man.") Butch had been working at the Galveston municipal golf course for the four months since he'd graduated from Lamar University in Beaumont. When he wasn't practicing, he fiddled and fidgeted behind the pro shop counter, hitting imaginary shots with invisible clubs while he waited on customers. The day after New Year's, Baird drove to Los Angeles. Two days later he teed it up on a Monday morning at South Hills Country Club in West Covina, one of the two courses used for qualifying. He looked around—and "saw a hundred individuals who could hit the ball as well or better than me." There were 396 aspirants—vacationing club pros from snowed-in golf courses in the north, golf bums, some down-on-their luck tour veterans, lots of local talent, and a few handfuls of rookies, like Baird—and only sixty-four spots available. The pros called this weekly qualifying contest, simply, "Mondays." Playing Mondays was torture. You could be low qualifier—as Baird was at Los Angeles, with 68—and still make no money that week—as Baird did not. He shot 75, 72, 76 in the tournament proper and missed the fifty-four-hole cut. Mason Rudolph, a Tennessean with a hilariously loopy swing, and Bill Parker, a club pro from New Jersey who wore glasses with thick, green lenses and an even thicker layer of fragrant hair oil, shared last-place money with seven others. They split two hundred dollars nine ways. Twenty-two dollars twenty-three cents each.

The next week, at Yorba Linda, thirty-five miles southeast of Los Angeles, Baird failed to qualify on Monday. Geiberger was still too sick to play. Jerry Barber won. Barber was an unlikely looking professional athlete: forty-three, bald as an egg, five feet five, about 140 pounds, not particularly strong. But he was feisty and unusually competitive, like a lot of small men, and the way he could putt made you believe in a Higher Power. Surely no one could putt like Barber without divine intervention.

Barber led Billy Maxwell by one shot with one hole to play. He stood on the green of the final hole, having played three shots to the putting surface of the par-five, the last from over a hundred yards. Julius ("Moose") Boros, the third member of the final group, watched with Barber as Maxwell played his third shot from fifty yards. "Congratulations, Jerry, you've got it won," the big man murmured to the little man. Barber would have none of it. "I said to Boros, I said, 'unless he chips it in.' And then he did. I predicted it. I thought it was going to be about three feet short, but it went in." The gallery had barely stopped reacting to Maxwell's brilliant stroke when Barber stepped up to putt from thirteen feet for the win. His putter, the same club he uses now, had a beat-up brass head, electrician's tape on the toe, and an almost perfectly upright lie, like a push broom. He gave it a wristy stroke and, of course, made it.

"I have a system," the world's greatest putter says. "I line it up and then I hit it hard enough to go in the hole. What else is there?"

The tour left the citrus district the next week for the cold and damp of Monterey Bay. The Bing Crosby National Pro-Am Championship—or, as everyone called it, The Crosby—was the most noticeable event on the winter tour, partly because of all the celebrities who played in it, partly because of the beauty of the three courses it was played on (Cypress Point, Monterey Peninsula, and Pebble Beach), and mostly because it was on television. This would be the third sucessive telecast, a record for a tournament that was not the Masters, U.S. Open, or PGA. The weather was almost invariably lousy, another perversely appealing aspect of the show; there is no particular drama in bright, sunny weather. Tournament host Crosby would interview the stars of stage, screen, and television on camera after they finished their long walk in the rain and wind. "I've never been so wet in my life," ex-swimming champion Johnny Weismuller told his host after his round. *And Lawrence Welk, how did you find the golf course today,* crooned Crosby. "Cheese, id wass horrble oud dere, Bing-a," the Champagne Music Maker replied cheerfully.

Geiberger made his debut in the Crosby and won a hundred dollars. Baird failed to qualify on Monday. Ken Venturi won, in, he said, "the worst weather I've seen in ten years of playing this layout. I thought the day would never end." He led by two shots after three rounds, and despite shooting 77 the final day, he increased his margin to three. Venturi was used to the course and the conditions. He grew up in San Francisco, an hour or two north of Monterey, and learned the game as a caddie. Like a lot of people who are attracted to golf, Venturi was something of a loner. He also had a bad stammer. His father, Fred, a ship chandler, sold net and twine to Northern California fishermen; when he made business trips south, he would bring Ken along and drop him off at Pebble Beach to make a buck carrying someone's clubs. As Venturi advanced as a junior and amateur golfer, the principal value of his growing reputation was that, he says, "I started to get the best bags to carry" at the Olympic Club and at San Francisco Golf Club, where he also caddied. Venturi met his muse in 1954. As a member of the 1953 Walker Cup team, he was invited to play in the Masters; he played a practice round with Ben Hogan. Soon he dressed like Hogan, practiced like Hogan, even played like Hogan. And, surprisingly, he became a member of an exclusive club: friend of Hogan.

"I played more rounds with Hogan than any other player," says Venturi with pride. "And I was the only one he'd practice with. He'd always hit behind me, never in front of me. One day I said to him 'you always stand behind me because you want to see what *I'm* doing. And you don't want me to see what *you're* doing.' He got a good laugh out of that." When Henry Picard, then the pro at Seminole, looked down from the clubhouse at Ben and Ken, he said he couldn't tell them apart until he could see the gray hair on the one and the black hair on the other.

Even more than Finsterwald and Littler, Venturi was preoccupied with winning a major championship, because he'd had two in his grasp and they'd slipped away like leaves in the wind. He was twenty-four and still an amateur in 1956 when he shocked the golf world by leading the Masters after three rounds. He was making his living then by selling Lincolns and Mercurys at a San Francisco car dealership owned by Eddie Lowery, a notable patron of amateur golf (Harvie Ward, the amateur star from North Carolina, was also an employee of Lowery Lincoln Mercury; he and Ken got to play plenty of golf). Lowery, who had caddied for Francis Ouimet when he won the 1913 U.S. Open, had also arranged for Venturi to take lessons from Byron Nelson. Venturi shot 66, 69, 75 at Augusta under windy conditions and led Cary Middlecoff, who stood second, by four shots. On the final day, the wind really howled. But Venturi committed a strategic gaffe, concentrating all his efforts at defeating Middlecoff. Meanwhile, Jackie Burke shot 71 and came from eight shots back to win. Venturi shot 80, with a 42 on the back nine, and lost by one. "I wasn't even watching for him [Burke]," he said after the round. "I was running away from Cary and it seems I ran into the door on the way out, doesn't it?"

He was a near-unanimous pick to win the Masters in 1958, but the second betting favorite, Palmer, led Ken by one with seven holes to play. They were paired together for the last round. Arnie hit over the green on the difficult par-three twelfth hole and his ball buried in the rain-softened ground. Palmer appealed for relief. Can't I lift it out of here? he asked. Arthur Lacey, the rules official on the scene, said no, the ball is only "half-embedded," you must play it. Besides, said Lacey, a member of the R and A (the British equivalent of the USGA), the ball actually appears to be in this sand bunker, and there is no embedded ball relief in a hazard. Palmer, furious, chopped at the ball and made five. Suddenly, Venturi led by one. Hold it, Arnie said, I'm going to play a second ball. He returned to the original spot, dropped a ball, chipped, putted, and made a par three. Which score would count? While Lacey went in search of a higher-up, Venturi and Palmer played the thirteenth hole, a par five. Arnie hit the green in two and was told unofficially before he putted that his three on twelve would count, not his five. "As if in celebration," wrote Mark McCormack in *The Wonderful World of Professional Golf,* "Palmer made his eagle putt." Venturi, unnerved by what he thought was an incorrect ruling, three-putted the next two holes. Palmer won, Venturi finished fourth.

"If they had had TV replay then, his score on twelve would have been five," says Venturi. "See, the rules say you're supposed to play a second ball *before* finishing the hole with the original ball. It has to do with the timing of your declaration. You can't play out and then say, 'I didn't like that score, I'm gonna play another ball.' What if your ball buries on the tee shot on a par-five? Do you play the hole, then walk back three hundred yards to play your second ball?

"I'm not bitter and I'm not saying I would have won . . .

[but] the 1958 Masters was a big deal because neither Arnold nor I had won a major yet."

There is another version of what happened on number twelve that day—the official version. Officially, Palmer told Lacey he intended to play two balls *before* he played his first ball into the hole (Palmer says he and Lacey worked out the two ball "compromise" before he played the first ball). "I have confidence that the committee went over the matter very carefully," says Masters and USGA rulesmeister Isaac ("Ike") Grainger, "and that Palmer's ball was not in the bunker, that it was embedded and that he proceeded in accordance with Rule 3–3." Grainger did not take part in that still-debated ruling, but he would help make another difficult—and crucial—rules decision at Augusta in 1960.

While Venturi obsessed about the Masters, now just weeks away, the rookies fought just to survive. At San Diego, Baird again failed to qualify on Monday. At Phoenix the following week, he came tantalizingly close to at least trying for a paycheck. He was the first alternate—that is, he would get to play if someone got sick or was injured—but no one did. "I had $185 to my *name*," recalls Baird, pushing back the wide brim of his trademark straw hat. A red-haired, fair-skinned man, he is allergic to direct sunlight, a unique affliction for a golf professional; he wears sunglasses and white cotton wraps on his arms when he plays. "I was about to quit," he continues, "but Charley Sifford says to me, 'You're out here to play golf, you're not out here to run home. You go play [the next tournament] at Tucson. It's on the way back to Texas, anyway.'" Baird went to Tucson and shot 71 on Monday, just good enough to qualify. His 72, 70 made the thirty-six-hole cut by three. "Next day, I shot 65. After thirteen holes on Sunday, someone mentioned to me that I was one shot out of the lead [held by Don January, the eventual winner]. I immediately bogeyed two holes. But I birdied eighteen." Baird tied for fifth and won $872.86. He gave his caddie, a local boy named Carlos, $60; daily caddie rates were $2.50. Carlos was thrilled. "He was rich and I was rich," says Baird, smiling at the memory. "That tournament catapulted me. I got to where I could say, 'Hey, I can play after all.' Up to then, I didn't really know."

Geiberger's breakthrough came in two parts. First, at San Diego, in front of family and friends, he shot a first-round 64, then held on to finish tied for fourth with Dave Marr and Billy Casper. He won eleven hundred dollars. Six weeks later, at Pensacola, he virtually repeated the performance: opening-round 64, fourth-place finish, one thousand dollars. "I'd been playing every week, which was stupid. The first lesson I learned was that you can only play three in a row," Geiberger says. "After Pensacola, I was on my way. I gave my sponsors back their money."

Geiberger played in the final group in the last round with Palmer. "I was awestruck," allows Al about Palmer's game. "I just thought, 'You can't do that in golf.'" Arnie played indifferently for eight holes, then entered a kind of golf Twilight Zone, a place where all putts go in the hole. On the ninth hole, twelve feet for birdie. He makes it. Tenth hole, fifteen feet. Birdie. Eleventh hole from twenty feet, for birdie. It's in again. Another birdie on fourteen. On the seventeenth tee he learned that he needed two more birdies to beat Doug Sanders by a shot. From seventeen feet on seventeen . . . yes. On eighteen, from thirty-two feet, of course, he holed it again. The Twilight Zone.

The Pensacola Open was the tenth tournament of the year and Arnie's fourth win. His first victory, at Palm Springs, had been upstaged by Joe Campbell's third-round hole-in-one, for which he was paid fifty thousand dollars. But Palmer had the spotlight to himself after he won three consecutive events, in late February to mid-March, at San Antonio, Baton Rouge, and Pensacola. MONOTONOUS headlined *Golf World* after his Baton Rouge win: "The PGA's winter tour, contrary to recent happenings, is not being played for the benefit of one Arnold Palmer, it only seems that way since he has won three events and gone to the bank with $22,211.86, an unprecedented amount for this early in a new year." Arnie played two more Florida tournaments—two fifth-place finishes—then left for Augusta, Georgia, a full week before the start of the Masters, the final event on the winter tour. He had decided to use a new putter at Augusta, and wanted time to break it in.

Palmer checked in at the tournament desk inside the big, white clubhouse at Augusta National and asked for and received registration number 13, because it was his thirteenth tournament of the year. While Arnie was obviously not superstitious about numbers, he did have two unvarying Masters rituals. He always broke in a new pair of golf shoes that week. And he always had the same caddie, Nathaniel ("Ironman") Avery. Said Ironman of his boss: "This man doesn't know what it is to play safe. It's let it go or blow it, all or nothing."

College buddies Jack Nicklaus of Ohio State and Deane Beman of Maryland met in Miami in March. Unlike most students on spring break, they eschewed the bars and the beach for the golf course, specifically the Orange Brook Country Club, where they were teammates in the International Four-Ball Championship. Both Nicklaus, the U.S. Amateur champion, and Beman, who had won the previous British Amateur, had received the most coveted piece of paper in amateur golf, an invitation to play in the Masters. This tournament would be their warm-up.

They were an odd couple, the large, powerful, ursine Nicklaus and the small, crafty, vulpine Beman. The Bear and the Fox. But they shot twenty-two under par for four rounds and won. They were ready.

Ben Hogan turned left off Washington Road onto Magnolia Lane. After a brief pause and a wave from the guard, Hogan guided his yachtlike 1960 Cadillac down the three-hundred-yard corridor—almost a tunnel—formed by the sixty-five 103-year-old magnolia trees bordering the drive. Mr. Hogan would be dining with friends at the club tonight. The early evening sunlight filtered through the trees and glinted softly, agreeably, off the hood of his car.

We know the number and age of the trees lining the entrance to the Augusta National Golf Club because they were planted in 1857, when the property changed hands. Up to then, Magnolia Lane was just Mr. Dennis Redmond's dirt driveway. Mr. Redmond owned the land—an indigo plantation—and had built in 1854 a graceful-looking, three-story, porch-encircled house on the highest point on the property. The building had an eleven-foot-by-eleven-foot cupola in its center, with windows on all sides, so, it was said, the master could overlook his fields and watch his slaves work.

A Belgian, Baron Louis Mathieu Edouard Berckmans (let's just call him Lou), bought the mansion and the acreage, and, with his son, Prosper Julius Alphonse Berckmans ("Julie") started the Fruitlands Nursery, the first commercial nursery in the South. Lou and Julie planted the trees *(Magnolia grandiflora)* that shaded Hogan's car a century later. And they imported scores of flowering plants and trees that had never grown in the area. In fact, if your yard has a privet hedge or wisteria vine *(Wisteria sinensis)*, it is almost certainly descended from Fruitlands, the first importers of these plants to the United States.

Lou died. Julie died. The old indigo plantation was for sale again. Bobby Jones, the youthful but recently retired king of golf, was shown the property with his friend, New York financier Clifford Roberts. "Perfect!" said Jones. "And to think this ground has been lying here all these years waiting for someone to lay a golf course on it." The hilly, 365-acre tract was sold to the Jones group in 1930 for seventy thousand dollars. The club Jones pictured would be for men only—no women's tees would be built—and would operate only during the winter season. It would be a *golf* club—no pool, no tennis; "one uncomplicated place," as Roberts put it, "where [our members] can feel completely at ease." Augusta National was formally opened for play in January 1933, and a small members' tournament was held to commemorate the event. To fortify the participants on that cold, wet day, Roberts had a keg of corn whiskey placed under tents on the first and tenth tees. "This being during Prohibition, good corn was better and safer to drink than scotch or bourbon whiskey available through bootleggers in Georgia," wrote Roberts in *The Story of the Augusta National Golf Club.* "However, some of those present had never drunk corn before, and did not know how strong it was until, let us say, it was too late."

Mr. Jones and Mr. Roberts decided to hold a tournament. They called it the Augusta National Invitational Tournament, while the rest of the world called it the Masters. It was conceived as a showcase for the best amateur golfers, with, as Jim Murray of the *Los Angeles Times* wrote in 1982, "a smattering of the most socially acceptable pros invited to play." The event succeeded, Murray wrote—indeed, was considered a major championship practically from its start, in 1934—"due to the presence of the incomparable Bobby Jones as inventor, founder and resident dreamer of the tournament, which was otherwise stuck away in a little hillbilly corner of Tobacco Road in North Georgia." But it was the golf course itself that made the Masters. Augusta National is a huge, hilly billiard table where the wind swishes and whispers through tall pine trees. In the spring, at Masters time, if the weather has been right, there are pink, red, white, and scarlet accents—thanks to the Berckmans' plantings of dogwood, flowering peach, and azalea. It smells good, too. Moreover, it is to golf course architecture what Man O' War or Secretariat were to thoroughbred race horses: a benchmark, a classic of its type, an improvement in the breed. Jones hired the best designer of the day, Dr. Alistair Mackenzie of Scotland, a former practicing physician. Jones helped. "Two great intellects," says Desmond Muirhead, one of today's foremost golf architects. "Augusta National is like a woman with a superb bone structure. That was Mackenzie's strength—structure. There have been few architects with sufficient ability to make great holes on the land as it stood rather than always reworking the land to make the holes. Mackenzie was one of them. He was an artist of consequence."

Mackenzie was a short hitter and abhorred rough; his short-comings as a golfer complemented Jones's mastery of the game. Both men admired the Old Course at St. Andrews above all others. The course they designed looks nothing like that an-cient, windswept links by the North Sea, but there are similar-ities. Both have large greens, open fairways, little rough, and just a few, key bunkers and hazards. Augusta has par-fives that can be reached in two—there are downslopes in the landing areas—if you can hit strong shots in the right direction. And if you can place your ball in the right spots, you get both a better view of *and* a better angle to the green. Muirhead believes Au-gusta to be Mackenzie's masterpiece, but adds "many of the greens have slopes that are really much too steep. If it weren't for the Masters, they couldn't get away with it."

As the only one of the four modern major tournaments to be held at the same site year after year, traditions evolved (or were created) at Augusta, an important part of its cachet. For ex-ample, the tournament was always held during the first week of April, or had been since 1940. Jock Hutchison, the 1920 PGA champion, and Freddie McLeod, who won the U.S. Open in 1908, always were the first players off the tee on Thursday, the tournament's opening round (actually, Hutchison and McLeod played together at Augusta "only" from 1935 to 1971; they were eighty-six and eighty-eight years of age, respectively, when this custom was retired). The defending champion always helped the new champion into a kelly-green Augusta National mem-ber's coat—these were always made by the Brooks Uniform Company of New York City—at a closing ceremony, a traditon since 1949, when rotund Claude Harmon held the jacket and Sam Snead poked his extra-long arms through it. And on Tues-day evening of tournament week, the previous winners of the Masters always got together for dinner in the Augusta National clubhouse.

As his car emerged from the sun-dappled shade, Hogan might have reflected that he himself had started the Champions

Dinner eight years before. He'd finally won the Masters in 1951, after narrow defeats to Byron Nelson in 1942, just before the war, and to Herman Keiser in 1946, just after it. Hogan made arrangements with the club, invited the other ten former champions (Nelson, Horton Smith, and Jimmy Demaret were multiple winners), selected the menu, and picked up the tab. Tonight, 1959 champion Art Wall would be the host of the ninth annual dinner. Demaret wore a bow tie and sat close to his pal, Hogan, a case of opposites attracting, and far away from Keiser, with whom he had a misunderstanding over a gambling debt, never resolved. Snead told stories, most of them off-color, in his mouthful-of-grits accent. He sat at the front table with Wall, Roberts, and Jones. Jones did not look well; in fact, he was gravely ill, and had been for more than a decade. He had syringomyelia, a rare, painful, crippling disease of the spine; since 1950 he'd had to use leg braces and canes to walk. Yet Jones smiled through the pain and indignity of his illness. To his right sat Gene Sarazen, celebrating the twenty-fifth anniversary of his 1935 Masters championship, smoking a big after-dinner cigar. Two of the group didn't drink: the thin, mournful-looking Wall, a teetotaler, and Palmer. Arnie had been sick with the flu for several days; this was his first day out of bed since Saturday. He still wasn't feeling well.

The talk that night was of the weather (cool and rainy), the relative slowness of the Augusta National greens, and of the changes Bob Jones and Cliff Roberts had made for that year's tournament. The traditional Wednesday long-drive contest had been scrapped; George Bayer would go in the books as the final Masters blaster, with a poke of 321 yards. In its place as a pretournament icebreaker would be a nine-hole contest on the club's two-year-old par-three course. There were new scoreboards, big ones, scattered around the course, ten of them now, and a new scoring system. Roberts explained: red numerals for under par, green numbers for over-par scores, and a green zero for even par. Caddies had started filling divot holes with a mixture of soil and seed they kept in the pockets of their white coveralls. They've been doing that in Japan for some time, Roberts said. And the winner of the 1960 Masters would, for the first time, be interviewed on TV by Jones.

While the past Masters champions dined below him, Jack Nicklaus lounged on his bed on the third floor of the clubhouse. The cupola room had been remodeled in 1945 into a small dormitory—kelly green carpet, beds for six, one bathroom—and amateur participants in the Masters were invited to stay there. The room was nicknamed "The Crow's Nest." Perhaps Jack was thinking about Bobby Jones. At the Wednesday evening Amateur dinner in 1959, when he was a first-time Masters participant, Mr. Jones had invited Jack and his father down to his cabin after the meal for a private conversation. Would he ask them to visit again? (He did, as it turned out.) Or, if form held, Jack *could* have been thinking about food. The year before, he and his Crow's Nest companion, Phil Rodgers, another full-figured fellow, had placed a major burden on the clubhouse kitchen. Meals were not free—accepting freebies of any kind endangered one's amateur status in the eyes of the USGA—but they were cheap, just a dollar for breakfast, a dollar for lunch, two dollars for dinner. "So Phil and I would order double shrimp cocktails, double sirloin steaks, and then we'd get a third one if we felt like it," Jack recalls with a laugh. "Finally they said to us, 'Fellas, if you're gonna eat more than one, we're gonna have to charge you another two dollars.'"

On Thursday, when the putts counted, Hogan had what must have seemed like a cruel pairing—Deane Beman. BB Eyes was an unimpressive ball striker who seemed to make every putt; Hogan, of course, was the opposite. Beman wore white socks and dark shoes and shot 71; Hogan, in a navy-blue cardigan, had 73.

Palmer also had an amateur partner in the first round, the ebullient Billy Joe Patton. Arnie birdied the first and second holes, holed a bunker shot for eagle on the eighth, then, his long, hooking drives catching Mackenzie's downslopes, birdied thirteen and fifteen. When he made a twenty-five footer on the final hole for another birdie, a round of 67 and the first-round lead, Patton delightedly slapped him on the butt, in the way some baseball and football players congratulate each other.

Mike Souchak went out in 34. Lots of pre-tournament attention had attached to him, partly because of his exceptional practice-round scores (70, 70, 70 and 68, a total good enough to win most Masters) and partly because of his vast potential. A number of knowledgeable people thought he was the likely heir to Hogan and Snead. "'Souch' looked like he could win anything, anytime," Venturi says. "He was going to be the next great player, no question," agrees Dave Marr, a Souchak friend from the few days they'd spent together as assistants at Winged Foot in New York. He was, like Palmer, an exceptionally strong man—he had arms and wrists like fence posts—with a gregarious nature. He could be somewhat coarse; he might clear his nasal passages *sans* handkerchief while on the golf course. Souchak slumped a bit on the second nine; his 72 tied the burly former college (Duke) football player with forty-year-old Julius Boros, the burly former accountant from Connecticut, and Gary Jim Player, twenty-five, the defending British Open champion, a South African who looked more like a gymnast than a golfer.

Palmer led by two over the 69's shot by 1948 Masters champion Claude Harmon (Souchak and Marr's former boss at Winged Foot); Jay Hebert, who looked and acted like what he was, an ex-Marine; Fred Hawkins, a very competent player who, incredibly, finished second in twenty-seven tour events (including the 1958 Masters, to Palmer) and won only once; and Finsterwald.

Dow Henry Finsterwald, a dead ringer for the Indian on the back of a nickel, had a personality as tightly controlled as his golf game. Brown shoes, brown pants, no smiles, frowns, or three putts. He was known more for finishing near the top than at the top, even though he had won nine times. His first-round 69 was built on an opportunistic short game; he lacked the strength of Palmer or Souchak to take full advantage of Augusta's design. And though Finsterwald was an expert in the sometimes ridiculously arcane rules of golf, Masters rules officials considered throwing him out of the tournament the next day.

The nine-hole leader was Finsterwald's playing partner, splay-footed, Hogan-hatted Ken Venturi. He lofted a feathery thirty-five-yard pitch gently into the cup on the second hole for an eagle three, while shooting a course record-tying five-under-par 31. He was still four under, with birdie holes ahead, when he duckwalked up the hill to the twelfth tee. The twelfth at Augusta has caused more dry mouths, wet palms, fluttery stomachs, and bad excuses than an IRS audit. It's like hitting from one rooftop to another. The green on the 150-yard hole is small, hard, and only a few yards wide; there's a stream in front of it called Rae's Creek, bunkers short of it and over it, unpredictable winds above it, and an Indian burial ground below it. "Terrifying," said Bobby Jones of the hole. Venturi hit a seven-iron a little too hard, slightly too low, marginally too far left. The ball hit the green surface, took a big bounce and buried in the steep slope over the green, just a few steps from where Palmer's ball had stopped in 1958. My ball's embedded, I get a drop from this, don't I? asked Venturi. No, the official on duty said, your shot landed on the green. That hole you're in was caused by someone *else's* ball. You'll have to play it. Venturi chopped, chipped, two putted. Double-bogey five. His confidence and momentum disappeared. He missed left from two feet on fourteen, missed right from six feet on fifteen (both were three-putt bogeys), and stumbled in with two more bogeys for a back nine of 42.

Palmer putted poorly—"like Joe Schmoak," he said, mystifyingly—the second day. He missed a shortish birdie putt on the long, difficult par-four eleventh. As his large gallery groaned, Arnie dramatically turned and looked at the muddy water in the pond behind him, then glared at the ball on the lip of the cup. He tapped in and slumped his shoulders. Finally he hitched up his pants with the heels of his hands and snatched his smoldering L&M off the ground. He seemed jumpy when he faced a similar putt for birdie on seventeen. Just as he was about to hit the six-footer, a self-absorbed gentleman in a straw hat strolled by. Peeved, Palmer uncoiled from his rigor mortis–like putting stance. He got set again, made it, and sighed heavily. He shot 73.

An additional worry for Arnie was his feet. His new footwear had caused a blister on his right heel. Midway through his round he tore off a piece of scorecard and inserted it into the offending shoe.

Hogan made his move. He shot 68, the best round of the day, but his round was in jeopardy when he hit in the water on twelve. But the ball looked playable, so he removed his right shoe and sock, rolled up his pants leg, and waded carefully into Rae's Creek. Hogan went about this business grimly, of course, but his water shot had a humorous antecedent. In the Masters of 1953, Johnny DeForest faced a similar shot. He studied the situation and carefully removed his left shoe and sock. The crowd murmured expectantly. Then DeForest stepped into the water—with his right, fully dressed foot. It brought down the house. Hogan got the correct foot in the water, splashed the ball out, chipped on, and saved bogey. Then he birdied three of the final six holes, while his caddie unaccountably began lying face down by the edge of the green when his boss putted.

Venturi rallied. "I don't think anyone, not even Ken's closest friends, expected he could come back from that echoing disaster [the previous day's second-nine 42, was the same back nine score he shot in the final round in 1956]," wrote Herbert Warren Wind in *Sports Illustrated*. "But there is a good deal of iron in this young man. He was back the very next day with a 69 that laid the ghost to rest right then and there. That was something to admire wholeheartedly. . . ."

Not withstanding Hogan's 68 or Venturi's 69, Finsterwald's 70 was the day's best round, because he played under the threat of disqualification from the first hole on. After holing out on the fifth green the day before, Finsterwald hit a practice putt. "I didn't see it. I was already walking to the next tee, I guess," says Venturi, who was paired with him. While practice putting is not against USGA rules, Masters officials had installed a local rule that prohibited it. "Otherwise, instead of getting through the round in three hours and forty-five minutes, they'd take *four* hours and forty-five minutes," says Ike Grainger. In the second round, on the first green, Finsterwald was about to practice putt again. *"No!"* shouted Billy Casper, his playing partner. I thought it was okay, said Finster, flustered. I did it yesterday, maybe a couple of times.

He turned himself in immediately. "I saw [Masters rules official] Ed Carter and told him what happened," recalled Finsterwald. "On number twelve or thirteen, they told me not to sign my scorecard and to wait by the scorer's tent after the round." By signing for a 69 the day before—when, with the two-stroke penalty for practicing he actually had 71—disqualification was automatic. But they were reviewing the situation; the whole thing was uncertain.

While Dow sat in a metal lawn chair by the eighteenth green, his head bowed, his elbows on his knees, Grainger and three other rules officials huddled behind him, under the TV tower. Their decision was unprecedented: two strokes would be added to Finsterwald's first-day score, disqualification waived. The Masters, you were reminded, is privately owned and operated. Since it is neither a USGA nor a PGA event, they do what they like with the rules. It seemed like a real break for Finsterwald—but was it? While he could have, perhaps should have been dismissed from the tournament, there is another way to look at it. In golf, as in law, there is something called detrimental reliance: if Smith receives incorrect information from Jones, Smith should not be penalized for relying on it. Finsterwald had asked on the first tee about any special rules in force and was referred to a mimeographed sheet, which said nothing about practice putting. The local rule on practicing was on the back of the scorecard, not the usual place for such information.

Without the penalty, Finsterwald would be leading the Masters at the halfway point. With it, Palmer's 140 led. Hogan, Harmon, Walter Burkemo, and Finsterwald were tied for second, one shot back. Casper and Venturi were another stroke behind. Nicklaus, with rounds of 75 and 71, had hit almost all the greens—and missed almost all the putts. Souchak was also stuck in the middle of the pack and, like Nicklaus, would stay there. Littler shot a horrid 82 in the second round and missed the thirty-six-hole cut. Hutchison and McLeod played their usual ceremonial eighteen holes and did not reveal their scores.

Third Round: Hogan had a fifteen-foot putt for birdie on the first hole—and *he left the pin in*. Putting at the flagstick, using it as a backstop, from the green surface was legal back then. But from five yards away, it was an extraordinarily defensive move, matching Hogan's exceptionally poor putting. A reporter had asked him the night before if he had noticed—as everyone else had—that he was taking an awfully long time to putt. "No," The Hawk replied, "actually I have less time to study the line anymore—it takes me so long to get the club in motion." He seemed to leave everything short, with, as Wind called it, "a timid, pushy stroke." Despite being a basket case on the greens, Hogan stayed in contention. He shot an even-par 72. He was hitting the ball better than anyone else, and putting worse.

Palmer, by contrast, was hitting his putts like a hockey player whacking slap shots past a goalie. On the fifteenth, Arnie's eleven-foot putt for birdie was hit so hard—and so dead center—that it hit the back of the cup, popped up four inches, and fell in. Although it's difficult to reconcile with his actual performance, Palmer felt his new putter was letting him down: "At the end of the third round, I was tempted to throw [it] away . . . It got so bad that I wasn't sure I could drop it in from three feet up, much let putt it in from three feet out." He shot 72 and led by one with one round to play. Tied for second were Hogan, Venturi, Finsterwald, Boros, and Casper.

Final round: Hogan, Hawkins, and Stan Leonard hit warm-up shots on the practice range, each with a cigarette in his mouth. It was impossible to tell if Hogan was tense a few moments before attempting to win his first major tournament since 1953. As usual, he was inscrutable. He seemed in control as he slashed a drive down the middle of the first fairway and hit the green in regulation. Then, suddenly, he seemed simply to be too old for all of this. He froze badly over his putts. You could almost hear the internal dialogue between Hogan and his hands. Hogan: "Hit it, dammit! Smoothly! Solidly!" Hands: "We're not ready yet. This putter doesn't feel right. And don't rush us. You're making us nervous!" He three-putted his way to a 76 and never challenged for the lead. Hogan missed fewer greens in regulation than anyone else in the field (only ten of seventy-two), but he also missed the most putts. He had seventy-five putts the last two rounds, worse than two per hole. "Not that this figure by itself conveys his thorough malaise on the greens," wrote Wind. "It is hard to recall a player of his class ever putting so poorly, though perhaps Vardon did in his 50s." (Harry Vardon, the great English champion of the early twentieth century, had age—and tuberculosis—to blame for his poor putting.) Hogan finished tied for sixth.

Nicklaus's day was similar to Hogan's. After a mediocre bunker shot on eighteen, he had a twelve-foot putt for 75 and a tie with Billy Joe Patton for the low amateur trophy. The pride of Ohio State and Phi Gamma Delta crouched over his ball (always a Titleist 5) and rapped it with a right-hand-dominated shove, like a softball being tossed underhand. He made it. Willie Peterson, his caddie, jumped a foot in the air in celebration. Jack tied for twelfth, ahead of such name professionals as Tommy Bolt, Bob Rosburg, and Souchak. This kid is a player, Chris Schenkel told the television audience. Color commentator Vic Ghezzi agreed.

Bob Hoag, smiling, clapped his young friend on the back and walked off in search of various pigeons, er friends, he had bet with. You pick any ten or twenty players in the field, Hoag

had told a number of bettors before the tournament, and I'll take
Jack Nicklaus. Who? You know, he won the U.S Amateur last
year. For every player you name that beats my friend, I'll give
you ten or twenty or fifty dollars. And for each of the players
you pick that Jack beats, *you* pay *me* the same amount. "We
[Hoag and a few of the other Nicklaus friends who came in from
Columbus] cleaned up on that bet for a few years, until people
knew who he was," Hoag recalls with pleasure. In 1960, Hoag,
Ivor Young, *et al. really* cleaned up.

Palmer snap-hooked his drive way, *way* left off the first tee,
into the ninth fairway. By the time he teed off, nearly an hour
after Venturi and Finsterwald, he had already lost the lead. Not
pairing the leaders in consecutive groups was a quaint and in-
convenient Masters tradition. The players didn't like it and the
television people hated it, but there it was. Was Arnie's lousy
first tee ball a clue that he was shaken by being out of the lead
for the first time all week? No. He muscled a long iron to the
green, between and around an intervening stand of tall pines,
a dozen feet from the hole. After he made the putt—was there
any doubt?—the air was punctuated with North Georgia–ac-
cented shouts of jubilation. "Yee-ha! Getcha some, Ahnie!
Yay-uh!" To the Yankee ear of golf writer Dick Taylor, the name
on everyone's lips sounded like "Ahno Pomma." His unusually
large, unusually vocal gallery ran between shots, or walked
very fast, like their hero.

Up ahead, Venturi and Finsterwald were playing flawlessly.
Ken regained the lead after Palmer's first-hole birdie with two
more of his own, and finished the front nine with a three-under-
par 33. Dow stayed close with a two-under 34. Venturi faltered
a bit to start the second nine, but saved par on ten and bogey
on eleven with perfectly played chip shots. Finsterwald bogeyed twelve, then birdied fourteen. The duelists were tied after fifteen holes at five under, one shot ahead of Palmer.

The sixteenth at Augusta is a 170-yard par-three over a pond
to a very firm green framed by three big sand bunkers. It may
be slightly less scary than the twelfth, but, as ever-cool Lloyd

Mangrum told reporters after he finished his final round, "Every time I get on the tee on that thing, I get tight. It cost me the tournament one of the few times I had a chance to win [in 1959]. I put it in the water there on both of the last two rounds." Finsterwald hit first and played a safe, sensible shot onto the fat part of the green, about thirty feet short of the hole. Venturi went for the pin, which was set on a narrow ridge, back right, by the bunker. His ball landed on the green, but rolled through it, into the sand. After Finsterwald putted up and made par, Venturi's next play seemed impossible. The shot itself was hard enough—downhill to a hard green, almost no room to work with. If he hit it too hard he could wind up in the bunker on the other side, or worse, the water. Shave it too fine and he's still in the sand. Moreover, the tournament was on the line, the tournament he wanted so desperately to win.

Despite everything—the shot, the crowd, TV, the high stakes involved, his own bitter history in the Masters—Venturi hit a wonderful shot, "Maybe the best bunker shot of my life," he said afterward. The ball landed gently, *just* over the lip of the trap, and dribbled to four inches from the cup. The tie for the lead continued to the final hole.

Palmer looked up at the big scoreboard by the eleventh hole and saw that he would probably need to play the last eight holes in no worse than one under to tie Venturi and Finsterwald. And on the corner of the scoreboard marked "messages," he saw

GO ARNIE

ARNIE'S ARMY

Venturi was safely on the last green in two, but Finsterwald bunkered his approach, then came out of the sand to about five feet. Venturi rolled his twenty-footer about a foot by; Finsterwald missed. Ken took a long time with his twelve-inch putt; after he made it, he stared into the cup for a long moment. He removed his white hat briefly, to acknowledge the applause. He did not smile. Several minutes later, he and his wife Conni were being escorted to the Roberts quarters by a convoy of Pinkerton security guards. There Venturi was briefed for his television appearance, in which it seemed likely he would be the star. He tried on a green jacket.

Palmer was running out of holes. He had lost ground with a symmetrical first nine of three birdies, three bogeys, and three pars. He made pars on ten, eleven, twelve, and fourteen, tough holes, but failed to birdie thirteen, a dangerous par-five, but one he could reach in two with an iron. The fifteenth at Augusta is another get-rich-quick par-five. You could make two there—as Gene Sarazen did in 1935, when he holed his Wilson 3 golf ball from the fairway with a four-wood for a double eagle—but you might also make a ten, as Walker Inman did in 1956, when he was the first native Augustan to play in the Masters. At this point, "I knew what I had to do," Arnie told the press afterward. "I watched the score board all the way around. I knew what I had to do to win."

Palmer's drive on fifteen was so-so, a little too far left, his lie not very good. A gusty head wind was making little waves in the pond fronting the green. Would he lay up short of the hazard, then pitch on, the percentage shot? He would not. He took a one-iron from Ironman and prepared to give it a rip. "Foolish," said Sarazen, to the TV back at the clubhouse. "Courage," said Inman, another fifteenth-hole expert. "To Arnold there was only one spot to play for. He's got to win."

The gamble didn't work, but, luckily, the ball missed the water and stopped under the TV tower to the right of the green. Arnie got relief from the tower, but chipped poorly. He tossed his wedge angrily to Ironman. The caddie glared. "When I saw Ironman's face I calmed down," Palmer said later. "It was the same look my father gave me when I was sixteen years old. I threw a club over a tree and Pap said to me 'If you ever do that again, I'll take your clubs away and you'll never play golf again.'" But he missed his putt for birdie. Only three holes left, none of them easy.

On sixteen, where Venturi had hit such a superlative bunker

shot an hour before, Palmer came off a four-iron, leaving a thirty-foot uphill putt for birdie. Uncharacteristically, he left the flagstick in. He wristed a hard slap shot up to the hole and *whang*, the ball ricocheted off the stick, just a foot from the hole. "It was a break," he conceded in the postmortem. "If I hadn't hit the flag, I'd have had a hard five-footer coming back for my par." Playing partner Casper saw it differently: "You'd have been putting out of the sandtrap."

Desperate now, still a shot behind, Palmer hit a drive and an eight-iron thirty-five disappointing feet short of the hole on the four-hundred-yard par-four seventeenth. He got over the putt—and backed off. Settled himself, took a deep breath, got over the putt—and walked away again. Spectators behind the green, directly in his line, were moving back and forth. A third try. The ball approached the hole, lost speed—and fell in. Ahno Pomma was tied for the lead. Everyone by the green—marshals included—jumped and shouted. Arnie, grinning, danced to the hole, removed his ball, and punched the air. He was tied for the lead.

Then, as several thousand overheated fans surged around him like floodwater around a tree, shouting in voices shrill or hoarse from the excitement, as a television camera showed a national audience each of the forty steps he took to the tee of the final hole, a curious thing happened. Arnie's mind went blank. "My mind played funny tricks," he remembered. "I couldn't think of anything 'til I got up to the eighteenth tee . . . it was just like the day in 1952 when I bought my first car. It was a forty-nine Ford but I thought it was a Rolls Royce. I drove it all around town to show it off to everyone I met. My feet never touched the ground that day, either."

Palmer felt a breeze in his face as he teed his ball. The crowd got quiet; his mind cleared. Like a mantra, he repeated the advice his father had given him thousands of times: *Start deliberate. Come back slow on the backswing. Then give it everything you've got.* Arnie slashed; his gallery whistled and shouted. He'd crushed it. The ball flew on a low trajectory up the hill, under the wind, away from the tall pine trees on the right. It hit and stopped in the center of the fairway, 260 yards out.

The eighteenth green at Augusta National is narrow, elevated, surrounded by large bunkers, and rises from front to back in three levels, on plateaus as distinct as stair steps. The flag stick this day was cut on the top step, a dangerous position, inhospitable to iron shots. Naturally, Palmer went for it. He selected a six-iron, inhaled smoke from his L&M, pitched the cigarette dramatically aside, hitched his trousers, exhaled. He repeated his mantra—with an added chant that said *keep your head down, keep your head down*—and swung. "I made sure that I never saw the ball in the air," he recalled. The ball almost went in on the fly. It spun by the hole and stopped six feet away. While Casper putted out, Arnie went to the side of the green and sat down next to his bag, his head bowed. Ironman sat on the bag. "I was thinking of the day Winnie and I got our marriage license. She was only twenty and we forgot to have her parents sign permission," Arnie told *LIFE*. "I sat down in the license bureau and waited for the clerk to say, 'I'm sorry.' I thought I'd hear those words again. But we got the license. . . ."

Palmer stood over his tricky, right-breaking putt to win. "The ball's scared of him," said Bob Rosburg, standing with a small group in front of a television in the upstairs locker room of the Augusta National clubhouse. "I guarantee he'll get it in the hole if he has to stare it in."

He stood like a crooked statue over the ball in his new shoes, jabbed delicately at it with his new putter. The ball rolled in, the crowd roared, Arnie danced briefly and shook Casper's hand delightedly. Venturi slumped. Palmer had finished three, three, three, with birdies on the final two holes, to edge the star-crossed Venturi by one. Finsterwald was third, two shots behind. Venturi's first-round, back-nine 42 and Finsterwald's two-shot penalty for a practice putt became mere bits of historical trivia. *LIFE* headlined the real significance of the week: AT MASTERS, PALMER REPLACES HOGAN, SNEAD.

▼

CHAPTER FIVE

I Shoulda Won the Open

Arnie was flying. High over Latrobe, above Hogan, Snead, Venturi, and Finsterwald, over this new kid Nicklaus, over all golf and all golf courses he soared, flying as high and as far and as often as he wanted. He'd bought an airplane.

"I love to fly," he said in *Go for Broke*, a sort-of autobiography written with William Barry Furlong in 1973. "It started when I was a little boy. If there was anything that could compete with my interest in golf, it was flying. . . . When I wasn't building, and breaking, model planes, I was running down the country club road to the airport. There was a flight room where some of the pilots would gather around an old pot-bellied stove, and I'd sit there listening to all the glories of the sky." He took his first flying lesson in 1956, and soloed in 1958. Now he could afford his own plane, a twin-engine Aero Commander.

Figuratively, too, Palmer's life took off. The national spotlight stayed fixed on him for weeks. He played golf with the President at Augusta the day after his thrilling, nationally televised Masters win ("I hear you're a good putter," Ike joshed Arnie in gigantic understatement). After the Masters concluded on April 10, the Palmers (Arnold, Winnie, and their two small daughters, Amy and Peggy) intended to take an at-home respite from the tour until the Houston Classic commenced on April 28. It wasn't much of a vacation. In the two weeks he was at home, Arnie was a guest on "The Perry Como Show"—twice—and appeared on another TV show called "Masquerade." He filmed a few commercials for L&M cigarettes. And *Time, Life,* and the *Saturday Evening Post* sent photographers and reporters to the Palmer abode. *Sports Illustrated* and *Reader's Digest* called, too.

Time:
As golf's new leader, Palmer is also the brightest star of a new generation of professionals. . . . The Palmer breed, now taking over, is that of the college-trained family man with an agent to line up fat endorsements and a cooler in the trunk for baby's bottle.

Win or lose, Palmer, with his daring, slashing attack, is fun to watch. He is a splendidly built athlete (5 ft. 11 in., 177 lbs.) with strength in all the right places: massive shoulders and arms, a waist hardly big enough to hold his trousers up, thick wrists, and leather -hard, outsized hands that can crumple a beer can as though it were tissue paper. . . . Palmer is anything but stolid during a round: he mutters imprecations to himself, contorts his face, sometimes drops his club and wanders away in disgust at a botched shot. On the greens, bent into his knock-kneed stance, he tries to sink long putts when many pros would prudently try to lag up to the cup. Says Palmer: 'I guess I putt past the pin more than most anybody. I always like to give it a chance. Never up, never in, you know.'

Life:
His latest success affirmed Palmer as the world's top golfer, the first man occupying the roost once ruled by the fabled Ben Hogan and Sam Snead. But this 30-year-old Pennsylvanian is a maverick among pros. He walks faster than some of them run, brashly gambles for eagles rather than settling for

safety, seems to want to shoot right through a tree rather than around it. His 270-yard drives and boldly stroked putts have won him five 1960 tournaments and a record $43,000.

Reader's Digest:
Palmer has captured the public's imagination to an extent unseen since the palmiest days of Bobby Jones, Babe Ruth, Jack Dempsey and Bill Tilden. Like those four, he has 'color,' that dramatic, magic ingredient which changes a sports contest from a mere game into an epic struggle.

Sports Illustrated:
The main point about the 1960 Masters, however, was that it marked the coming of age of our young professionals. . . . From the outset, Palmer, Venturi, Finsterwald and later on, Casper—were the people to watch. As the tournament moved on, they became increasingly dynamic figures in the eyes of the huge galleries.

With fame came fortune. McCormack could now get Arnie one thousand dollars for an eighteen-hole exhibition, up from the $350 to $500 he had been getting. Television appearances by the new Masters champion now went for twenty-five hundred dollars. Wilson Sporting Goods Company—Palmer played their clubs and balls—kicked in a thirty-five-hundred-dollar bonus on top of his annual salary of sixty-five hundred dollars. And Laurel Valley Golf Club in Ligonier, Pennsylvania (near Latrobe), paid him five thousand dollars to sew its name on his red-and-white Wilson golf bag. "There was not a hotter commodity in sport than Arnold Palmer," wrote his agent in his 1967 book *Arnie.* "The offers came pouring in, and soon Arnold himself realized that his life was going to become more complex, like it or not. One big reason was that we were approached by a man named Jack Harkins."

Harkins was president of the First Flight Company of Chattanooga, Tennessee, a second-tier manufacturer of golf equipment (Wilson, MacGregor, and Spalding were the first tier). *Heard your contract with Wilson expires this year, Arnold,* said Harkins on the phone the day after the Masters. *We think we can do better for you—a lot better.* McCormack and Palmer agreed to meet the man from First Flight when Arnie rejoined the tour in Houston in two weeks.

Arnie's only nongolf endorsement up to then had been for ketchup. He had committed to the condiment print ad casually, without advice from counsel; McCormack called him "the man who can't say no." He got five hundred dollars for posing with a steak, a waitress, and a bottle of "thicker, richer, Heinz." The ad was in black and white, except for a blazing scarlet ketchup bottle; the effect was bizarre. Soon after the Masters, McCormack evaluated other endorsement deals—for shirts (accepted), pants (accepted) and Wonder Bread (rejected). The baker would pay three thousand five hundred dollars for one television commercial, which was fine, and the Masters champion would tell the camera that "Wonder Bread tastes great . . . and toasts great, too," which was also fine. But the ad copy mentioned Winnie, Peggy, and Amy. Not fine. Arnie did not believe in using his family in any advertisement.

As more and more businesses tried to hitch themselves to the Palmer star, it soon occurred to McCormack that his client was more than just an exceptionally good athlete/spokesman: *he was himself a brand name.* Thus, McCormack wrote, "No field was not feasible for an Arnold Palmer franchise. Nothing would, by definition, rule out Arnold Palmer soap, florists, Christmas trees. . . ."

This revolutionary idea would make them rich.

Jack Nicklaus painted wide, white designs on his chest, face, and stomach, wrapped a flowered bed sheet around his waist, and placed yellow and pink leis around his neck. There. Ready for a day of fun.

It was spring quarter at Ohio State University, and for the brothers of Phi Gamma Delta that meant the biggest celebration of the year: the annual Fiji Island Party. They made a week of it. The Phi Gams—they called themselves Fijis—rented (or borrowed) a farm outside Columbus, as they always did, and spent a few days with their dates, building grass huts and decorating the area in a midwestern university/South Sea island motif. The party started at noon on Saturday. A Fiji Island queen was crowned. The winner, wearing a sarong and a garland of daisies, was Jack's intended, Miss Barbara Bash of the Kappa Alpha Theta sorority. Fresh pineapple and fried chicken were served. Vodka was consumed, in native drinks such as the Screwdriver and the Purple Passion; as day became night, some over-served partygoers began to speak in Melanesian, the native language of Fiji. Nicklaus remembers those days fondly. "I loved it," he says.

Of course, life was not just a luau for Jack. He was near the end of his penultimate year of college and was just a few months from marrying Barbara; he was concerned about the future. How would he make his living? Pharmacology—and the pharmacist's life—had lost their appeal. It had gradually dawned on him that golf would always be a part of his life; his excellent performance at the Masters had brought this home with some clarity. But he wanted to remain an amateur, like his hero, Bobby Jones. Jack looked around for someone who made a good living and got to play a lot of golf, and he saw his friend Bob Hoag. Hoag sold insurance. He talked it over with Barbara and with his father, Charlie. Insurance it would be. He decided to change his major in the fall to the College of Commerce to prepare for his new career.

Soon after his return from Augusta in April, Jack Nicklaus, the United States Amateur champion, the low amateur and twelfth-place finisher in the Masters, the greatest player of his age in the world, made his debut as a college golfer. No one noticed much. College and amateur golf in 1960 were about as popular and newsworthy as fencing or cross-country. "I remember when I first began to do well in the Open and the Masters, well enough so that a few reporters would come over and ask me about myself," Nicklaus recalled in *The Greatest Game of All*. "Well, the moment I'd refer to some round I'd played in the NCAA, the Big Ten, the Trans-Mississippi, the North and

South, or even the U.S. Amateur, the reporters' eyes would glaze over; some of them would begin to yawn, others would edge away and light up a cigarette, and I felt like the biggest bore in the world."

But the perception of college golf as an innocuous, somewhat boring pastime of unathletic undergraduates at Harvard or Yale was changing, and Nicklaus himself was changing it. Whenever someone did a newspaper column or magazine piece about "pudgy Jack Nicklaus, the amateur who can beat the pros" (scores of such stories were written), he was inevitably identified as an Ohio State student. While most of the ex-caddies and part-time club pros on the tour of 1960 had never darkened the door of a college classroom, the writer would usually notice that, by George, a lot of the younger, better players had gone to college and played on college golf teams: Palmer at Wake Forest, Souchak at Duke, Finsterwald attended Ohio University, Venturi went to San Jose State, Littler was at San Diego State, and so on.

But the truth is, college golf was a little beneath Nicklaus in April and May of 1960. During the spring break between quarters, the team did not take a trip to Florida or Texas, someplace warm, as northern college baseball teams had for years, to play matches or in a tournament to prepare for the season. Jack took two such trips on his own, when he won the International Four Ball with Beman, and his outing at Augusta. He was the national amateur champion, and a Walker Cup player; his teammates and most of the players he would compete against were dilettantes by comparison. "My golf record at Ohio State was respectable, but I could never really get enthusiastic about college golf, since my general golf horizon was expanding so fast," wrote Jack in his book in 1963. "However, the two years I did participate in college golf, I enjoyed it very much."

Compared to the Masters or the Walker Cup or even the Rubber City Open, college golf was decidedly low-key. For example: practically every week in the spring, the OSU coach, a big, easygoing gentleman named Bob Kepler, would ask Jack and a few other Ohio State golfers if they wouldn't rather just put away their clubs for the afternoon. Then they'd pile in "Kep"'s car and drive an hour west, to the Zanesville Rod and Gun Club. Soon fly fishing became Jack's alternative sport of choice and his favorite way to relax. Back at the course, Kepler would not tinker with a player's swing, unless he was asked for help; most of his charges had their own teachers back home. Jack, for instance, could consult with Grout at Scioto whenever he needed to.

Nicklaus's teammmates were Richard Butler, Frank Carr, Fred Ebetino, Allen Jones, Jim and Bill Muldoon, Robin Obetz, Mike Podolski, Frank Kurtz, Russ Jimeson, Pat Meadows, and Don Stickney. Obetz was his best friend on the team; Podolski was, other than Jack, the best player. Nice guys, but the best part of being an Ohio State golfer was the thirty-six-hole university-owned golf facility. The Scarlet and Gray courses at Ohio State were designed by Alistair Mackenzie, the architect of Augusta National. The Scarlet was and still is the best college golf course in the country; it is Augusta with more rough, colder weather, and no dogwoods, a perfect place to build a champion's golf game.

Matches were on Saturdays and were contested over thirty-six holes. It was significant exercise: a ten-mile forced march over a long, rolling course like Scarlet or the University of Michigan course, its turf softened by spring rains, with periodic pauses to hit three-wood or two-iron second shots into par-four greens. And, of course, the players carried their own clubs. Nicklaus and company won their first match, against an alumni team, then beat Ohio University, tied Purdue and Indiana, beat Michigan, got thrashed by Purdue, won the Ohio Intercollegiate tournament, lost to Indiana, and beat Western Illinois. The short season concluded in late May, just before final exams. The 1960 Big Ten conference championship was held at Michigan State. Each team brought six players; the low five scores each day counted. Purdue won, Ohio State finished third. John Konsek of Purdue was the individual winner, for the third time in a row, with 282. Jack was second, with 284. He had no regrets; the college golf season had been, in a way, mere preparation, not an end in itself. Jack was building for something bigger, honing his game, trying to bring it to a peak.

The U.S. Open was in three weeks.

Palmer picked up the tour in Houston, as scheduled, and had his meeting with Jack Harkins and McCormack. *One hundred fifty thousand dollars minimum for five years*, the First Flight president was saying. *You'll be on the Board of Directors. Stock options, probably worth a half-million dollars. Your bonus for winning the Masters or the Open with our equipment will be five thousand dollars. What does Wilson pay you—a thousand?* (Wilson paid one thousand to any Wilson player for winning the Masters, two thousand for winning the U.S. Open). *And you know, Arnold, these cheap clubs with your name on them that Wilson sells through department stores don't really do you or your profession justice. Now, what we'll do . . .*

Arnie and the agent were somewhat awestruck at the big numbers: "Everyone feeling the excitement of perhaps entering into a new kind of adventure together," wrote McCormack. "[And] Arnold daydreaming about having some superb golf clubs with his name on them that he would design." Harkins and McCormack agreed to get together later and get all this in writing.

Palmer shot 66 in the first round at Houston, despite not having played eighteen holes since his victory lap at Augusta National with President Eisenhower. Time and weather had permitted him to play only nine holes at Latrobe Country Club since then. Yet there it was, a six-under score and the first-round lead on the 7,122-yard Memorial Park municipal course. Perhaps he was buoyed by his increasingly rosy financial outlook. Or maybe it was the crowds. Thirty thousand spectators, the largest gallery in Texas golf history, came out in iffy weather to watch the third round; fifteen thousand watchers, a first-day record, appeared on Thursday. No one thought the unprecedented stampede of Texans was caused by Porky Oliver, Freddie Haas, Bill Collins, Fred Hawkins, or any of the other contenders. Home-state heroes Ben Hogan and Byron Nelson were not playing. It was Arnie the people wanted to see. They had watched his fantastic finish at the Masters on TV and had been surprised to learn from sports page columnists since then that this was part of a pattern, the continuation of a streak. *Did you know,* they wrote, *that earlier this year Palmer shot final rounds of 65 at Palm Springs, 68 at Baton Rouge, and 67 at Pensacola—and he won all three events?* He did? Incredible. Got to see this guy.

The unusual thing about Palmer was not that he brought people out, but that he kept them out. He made fans for life. For all that has been said and written about the sociological, psychological, and subtle nature of Arnie's appeal, the basis of his attractiveness was not hard to figure; it hit you over the head the first time you walked in his gallery. Over here you had Hogan—or, more likely, several score of golf professionals trying to look and act like Hogan (or Humphrey Bogart). Hat. Cigarette. Cool, controlled, self-contained; scientific, even. Unemotional. They played golf like chess. Percentage players. And over here was Palmer. He was a riveting figure, with stage presence any actor would envy. He was magnetic; the people strained against the gallery ropes and stared at him, and Palmer, an inveterate crowd checker, looked right back. He had the cigarette but (usually) no hat; he wasn't hiding from anybody. He smiled! He anguished! He was jubilant or affable or disgusted or humble or grimly determined, and it was no act. It's a chicken-or-egg question: did Arnie's emotions bring out the crowds or did the crowds bring out his emotions?

Then there was the *way* he played golf that people found so refreshingly different. He swung out joyously, with abandon; Hogan and his legions were usually pretty grim about the whole business. Hogan hit the ball hard with his technically perfect swing but Palmer seemed certain to rupture himself on each drive, so furious was his inartistic thrash at the ball. Until 1960, when he started to win tournaments in bunches, Palmer played, wrote Dan Jenkins, "with all the finesse of a dock worker lifting a crate of auto parts." He made a hard game look hard. People loved that. "He was Everyman fighting a hook," said Peter Andrews in *Golf Digest*. "We cannot play his game, but he plays ours."

There is, of course, another explanation for the sudden, startling popularity of Arnold Palmer in the spring of 1960. According to this school of thought, it wasn't just the way he acted, the way he played, and the fact that he won—on television. This is the psycho-socio-political interpretation of Arniemania. One version of this appears in *Go for Broke!* and you hope to hell Arnie didn't really write this:

> It was a moment that cried out for somebody—anybody—who could not merely challenge defeat but charge boldly after victory. What I did in golf in 1960 was, mysteriously, to touch the temper of the times. For we all know now that the basic drama of the 1960s—the whole insistent pulse of life, from the civil rights marches to the reach for the moon—was a reflection of the feeling that man must not only define his life but control it. No matter how enormous were the odds. If 1960 was anything, it was the beginning of one of those historic moments when it seemed important—personally, and as part of the nation—to go for broke. And it was a time when a symbol, any symbol—even this compelling, obsessive, utterly maddening game called golf—might come to reflect, however vicariously, the emerging style of our times. It was my fate, and extraordinary good fortune, to become part of that symbol. . . . It was important that I won against the odds. That I clearly enjoyed bucking the odds. And that I did it time and time again.

This is baloney. And it is pretentious baloney, so one hopes that Palmer didn't write it because he is a man without pretense. "Touch the temper of the times"? When have we *not* liked to watch the emergence of an appealing young athlete? When did we not like an upstart winner? "Symbol of the emerging style of our times"? Excuse me, but did we "go for broke" in

Vietnam? Palmer was no mere symbol in or of 1960. His popularity was due to his timing, not the time. And not to diminish Arnie and his accomplishments, but several other golfers *could* have been as universally known and liked, but their timing was off. Walter Hagen and Bobby Jones, certainly; Jimmy Demaret and Tony Lema, maybe. Arnie was flesh and blood, he was exciting—and he was on TV. That's what fed the Palmer phenomenon.

At Houston, Arnie backed up his 66 with rounds of 71 and 70, then birdied two of the final four holes to tie for first with Bill Collins. Collins had been one of the best players on the tour in the first third of the year. He had finished second at Los Angeles, and second again at Phoenix, when he took three shots from the edge on the last hole, then lost a playoff to Jack Fleck. Collins is a big man—six feet three inches, 220 pounds. After he got out of the service in 1948, he worked the graveyard shift at the Fisher Body plant—he was a metal finisher—so he could play golf when the sun came up. He married in 1949, turned professional in 1951, and landed an assistant-pro job in Philadelphia. He worked on his game, saved his money, and joined the tour full-time in 1958. He won a tournament, the New Orleans Open, in 1959. Collins was a comer.

"Palmer was the best then, no question," he says now, in a voice that could cut glass. "He thought he could hole out anything under 140 yards." What about before 1960—who did Collins think was heir to Hogan? "I thought Venturi would be the next great player. . . . Tommy Bolt hit the ball more solidly than anyone. . . . Casper was the most underrated player. He was as good as or better than the Big Three (Palmer, Player, and Nicklaus). . . . I played with Palmer in his first tournament. He had to use a three-wood off the tee to get the ball in play. He hooked the shit out of the thing."

Collins pauses, drags on his filter cigarette, and considers another question. No, he didn't know Nicklaus in 1960, but they got to be friends a few years later. "Jack and I would play Palmer and Finsterwald or Palmer and [Bo] Wininger during practice rounds at Doral and Augusta. I remember once we were paired together at Desert Inn—Jack was heavy then—and Palmer's group was right in front of us. They teed off and almost all of this huge gallery around the first tee went with him. Jack looked at me and said, 'Someday, *I'm* gonna have a gallery like that.'"

On Tuesday, May 3, Collins won the playoff with Palmer, 69 to 71. Big Bill won fifty-three hundred dollars, Arnie got thirty-four hundred dollars, and they split the extra-day gate receipts. PALMER DEFEATED headlined *Golf World*.

"Next to play, the defending champion," called out a man with a clipboard and a red plaid jacket and matching tie. "Winner of the 1946 and 1948 PGA Championships, winner of the Masters in 1951 and 1953, the British Open champion of 1953, the United States Open champion of 1948, 1950, 1951, and 1953, and a five-time winner of the NIT. From Fort Worth Texas. Ladies and gentlemen, Ben Hogan." The hometown crowd around the first tee at Colonial Country Club applauded appreciatively and were acknowledged briefly by the small, gray man with a golf club. If Ben Hogan would not come to the tour, the tour would come to Ben Hogan. Two weeks after the Houston event, the pros came to Hogan's home course. He had won so much here—five of the thirteen Colonial NITs (National Invitation Tournaments) contested up to then—that the press called the place "Hogan's Alley." With the exception of Snead at the Greater Greensboro Open (seven wins), no one owned a tour event like Hogan owned Colonial.

Since the Masters a month before, The Hawk did what he always did—he worked early and he hit golf balls late. By eight A.M. he would stop his Cadillac in front of a little white sign in the parking lot at the Ben Hogan Company marked "Reserved For Mr. Hogan." Then he would limp through a back entrance directly into his office, a large square room with pale brown carpet and brown wood paneling. Invariably he wore a business suit as muted as the colors in the office. A color map of the world was on the wall behind his desk; in front of the map, on a table, was a flattering head-and-shoulders photograph of his wife, Valerie. On the walls were two paintings of unsmiling, old, bald, white men. "To Ben Hogan, With warm regards from his old and devoted friend. Dwight Eisenhower" was inscribed on a portrait of the president on the wall to the left of his desk. On the opposite wall was a painting of Marvin Leonard, his benefactor, business partner, and good friend, the man who founded Shady Oaks and Colonial Country Clubs, started the NIT, and helped to start the Ben Hogan Company.

On occasion Hogan would forego his afternoon practice session at Shady Oaks and actually play the game. He and Leonard or Gary Laughlin, another business associate/friend, would go to one of the more private private clubs in Dallas or Fort Worth and play a "casual" match against two members of the host club. For Hogan, of course, the matches were not casual, whether the stakes were modest or significant. "We would play five-dollar Nassaus," Laughlin says—twenty dollars might change hands in such a bet—but others say the wagers in those games were often far higher, and several thousand-dollar increments could pass from one wallet to another at day's end (after golf, Hogan and company might play the time-honored game of "get even or get farther behind" called gin rummy). "My job was to play well on the holes where I got [handicap] strokes," recalls Laughlin. "If I didn't, the ride back to Fort Worth would be awfully quiet."

The 1960 Colonial was significant not only for the reappearance of Hogan: some saw the tournament as an annual Open Omen. "In eight of the last 12 years," wrote Dan Jenkins in *Sports Illustrated*, "the winner of the U.S. Open has been among the top five at Fort Worth. Colonial CC is Ben Hogan's home course, and Hogan has accounted for four of the Open victories. But Lloyd Mangrum, Ed Furgol, Dick Mayer and Tommy Bolt have helped the tradition." If Colonial was a harbinger, then Julius Boros, the winner, and Gene Littler and Kelvin Nagle of Australia, the runners-up, would be good bets in the Open, along with Ted Kroll, who was fourth, and Mike Souchak, Ken Venturi, and Jerry Barber, who tied for fifth. Hogan finished another stroke back, five shots out of first. And if top-five-at-Colonial-do-well-at-the-Open form held, then Palmer would not be a factor at Denver in June. He finished twenty-second. "If Palmer's performance was disappointing to the masses who followed him, he was not particularly distraught," Jenkins wrote. Palmer admitted that "the constant pressure of contending seemed to catch up to me." Another admission was more startling: he had tried out some new irons at Colonial, his *third* such switch of the year. Some players went years—even careers—without changing clubs. Guys who were winning almost never changed.

Hogan was unhappy with his performance. Just as in the Masters, he had hit more greens in regulation than anyone else in the field and took more putts. He didn't feel ready for the biggest—and perhaps his last— tournament of the year. He decided to do something about it. The *Fort Worth Star Telegram* heard about it two weeks later.

SPORTS REPORT
By Jim Trinkle

A letter was opened in Memphis, Tenn., last week and its contents set off one of the wildest Beale Street celebrations. . . . The letter, from Fort Worth, contained Ben Hogan's entry in the Memphis Open beginning Thursday. . . . What his presence in the field means in gate receipts is open to speculation, but it will be plenty. . . . As a golf club manufacturer hard-pressed to keep customers supplied with enough sticks (they all want 15 now, like Sam Snead), Hogan's appearances have been limited to only the bluest of blue chip events.

It is only 16 days until Hogan and a small army of 150 other golfers take up arms against a common foe—Denver's Cherry Hills Country Club, which will defend under the banner of the United States Golf Association.

The occasion is the annual summer pilgrimage known as

the National Open, and this explains Hogan's presence in Memphis. He needs the competitive work to prepare for the one tournament he covets most.

Each year since 1953, when he won (at) Oakmont in Pennsylvania, Hogan fans experience similar sensations as time grows short until the Open. There is a tightening in the chest, runaway pulse and nightmares in which their hero gets the yips on a 12-inch putt. In 1955 it looked as if their prayers were answered and Hogan would reach a goal no man ever crossed—winning five National Opens.

A lean and somber man with a magic putter—his name was Jack Fleck—sent their dream castles a-tumble.

Hogan shot 66–66 in the first two rounds in Memphis and was tied for the lead with Bob Rosburg and J. C. Goosie. As he sat in the locker room afterward, a *Golf Digest* writer watched as Tommy Bolt "juggled the ice cubes in his glass and addressed Mr. Hogan as only Bolt would dare:

'Say, Ben, what's all that jazz you go through when you putt. You stand over that ball for hours.'

'I always putt like that,' Hogan replied. 'If I was alone I would putt like that.'

'Well, I don't get it,' Bolt said. 'I been wondering about that putting of yours and even tried it today. I stood over the ball longer than I ever have before. When I hit it my club felt like it weighed a ton. . . . Why don't you just walk up to the ball, find the line and hit it.'"

Hogan did not have much of a reply, so he tried a little offense: "Say, where'd you get those pants, Bolt? Skin a rattlesnake?"

Bolt blazed after bantering with Ben. He shot 65 in the third round and, as he prepared to play the sixteenth hole on Sunday, he needed two birdies on the final three holes to tie for first. A tournament official stopped him on sixteen. "Uh, sorry, Tommy," he said. "Your wife had to be taken to the hospital this afternoon—she's at Saint Joseph's in Memphis—and they had to operate." (Mary Lou Bolt was bleeding internally.) Bolt got his birdies despite the upsetting news. There would be a Monday playoff with Bolt, Gene Littler, and the tour's best part-time player, Hogan.

Bolt hit two of the two thousand playoff spectators with wild second shots—a woman on the fourteenth hole on the back of the neck and a boy on the sixteenth, affected anatomy unrecorded. But he had built up a big early lead and was able to hang on to defeat Hogan 68 to 69 (Littler shot 71). The winning shot was Bolt's two-iron to the par-three seventeenth; it set up the clinching birdie. "I knew when I hit it off the tee it was going to be somewhere around the pin," said Bolt. "The Hawk said 'Good shot,' and that's like him writin' you a letter three pages long. He don't say much." *Memphis Press-Scimitar* sports columnist George Bugbee was almost overcome by it all: "Ben Hogan came, was seen by awe-stricken multitudes, and conquered hearts in a golf tournament that had everything," he swooned. "Bolt and Littler added flamboyant touches to the battle. . . . But it was, in the final analysis, the little figure of Ben Hogan who dominated this show from start to finish, an immortal who here added, by his incredible skill and valor, new inches to his matchless golfing stature."

Hogan felt much better about things. "I've played better than this, of course, but I was pretty encouraged about it all. I'm glad I played here and I'm glad I had to play that extra day, although I'm awfully tired. I think it will help me get in shape for the Open, both mentally and physically." Commented Bolt: "The National Open is coming up and The Little Man is playing very well. I better get my money down on him."

The U.S. Open was now just ten days away.

Wilson would not let Arnie go. McCormack made the unpleasant discovery at a meeting at the giant sporting goods company's headquarters in River Grove, Illinois. Arnold and Winnie attended. They met the new president of Wilson Sporting Goods, Bill Holmes, who knew both that Palmer and McCormack were talking with First Flight and that Wilson had an option to renew the contract for three more years. Would you, based on previous assurances from other Wilson executives, release Arnold from his contract? asked the agent. Long silence. "No," said Holmes. "We would not." Longer silence.

While McCormack must have pictured a check for $150,000 suddenly sprouting wings and flying out the window, Palmer was not all that disappointed. The deal with Harkins was a bit of a flier anyway; Wilson was much more established. Besides, Holmes had agreed to renegotiate the contract. "Boldness is what Arnold brings to the golf course, but I think he must exhaust it all there," McCormack wrote. "Careful planning, orderliness and security are the things he looks for elsewhere."

Palmer played in two more tournaments after Colonial and before the Open. He missed the thirty-six-hole cut at the 500 Festival Open, his first missed cut in two years. Doug Ford won that bizarre event, held on the easy golf course built on the infield of the Indianapolis race track. The noise was terrific, from the practicing Indy cars and from the carburetion-testing garage nearby. "You could play a brass band behind me and I wouldn't care," recalls Ford. "Nothing ever bothered me once I got over the ball—except my swing." Arnie skipped Memphis, then played—very well—at Oklahoma City the following week. Littler won, with birdies on the last three holes. Art Wall was second, and Palmer was third, three strokes back.

The United States Open was next.

The surest sign that the U.S. Open was approaching was the annual appearance of sports page or golf-magazine stories titled *Will Snead End Open Jinx?* It seemed they'd run the same story for twenty years. *Experts agree Snead is the greatest player never to win the Open,* the stories would say. *Snead still a threat to win despite his age—he turned forty-eight on May 27* (he is three months older than Hogan). *Snead is playing great—he won DeSoto Open and Greater Greensboro Open earlier this year, the seventy-eighth and seventy-ninth wins of his fabulous career, an all-time rec-*

ord. He has won the Masters three times, the PGA Championship three times and the British Open once, never the Open. His jinx in the Open started in 1937 and continued in 1939, 1940, 1947, 1949, 1953 . . .

It must have been a trial for Snead to be reminded that, through a bizarre combination of bad judgment and worse luck, he had never won golf's biggest tournament. In 1937 he shot 283, just one over the U.S. Open record. Then Ralph Guldahl, a tall, silent, round-shouldered Norwegian from Dallas, surged on the final nine holes to win by two. Big Ralph's key stroke was a successful bunker shot on the third-to-last hole. A cigar butt lay against his ball; he exploded both ball and butt onto the green and made the putt. Then, in the prescoreboard year of 1939, Snead thought he needed a birdie four on the final hole to win. He didn't; a par would do it. He tried a high-risk second shot, a brassie from a grassy lie. His two-wood shot dribbled a hundred yards into a fairway bunker. From there Sam hacked his way to an eight and again lost by two (Byron Nelson won in a playoff with Craig Wood and Denny Shute). But his most galling Open defeat had to be that disaster in 1947 at St. Louis Country Club. Snead and Lew Worsham came to the final green of their eighteen-hole playoff for the title tied. Both had two-and-a-half-foot putts for par. Sam's putt was downhill, with a left-to-right break, and he wanted to get it over with; five thousand people were watching, and he'd already read enough "Snead's Open Jinx" stories. He stood over the putt and was about to hit it . . . .

"Wait a minute," called Worsham, whose putt from below the hole was much easier than Sam's. "Are you sure you're away?"

Snead stopped. A discussion ensued. Ike Grainger, the USGA official refereeing the match, told the combatants that Snead could putt only if he was furthest from the hole. A USGA staffer produced a heavy steel measuring tape, Grainger measured, and it turned out that it *was* Snead's turn, his ball being thirty and one-half inches from the cup to twenty-nine and one-half inches for Worsham. Sam, flustered, missed. Worsham made his putt and won.

"I think Snead was upset that there was a contest over who would putt first and he was upset with himself and with Worsham," says Grainger, "but he was a hell of a good sport about it. At the presentation ceremony, he was Sam Snead at his best."

Snead had more ham in him than a prize pig; he loved nothing more than a microphone and an audience. He did dialect, which sounded hilarious in his backwoods accent, and he preferred off-color stories, the smaller the group, the offer the color. "Rabbi Snead" is the punchline to one of his favorite jokes. He told a group recently that he knew someone "tryin' to get that little hitch, little flick, little flick out of his backswing . . . but that didn't work and then he couldn't get the flick back." His audience guffawed. "You know, golf's a funny game. One day you're on cloud nine, the next day you couldn't scratch a whale's back. . . . The golf swing is all rhythm and timing, rhythm and timing, rhythm and timing. . . . I had a hole in one with every iron in the bag, from the one-iron on up. Did you know that Bob Jones and Hogan never made a hole in one?" (which, incidentally, is not true. Hogan has made several holes in one).

The press loved Snead. "He's a genuine, dyed-in-the-wool-hat American legend," wrote Jim Murray. "Dan'l Boone with a one iron, Huck Finn in a hat." Fans were enthralled by the rhythmic grace and power of his swing and by his durability; he started winning in the thirties and now, in 1960, he was still winning. "Someone asked me," Sam says, "what two brothers won the most tune-a-ments. Well, I don't know and he says 'you, you dumb cluck, you and *your* brother. And he never won one!'"

Samuel Jackson Snead was born to rural poverty in Ashwood in western Virginia, not in West Virginia, as has been frequently written. Ashwood is about fifty miles north of Roanoke in the Applachian Mountains, near the towns of Hot Springs,

Warm Springs, and Healing Springs. Hot Springs had a golf course.

"The first golf I played was on the Goat Course, which was called that because it was built straight up and down a mountain," recalled Snead in 1965 for *Golf*. "We made clubs from hickory sticks, leaving the bark on at the top for a grip. The club heads were knots of wood nailed to the shaft. When the course cops weren't looking, we'd pop out of the woods, play a few holes, then duck back in again.

"I never had a golf lesson from anybody. It just came natural. About the time I was sixteen, I entered a long drivin' contest against men. Won it, too, with a knock of 318 yards."

Snead went to work at Hot Springs at age nine, as a caddie. He was promoted to "apprentice club maker" at age sixteen. About then, the stock market crashed. "Hell, I couldn't make enough to keep my clothes clean—$20 a month," Snead said. "Later on, though, they made me assistant pro. That paid $10 a week. Man, I was swole up with pride. Only trouble was, I had only one set of irons, some sprung woods and no golf bag. I found an old ripped-up bag that somebody had thrown away and patched that up. Oh, I tell you, I was a hot-lookin' pro." Within a week, the new assistant pro broke the course record.

His humble origins became legend. So did his frugality. It was said he never bought anyone a drink—"Why should I help your bad habit?" he'd say. Caddies were not anxious to work for him, because on the one hand he was a lousy tipper and on the other he was inclined to be disagreeable and fault-finding when he wasn't playing well. It was said that he didn't trust banks. "Old Sam puts his winnings inside tin cans and buries them in his backyard" was repeated so often that it began to have the ring of truth. "Jimmy Demaret started that story," says Snead. "After it got in the paper a few times, I came home one night and found a man with a hoe, a rake and a lantern in my backyard."

Snead had been involved in three well-publicized controversies in the spring. He "threw" a television match against Mason Rudolph after he discovered he had an extra club in his bag. He criticized the condition of the Starmount Country Club, the site of the Greater Greensboro Open, so sincerely and so publicly that the owner of the club felt compelled to ban him from the grounds—and this after Snead had won the tournament on the awful course. And a third brouhaha erupted when a reporter overheard Boros say he was sure Sam accepted appearance money to play at Greensboro, and that Casper, Venturi, Rosburg, Middlecoff, and others avoided the event because Snead was getting a thousand dollars or fifteen hundred dollars just for showing up (the best players might also have skipped the Greensboro tournament because it was inconveniently scheduled, right after the Masters). Taking appearance money was against PGA rules. "Let him prove I've accepted money to play here," Sam said. "They owe me a lot of money because I've been coming here twenty-two years and haven't received any of it yet."

Depending on your perspective, these spats either detracted from Snead's good image or proved his tendency to be petty. Either way, he had never enjoyed the formidable reputation of his colleagues Hogan and Nelson, even though he had won more tournaments. No one ever talked about the "Snead Era"—the "Hogan Era," the "Age of Nelson," yes, or "Hogan, Nelson, and Snead," but never Snead alone. Why not? Perhaps it was the sheer length of time that he was at or near the top of the sport; his "era" spanned several smaller eras. Possibly, it was his failure to win the Open. Would this be the year Snead beat his Open jinx?

The air was fresh and clear. The sun glinted pleasantly off the snow-capped mountains in the distance. The grass was green and lush. The lakes were shimmering blue. And Tommy Bolt was mad as hell.

He had driven out of bounds on the eleventh hole and had hit into the water on the par-three twelfth, taking a triple-bogey six. On the eighteenth hole, Bolt boiled over. He pulled his tee shot into the large lake left of the fairway. His color deepened. Muttering, he teed up another ball. Again, the water. That did it. He hit a third ball, which found dry land at last, then, with a fearful cry, Bolt drew back his driver with both hands, over his right shoulder, sort of an ax-murderer stance. His playing partner, Claude Harmon, recoiled, instinctively throwing his arms up to protect himself. Then Bolt heaved the club into the water. Nearby spectators became uncomfortably silent. Such a display . . . Then a ten-year-old boy dove into the lake. He emerged a minute later with the club, and the crowd cheered, the tension broken. Bolt approached the dripping child to thank him for retrieving his club, but the kid gave the golfer a fake and ran right around him; he'd decided to keep it.

Welcome to the first round of the 1960 Open Championship of the United States Golf Association. "This was, to put it mildly, the wildest Open ever," wrote Herbert Warren Wind in the next week's *Sports Illustrated*. To wit:

The tournament favorite, Arnold Palmer, was in trouble after one swing. He hit a horrid drive on the first hole into a little, fast-flowing stream right of the fairway. Palmer walked to where he thought the ball would be, only to find that the Rocky Mountain spring water had carried it at least thirty yards downstream, to within about forty yards of the green. Then, to complicate matters further, a boy waded into the water, plucked the ball out, and threw it on the bank. Where should I drop, Arnold asked a USGA official. How about up here? No, sorry, Mr. Palmer. You must drop opposite where the ball entered the water (or, in golf legalese, "where the ball last crossed the margin of the lateral hazard"), not where it stopped. Arnie dropped, chopped, chipped, chipped again, and had to make a ticklish putt for double-bogey six. Charge.

It could have been worse—he could have tried to play his ball from the babbling brook, as poor Ray Ainsley had done. Ainsley, a professional from Ojai, California, attempted this difficult feat in 1938, during the first Open held at Cherry Hills. He hit his second shot on the sixteenth hole of the second round into Little Dry Creek, which was not dry and did not seem little to the misguided Mr. Ainsley. He waded into the brook and watched as the lively current carried his ball erratically downstream, away from the hole. He decided to try to play the bouncing ball. Bad move. The water "swirled him about and threatened to sweep him into the whirlpool. He ignored the dangers of boulders and seaweed and the incoming tide," wrote Henry McLemore of the United Press that night, having fun with it. "Sharks nibbled at his ankles but still he kept whacking away. Passing ships sent lifeboats but he waved them aside. . . ." The *Denver Post* headline read HE TAKES 19 STROKES ON HOLE AND BECOMES NATIONAL HERO. Nineteen shots on one hole is an Open record that survives today.

Back again to 1960, up ahead of Palmer on the eighteenth tee, Doug Sanders was preparing to drive. He was working on a great round; a par-four on the uphill, 468-yard hole would give him a 68 and the lead. Just as he was about to pull the trigger, a fish jumped out of Bolt's Lake and loudly splashed back in. "I thought for a minute someone was unloading a truckload of empty beer cans," Dougie said. A *Sports Illustrated* photographer caught the dumbstruck Sanders just at that moment. The caption for the photograph in the magazine the next week read "STARTLED SANDERS, transfixed in act of addressing shot, stares at bubbles where fish has disappeared in pond." Unfortunately, he did not reset and gather himself; he held his ground, swung, and almost missed. The ball quick-hooked into the pond with the fish.

Sam Snead did better with the Cherry Hills water. He skipped his ball across the moat guarding the seventeenth green and got a birdie.

Back to Palmer, now on the second hole, as recalled by his playing partner, Jack Fleck: "I noticed that Arnold and his caddie were squawking, arguing about clubs or yardages or something. I walked over to him and said 'Arnie, it's just the beginning of the tournament, you've got to settle down.' Maybe

I should have kept my mouth shut." But Palmer did settle down, and shot 72.

Ben Hogan shot 75. On the ninth hole, his snap-hooked tee shot hit a man in the stomach. This, reported *Golf World*, "seemed to unnerve him."

The first round was not all chaos and pratfalls, however. Jerry Barber putted his way to a 69. The U.S. Amateur champion, Jack Nicklaus, also played well, as expected. He shot even-par 71. And Mike Souchak shot a neatly organized 68—with only twenty-four putts—and had the lead to himself. Souchak, age thirty-three, was a former college football player (All-Southern Conference as a defensive end and field-goal kicker)—and looked it. With his heavily muscled upper body, he hit the ball a long way, which you'd expect, but he also had a nice touch around the green, which you might not expect. "Best player never to have won a major," says his pal, Dave Marr. A number of his contemporaries thought "Souch" would prove to be, if not another Hogan, at least another Palmer. Like Arnie, he was from Pennsylvania (Berwick, down the road from Scranton); he was an aggressive player and a likable guy; and he was capable of bursts of low scores that were almost unbelievable. He had won at San Diego early in the year, the tenth victory in his eight years on the tour, with rounds of 67–68–67–67. But that was nothing compared to what he did when he won his first tournament, the 1955 Texas Open.

Souchak played three spectacular rounds (60–68–64) at Brackenridge Park Golf Club, a municipal course in San Antonio. Brackenridge was famous for not having grass on its tees—players had to hit from rubber mats. "Then, in the fourth round, a norther blew in," recalls Marr. "I was gonna quit after nine, it was so cold. Everybody was putting on gloves and overcoats. . . ." In chimes Bob Rosburg: "And the mud. We used to steal knives from restaurants to scrape the mud off our shoes at Brackenridge." Souchak played the final round in twenty-eight-degree temperatures in 65—with gloves on. He birdied the final two holes for a four-round total of 257, by two shots the lowest ever. In his first-round 60, he played the second nine in eight-under-par 27, another all-time best. "I eagled the thirteenth and birdied in," he recalls. "Three, three, three, three, three, two, for 27. I shot my age for nine holes."

The knock on Souchak was that he was not exactly fanatical about golf. "Mike would win a tournament in August by eleven shots, then quit for the year," laughs Marr. The attractions at home were his wife, Nancy; six-year-old Michael, Jr.; Patricia, three; and Frank, six months. Souchak had his detractors. One was Claude Harmon, the head professional at Winged Foot Country Club in New York, Souchak's former boss. Big Mike announced one day that he was quitting his assistant-pro position to join the tour, and gave short notice. Harmon, bitter about being left in the lurch, called around. This would not be an easy job to fill, or rather, it would be too easy. Winged Foot was the best assistant's job in the country, because of Harmon's ability to land his thoroughly trained apprentices the most desirable head-professional positions. Jack Burke, Jr., the Masters and PGA champion of 1956, recommended his cousin, Dave Marr. Harmon hired him. ("I had to tell them I was twenty-five," says Marr. "I was only twenty. That's why a lot of Winged Foot members think I'm sixty-six or whatever.") Marr reported for duty before Souchak left and they became friends. Harmon, Marr noticed, would "say things" to members about Souchak, things like "I don't think he's gonna make it." There were other doubters. "I didn't think he was another Palmer," says another touring pro of the same vintage. "He didn't have it up here like Arnold did. He had the mentality of a football player. I didn't think he had enough imagination to play from trouble or to play from behind."

After two rounds, any question of Souchak's ability to play from behind or from trouble were still unanswered. He had not been in trouble (unless you counted his second-round shot on the eighteenth hole, when his ball rolled over the green and stopped on a pile of Dixie cups; from there, he made his only bogey of the day). And he certainly had not been behind. He shot 67 and led the closest challenger by three. Souchak's two-round total of 135 was a new record, surpassing Snead's 138 at Riviera in 1948. Rex Baxter and Hogan also shot second-round 67's, Sanders and Johnny Pott had 68's, and Boros, Finsterwald, Snead, and several others shot 69. Here, at last, were the low scores that had been predicted. "There were lots of short holes at Cherry Hills," recalls Walker Inman, Jr. "You felt if you played good you could shoot a good score—unlike, say, at Olympic [in San Francisco, the 1955 Open course], where the rough was up to your waist." It had been agreed before the tournament began that this was a short golf course, despite its 7,004-yard length. It was, after all, a mile high. *The ball travels 6 percent farther in our thin air compared to sea level,* pronounced the host profes-sional, Rip Arnold, with seemingly foolish precision. Hogan shot two 67's in practice and predicted his Open record of 276 (set at Riviera in 1948) would fall. "Cherry Hills has great char-acter and it's a very well-used piece of ground. But it's short, considering its altitude," says golf architect Desmond Muir-head. "It is a course that rewards adventurous shots, not merely the most accurate shots."

"It was the easiest Open course I'd played on to that point," says Marr, but adds, "As Middlecoff said, 'you don't win the Open—the Open wins you.' It's the hardest tournament in the world to win."

Hogan's charge into contention was spectacular. His 67, said playing partner Finsterwald, "was one of the greatest rounds of golf I ever saw." Dow played well himself, despite a shocking confrontation with his caddie. On the sixteenth, a 402-yard par-four, he asked the bag toter for his opinion on the correct club for the second shot. "Why should I tell you? You've asked me twice already today and didn't use my advice," quoth the caddie, a forty-year-old man who perhaps had been in the mountain sun too long. Finsterwald frowned, grabbed a club, and was about to hit, when the disgruntled baggage handler called out "not enough club." It wasn't; Dow came up short.

Angry words were exchanged. The employer/employee relationship was terminated forthwith. A Portland, Oregon, television broadcaster named Charlie LaFranchise carried Finsterwald's clubs the final three holes.

Since extreme length and strength were not required to play Cherry Hills well, the excellent start of Sanders should not have been a surprise. He was a relatively short hitter, but was very accurate. Sanders, twenty six, was a native of Cedartown, Georgia, a little town between Atlanta and Chattanooga. He won the 1955 Canadian Open, a PGA tour event, while still a student at the University of Florida; no amateur would win again on the tour for the next thirty years. And Sanders had been playing very well in 1960: he had been second twice (both times to Palmer), fourth twice, and fifth once.

His swing was bizarre. He set up in the widest stance on the tour, wide enough for a man pounding railroad spikes, with his feet at forty-five-degree angles to his body. For long seconds he simultaneously gripped and regripped the club, milking it, while tapping his heels into the ground, up and down, up and down. . . . Come on, hit it Doug. Suddenly, it was over. His wristy swing was so short and quick that it was almost invisible.

No one could play like Sanders—and his golf game was good, too. He was the heir to Walter Hagen as the hardest partier and most successful ladies' man in sport. A pro shop assistant was once instructed to take Mr. Sanders to the airport after a tournament. "Here, son, hold these," Sanders said, handing the young man two water glasses almost filled with scotch. "Christ, I hope he doesn't expect me to drink one of these things," the driver said to himself. He didn't. Sanders drained both glasses. "God *damn*, I'm a lucky man," he says today. "At the Bob Hope tournament, Bob always let me pick the queens, and I'd wind up dating them that week, seeing them, you know. . . . Jill St. John . . ." (another Sanders inamorata was Donna Douglas, the television actress who portrayed Elly May Clampett on "The Beverly Hillbillies"). Dougie's voice trails off dreamily. He speaks in a sort of sing-song and is apt to hold your arm and put his face very close to yours when he reminisces. He doesn't want you to miss a word.

"The world was looking for a hero, and Arnold Palmer won like a man, going for it all the time, and he never forgot how to be a champion. . . .

"I was at the Oak Manor Motel in Baton Rouge, goddamn, it was like yesterday . . . I was sitting there having a beer with Gary Player. I said, 'If I could give you $250,000, would you stay an amateur?' and he said 'Laddie, I'm going to come back next year and I'm going to win everything. . . .

"Did you ever read *Dead Solid Perfect* by Dan Jenkins? That was about *me*. . . .

"Not many people can say what I'm about to say. . . . If I died today and could come back as anyone else, I'd come back as me.

"I was having dinner with Mr. Frank Sinatra, and we were drinking a fifty-nine Chateau Lafite, and Frank said, 'George'—that's my real first name—my close friends call me George—'you, W. C. Fields, Errol Flynn, me—there are only a few of us who can say—I Did It My Way.'"

Two shots behind the Georgia playboy, three players were tied for third: Barber, Finsterwald, and the 1955 Open champion, Jack Fleck. Fleck, perhaps more than most, would prove something by winning this week. His defeat of Hogan in a playoff for the 1955 Open at Olympic in San Francisco was widely viewed as a fluke. Mention of the f-word makes Fleck slightly testy. "Fluke? What is a fluke? The possiblity that winning the Open was a fluke never occurred to me," he says. "What about Andy North? Orville Moody—was he a fluke? [Both North and Moody were upset winners of the Open.] And I won two other tournaments on the tour, you know."

Fleck—Hogan; their names have been linked since Fleck's shocking playoff victory. But their ties actually began several months earlier. "I wrote to the Hogan Company early in 1955 and told them I was interested in trying their clubs," he recalls. "Hogan wrote back and said, 'Send us your specs.'" At this

Arnold Palmer (*courtesy of Arnold Palmer*)

Arnold Palmer (*courtesy of Arnold Palmer*)

Ben Hogan (*courtesy of Texas Sports Hall of Fame*)

Ben Hogan (*courtesy of Texas Sports Hall of Fame*)

Jack Nicklaus (*courtesy of Jack Nicklaus*)

Jack Nicklaus
(*courtesy of Jack Nicklaus*)

Mike Souchak (*USGA*)

Julius Boros (*USGA*)

Tony Lema (*USGA*)

Dow Finsterwald (*USGA*)

Deane Beman (*USGA*)

Ken Venturi (*USGA*)

Don Cherry (*USGA*)

Sam Snead (*USGA*)

Bob Brue (*courtesy of Bob Brue*)

Mark McCormack (*courtesy of Mark McCormack*)

Butch Baird (*courtesy of Butch Baird*)

Jack Fleck (*USGA*)

Gary Player (*USGA*)

Doug Sanders (*USGA*)

Moe Norman (*courtesy of the Royal Canadian Golf Association*)

Jay Hebert (*USGA*)

Billy Casper (*USGA*)

Charlie Sifford (*courtesy of Charlie Sifford/Roisman Pro-Rep*)

Chi Chi Rodriquez (*USGA*)

Kel Nagle (*USGA*)

Al Geiberger (*USGA*)

Arnold Palmer (*courtesy of Arnold Palmer*)

point, his factory had produced exactly one set of clubs Hogan was happy with—the set he used. So Fleck sent in his preferences for loft, lie, length, grip material, and diameter. When the tour came to Hogan's Alley in May, Fleck shot 69 and 72, then caused a stir when he announced to the press, "I'm switching to Hogans tomorrow." Fleck picked up the irons that afternoon. The wedges weren't ready, so Hogan promised to deliver them himself at the Open.

At Olympic, Hogan holed out on the final green and handed his ball to Joe Dey of the USGA. "Here's one for Golf House," he said, referring to the USGA museum and headquarters. Hogan had apparently won an unprecedented fifth U.S. Open. The only player still on the course with a chance to tie or beat Hogan was this tall, intense guy with new clubs, and he was just a club pro from Bettendorf, Iowa; he'd never won anything on the tour, much less the Open. If Fleck could play the final nine in one under, he could tie The Great Man. Which, of course, he did, dramatically, with a birdie on the final hole. Then he outplayed the tired, limping Hogan in the playoff, 69 to 72. It was no fluke. "A lot of guys thought Hogan hated me afterwards, but I never thought that," says Fleck.

1960 had been Fleck's best year since winning the Open. He had finally won again, at Phoenix; was second at St. Petersburg, when George Bayer pitched in over a mound to win their playoff; and finished a close third at Houston, one shot out of the Collins-Palmer playoff, when he missed a twelve-inch putt in the last round. "I should have won five tournaments that year," says Fleck.

He hit his drive off the fourteenth tee at Cherry Hills, then stood and watched a man who *had* won five 1960 events. Arnold Palmer addressed his Wilson Staff, "the Long Ball," preparing to do it extreme violence on the 470-yard par four. He whacked it. He watched it. The ball cut through the thin Colorado air in a lovely arc, a small diminishing dot in the brilliant blue sky, and landed soundlessly in a field, fifty yards out-of-bounds to the right. But this was not the tragedy it would ordinarily be, for the free thinkers at the USGA had changed the out of bounds penalty to no penalty at all. Arnie hit another ball—on the course this time—and lay only two, not three, as he would have in years past.

The no-penalty o.b. ball allowed Palmer to be eight shots behind Souchak after two rounds, instead of nine. Big deal. Arnie was one over par, Souchak was seven under. He was out of it. But a charge by Palmer from eight shots back seemed no less likely than a challenge from the curious collection of five players tied for sixth at one under. There was Snead, who was self-destructive in the Open; Casper, the defending champion, was a possibility, but his forte was conservative play, not the kind of slash-and-burn golf that would be required to catch Souchak; neither Ted Kroll, forty, the pro many of the pros went to for swing help, nor Bruce Crampton, twenty-four, an unhappy-looking Australian, had ever won a major championship. The fifth member of this group, Don Cherry, was the longest shot of all.

Cherry, thirty-five, was one of the very best in the relatively anonymous world of amateur golf. At the same time, he was, in a way, better known than anyone in the field. More people listened to him when he opened his mouth than Palmer, Hogan, and Snead combined. Cherry was on the radio, on TV, on records, in nightclubs. He was a singer.

"It's a weird thing that anybody could play golf and sing," Cherry says now, "because one is nighttime and the other is daytime. . . . The biggest thing I got was respect for being able to do both." He would book nightclub gigs in whatever city the tour was in on a particular week, play in the tournament (as an amateur, accepting no prize money) and sing at night. He liked the guaranteed pay that being an itinerant musician provided—usually five or six hundred dollars a week—but did not really enjoy performing. And he couldn't abide hecklers at all. Naturally, after his pals on the tour discovered Cherry had a thin on-stage skin, they made sure to taunt, confuse, annoy, and interrupt his performances. Once, Demaret smuggled an air horn into an Evening With Don Cherry somewhere, and honked the noisemaker loudly just as Don was putting the big finish on some romantic ballad. Another time, Demaret got a big group of pros together to go to the small theater where Cherry was singing. He met each golfer at the door and handed him a box of a dozen unwrapped golf balls—steel-centered First Flights, presumably, since Demaret was the main spokesman for the company. "On my signal," Sunny Jim told the giggling golfers. Perhaps Cherry was in the middle of "Mona Lisa" when Demaret gave the sign, and a dozen dozen golf balls clattered down the hard theater floor toward the stage. Hilarity filled the air. Cherry headed for his dressing room in a huff. "I walked off the stage a number of times," he recalls. "I'd argue with the audience. . . . I'd say 'Fuck you, I'm out of here.'"

Hecklers made Cherry mad, but golf made him furious. "I had the worst temper the world had ever seen. I think it was the result of being suppressed as a child," he speculates. Cherry had the classic golf game of the easily angered; he played exceedingly well from tee to green but then, it seemed, he never made a putt. It didn't seem fair. He had a worse temper than his friend Bolt, Cherry says, but not quite as bad a disposition as the volcanic Lefty Stackhouse, another Texan from an earlier era. "Lefty was my hero," he says. "I watched him skull a chip across the tenth green at Lakewood Country Club in Dallas, then punch the trunk of a hackberry tree. Broke every bone in his hand."

Cherry was a baffling man, a walking contradiction. He recorded a half-dozen hits in 1955 and 1956 ("Band of Gold" and "I Believe" were two of the biggest) but wasn't able to build on these successes because of his mistrust of agents. He was both an entertainer and "a complete introvert." He inherited a strong moralistic streak and was a self-described family man, but had four marriages and four divorces (he married a former Miss America, a Miss Nevada, and a "mis-take," as well as a girl from Claremore, Oklahoma, for four hours—long story). He'd wear a toupee for one wedding or club appearance but not for another. He didn't smoke or drink, but his best friends—Dean Martin, Phil Harris, Bobby Layne, Mickey Mantle, and Demaret—most assuredly did. He was drawn to golf, but it usually made him livid. Could a man like this win the U.S. Open?

The other amateur in the Open, Jack Nicklaus, was even par, a stroke behind Cherry after two rounds. He felt optimistic; his swing felt great. "The sensation I had was that I was getting into the proper position on my backswing with a very restrained turn," he remembered later. "There was no way the ball could go left; if I didn't hit the ball dead straight, I'd block it out a shade to the right. I was hitting my shots a little like Hogan, in fact."

The purity and consistency of Jack's ball striking was completely lost on one member of his gallery, a large, bull-necked, enthusiastic man with a red baseball cap pulled down so tight on his head it made his ears stick out. Wayne Woodrow ("Woody") Hayes, the head football coach at Ohio State, had been attending a coaching clinic in Colorado Springs, an hour or two south of Denver. He heard that a certain OSU golfer was doing well in the Open, so he dropped in during the second round and walked the course with Charlie Nicklaus. "Woody didn't know anything about golf and he really didn't like it," recalls Paul Hornung. "But he liked Jack. He called the *Dispatch* office at six A.M." Hayes spoke with a slight lisp. "I didn't see a single reporter from Columbus," he told Hornung. "Now, I have notes from the fifth hole on. . . ."

"Open Saturday" is a term you don't hear much anymore. It used to be one of those phrases like "first love" or "boot camp" that cause the mind to turn on and whir like an electric fan. Until 1965, when the practice was abandoned, Open Saturday meant a double-round, thirty-six holes, ten miles of fatigue wedded to eight or nine hours of mental stress. One pictures Hogan limping to the finish at Merion in 1950 or Venturi, near collapse, holing the winning putt in the heat at Congressional in 1964. The biggest tournament in golf had the toughest final day.

The cloudless sky above Cherry Hills on that June Saturday morning was a brilliant blue. On the western horizon, Pike's Peak and the brown, snow-capped Rockies were vivid in the thin, clear air. Two other natural wonders would spend the day together: William Ben Hogan, forty-seven, the four-time champion and the greatest player of his age, and Jack William Nicklaus, twenty, whose day was still to come.

"Several golfers I knew had previously told me that Hogan was hard to play with," wrote Nicklaus/Wind in *The Greatest Game of All*. "He was cold, they said, and he concentrated so explicitly on his own game that he was hardly aware that anyone else was on the course. This, I discovered early in the day, was absolutely wrong. Ben couldn't have been pleasanter to play with. . . . In a word, he treated me like a fellow competitor, and I liked that. . . . I have never been partnered in a championship with a man who was in a contending position, as Ben was at Cherry Hills, who was so enjoyable to play with."

Woody Hayes stayed over to watch the conclusion of the Open. "Woody became an unofficial gallery marshal," recounts Paul Hornung, with a laugh. "A pretty big crowd came out to see Hogan. Woody would hold his hands up and 'shoosh' if they were noisy while Jack was trying to hit. And he'd say 'How about letting Jack Nicklaus's father in to see his son.' Charlie was embarrassed to death, but he got to see a lot of that tournament."

Jack and Ben apparently fed off each other that day, the good play and considerate demeanor of each enhancing the performance of the other. Hogan, Nicklaus noticed, hit every fairway and green in regulation. Both shot 69, the best scores of the third round (except for the 68 shot by Boros). The crewcut youth and the balding, gray-haired man were now two under par.

Palmer, paired with Paul Harney, played in relative solitude. Jim Stadler, a Cherry Hills member, was in the tiny congregation. "It's unbelievable now, but he didn't have a gallery of thirty," Stadler recalled. "He was in the rough all day. I followed him down to the tenth hole [a straightaway par-four of 444 yards]. He knocked the ball in the right trap; the pin is down in a very easy location, down on the flat towards the golf shop. He takes a swing and leaves it in; he takes another, and barely gets it out, but it sort of hangs on the fringe, and then rolls on the green about six feet. He's got a twenty-foot downhiller, he's taken four strokes now, and most people would figure that [he is] going to wind up [with] seven for the hole. But he made it with the fifth stroke. Most people remember what Palmer did Saturday afternoon—but that bogey in the morning was pretty important, too." Arnie had five birdies to offset six bogeys and finished with a 72, two over after three rounds, seven shots out of the lead. He signed his scorecard and walked unhappily into the locker room for lunch.

Souchak played the perfect front-runner round—for seventeen holes. On the eighteenth tee, scene of the first-round tragi-comedy starring Bolt and Sanders, some unnamed and unmourned spectator noisily started his smuggled-in movie camera *just* when Souchak was at the top of his backswing. Big Mike flinched and drove it out of bounds right. His resultant double-bogey six gave him a third-round 73. "I was paired with Mike the first two rounds, and he played as well as a man could play," comments Rosburg. "But he was paired in the final two rounds with someone he didn't like." That would have been Doug Sanders.

Souchak's lead was down to two shots over Finsterwald, Boros, and Barber; three over Hogan, Nicklaus, and Fleck; and four over Cherry, Johnny Pott, and Gary Player. Sanders (77), Kroll (75), Crampton (75), Snead (73), and Casper (73) shot their way out of contention.

Fourth round: The Famous Hamburger Incident took place in the men's locker room between rounds. Present were Rosburg, Venturi, and Palmer, three rather disconsolate golfers—they were all out of the running, it appeared—and two

writers, Bob Drum of the *Pittsburgh Press* and Dan Jenkins of
the *Fort Worth Star Telegram*. This vignette has been told and re-
told so many times it has become a bit worn out. Following are
four versions of what happened:

> I was very disappointed after shooting a seventy two in
> the morning round. . . . I was seven shots off the lead and
> fourteen players were ahead of me. . . . I was having a ham-
> burger when Drum came by. I was sitting between the rows
> of lockers when I said 'I think I'll go shoot sixty-five,' and Bob
> said, 'You better, and even that probably won't do you any
> good.' That made me mad. I didn't even finish the ham-
> burger. I went out and hit some balls. I drove the first green
> of the 346-yard first hole and two-putted. . . ."
>
> —Arnold Palmer, March 1991 *Golf Digest*

> I was trying to find a way to pep him up. He asked,
> 'What would a sixty-five do?' I said, 'Nothing for you.' He
> said 'Sixty-five is 280 (four-round total), and 280 wins
> Opens.' He was so mad, he didn't even finish his hamburger.
> But that's what I was trying to do, get him mad. . . . He drove
> the first green and two-putted for a birdie."
>
> —Bob Drum, in same magazine article

> He thought he could drive the green, but in three previ-
> ous rounds he had not done it.
> 'It really makes me hot,' he said. 'A man ought to drive
> that green.'
> 'Why not?' I said. 'It's only three-hundred-and-forty-six
> yards through a ditch and a lot of high grass.'
> 'If I drive that green I might shoot a hell of a score,' he
> said. 'I might even shoot a sixty-five if I get started good.
> What'll that bring?'
> 'About seventh place. You're too far back.'
> 'Well, that would be two-eighty,' Arnold said. 'Doesn't
> two-eighty always win the Open?'
> 'Yeah,' I said. 'When Hogan shoots it.'"
>
> —Dan Jenkins, in *The Dogged
> Victims of Inexorable Fate*

> It was a cheeseburger.
>
> —Robert Sommers, in *The U.S. Open,
> Golf's Ultimate Challenge*

Palmer's swing on the first tee of the final round of the 1960 U.S. Open looked to be his normal slash—no harder. He teed the ball low, and took a cut at it with his driver (extra-stiff shaft, D-9 swing weight, about the stiffest and heaviest club on the tour). Grass from his small divot flew up in front of him while he followed through, his left elbow unclassically akimbo. He watched the flight of the ball earnestly, with his characteristic side-to-side movement of the head, like a dog that doesn't quite hear or understand you. The ball took off on a low line, landed in tall grass (dried out from ten days of no rain), jumped out, and ran up to the small green. The large first-tee and first-green galleries let out a shout that everyone on the golf course could hear.

Actually, he did not drive the green. Arnie's ball stopped in the fringe, about two paces from the putting surface. And he did not almost make his eagle putt, as some accounts have it. "It [the ball] was pin high, exactly pin high," Palmer recalled. "I was putting right to left [from about thirty feet] and damn near three putted. I got nervous, but then made that. . . . The fact is, I knew that I was in the tournament."

More important than the birdie was the feeling his heroic drive gave him. He'd been trying all week to reach the green with a driver, while virtually the rest of the field played more cautious tee shots with fairway woods. Arnie now felt vindicated, energized; he began to walk fast.

He chipped in from thirty-five feet on the second hole, hit a wedge to a foot on the third, made an eighteen-foot putt on the fourth . . . four birdies in a row. He made a twenty-five-footer with a big break on six, threw his visor in celebration, and cakewalked to the hole. Now people were running from all over the golf course to see this wondrous exhibition. Drum, a rotund man, had arrived at the sixth tee in some cardiovascular distress. As he stood by the gallery rope huffing and puffing, Arnold looked over and said "I knew I'd have to do something sensational to get your fat ass out here.'"

Palmer's run—he made two more birdies and a bogey for a

five-under-par, first-nine 30—did not settle anything; it only muddied the waters. For a while, *nine* players were at two under par. The lead changed hands twelve times during the last round. There was a five-way tie for first for a few minutes. When it was over a few hours later, most of the exhausted, sunburned dozen would probably have told you, "I shoulda won."

> *"Souchak cracked."*
> —Robert Sommers, author of *The U.S. Open, Golf's Ultimate Challenge*

The barrel-chested, curly-haired, broad-faced Souchak had been remarkably poised under the pressure of leading for three rounds, but he made a strategic mistake to begin the final eighteen. He noticed that the big crowd around the first tee, *his* gallery, was diminishing; he knew from the scoreboard and from periodic sonic booms that Palmer was making birdies in bunches; and, of course, he had heard that Arnie had driven the first green. So Big Mike took out his driver, though he'd played a four-wood off this tee without incident the previous rounds. If Arnie could do it . . . But he left his drive out to the right. The ball ended up in the same ditch Palmer had hit into on his first shot of the first round, and he made a double-bogey six. Souchak fought back with a couple of birdies, but when he bogeyed the ninth, he lost the lead—for good.

> *"I'll tell you who could have won it—Don Cherry."*
> —Bob Rosburg

Cherry stood in the fairway of the par-five seventeenth hole and weighed his options. Despite having missed several makable putts, he was three under par, one shot out of the lead. He could lay up short of the water that surrounded the island green and hope for a pitch-and-putt birdie. Or he could roll the dice, go for the green in two, and perhaps make a birdie to tie or an eagle to win. But the green was small and hard to hold from fifty yards, much less two hundred and fifty. . . . Cherry uncovered his three-wood—he was going for it. Here was a gutsy move, a mere amateur trying a bold, low-percentage shot, putting putting everything into winning, not content with just finishing well.

He didn't make it. His ball rolled into the hazard. Double bogey.

"One by one, the others wilted."
—Tom Flaherty, in *The U.S. Open, 1895–1965*

Maybe Cherry Hills was tougher than it looked. As the long, hot afternoon wore on and TV coverage began, the greens seemed to get faster, the fairways narrower, the rough, sand, and water more magnetic. Only eight players broke par; Hogan's record 276 was not challenged.

First, Finsterwald. "I drove it under a pine tree on nine and made [double-bogey] six and I three-putted ten," says Dow now, without apparent bitterness. Boros, whose U.S. Open record in the previous decade was second only to Hogan's, made bogeys from the bunkers on the fourteenth and eighteenth holes and missed a three-foot birdie putt on seventeen. Barber slumped to a 74, Pott shot 75, Player had 76. And Snead, who needed a 65 to win his first Open, shot 75.

Two players who did not wilt—but did not win—were Kroll, with a final-round 67, and E. J. ("Dutch") Harrison, the tour's best hustler, who shot 69.

"If anyone blew it, I did."
—Jack Fleck

"I played the last thirty-six with Dow," Fleck says. "Arnold was two groups in front of us.

"I birdied five of the first six, but then I missed from six feet for birdie on seven. I bogeyed the eighth [he was tied for the lead at this point, at four under par]."

Now, just when he wanted it the most, Fleck's putting touch deserted him completely. "I three-putted from seven feet on the thirteenth, three-putted the sixteenth, missed a three-and-a-half foot birdie putt on seventeen, and missed from four feet on the last hole and made bogey.

"I *gave* him [the eventual winner] that Open," Fleck says ruefully.

It all came down to Nicklaus, Hogan, and Palmer, future and past versus present.

"I played thirty six holes today with a kid who should have won this thing by ten strokes."
—Ben Hogan

Robin Obetz, Nicklaus's Ohio State golf teammate, called his father Friday night. He had a feeling.

"Dad, Jack's at even par. He's gonna win the Open as an amateur."

"You want to go watch?" his father replied. They got up in the dark the next morning and flew from Columbus to Denver via Chicago, and walked the final twenty-seven holes with Charlie Nicklaus and Woody Hayes.

It's helpful to think of Nicklaus as being ten years older in maturity than he was by the calendar. This device helps explain how he had won the Ohio Open (he was "twenty-six," not sixteen), how he won the U.S. Amateur (he was "twenty-nine," not nineteen), and why, at age twenty, with six holes remaining, he led the U.S. Open.

"I learned from the small field scoreboard on the thirteenth that I was the only player who stood five under," he wrote. "I had moved into the lead a stroke ahead of Boros, Palmer, and Fleck. The prospect of possibly winning the Open didn't awe me at all. All I had to do, I said to myself, was to continue hitting my shots well and let the rest take care of itself."

While Nicklaus was mature beyond his years, he was not— compared to Hogan and Palmer—experienced. This would cost him. On the thirteenth, he hit a twelve-foot birdie putt a foot and a half past the hole. But before he tapped in this short one, he noticed a half-repaired ball mark directly in his line. He hesitated. "I remember well my thoughts at that moment," Jack wrote three years later. "'I'm playing good golf and I'm twenty years old,' I said to myself, 'and I'm scared to ask the officials if I can refix the ball mark, though I know I shouldn't be.'" He could, of course, legally repair the mark, but he didn't. The ball hit the slight indentation, and it was just enough to cause it to miss. He missed three more reasonable putts down the stretch—from seven feet for par on fourteen, a five-footer for birdie on sixteen, and from twelve feet for birdie on seventeen. These hurt, certainly, but again, it was inexperience that did Nicklaus in on the final hole.

"I remember our slow walk together up the hill to the last green," he wrote. "I was nowhere near as exhausted physically as Ben was, but my concentration was gone. . . . I had no clear idea of how I stood in relation to the leader. I simply assumed I was out of the tournament."

He wasn't. Jack chipped from the right rough to six feet below the hole. You could have noticed, as he crouched over his putt, that his pants weren't big enough in the hips; the white cloth of his pockets stuck out like little flags. He missed the putt, tapped in, and wearily picked his ball out of the hole. Had he realized that a par *could* have won the tournament, it seems likely that he would have hit a better chip and a better putt. His 282 for the seventy two holes was a new amateur record for the Open. Jack signed his card and made his way to a chair in the clubhouse, where he watched the tournament's conclusion on tv.

> *"Hogan was the best player—he just blew it."*
> —Robin Obetz

Hogan took a share of the lead on the fifteenth. He hit an iron twenty feet from the hole on the 205-yard par-three and, wonder of wonders, made the putt. On a day when he had hit every fairway and every green in regulation, a fantastic feat on an Open golf course, this was by far the longest putt he'd made. He was now tied at four under with Palmer and Fleck.

He parred sixteen, missing from twelve feet for a birdie. On the par-five seventeenth, Hogan gave no thought to trying to reach the water-guarded green in two. He laid up short in the center of the fairway, facing a third shot of between thirty and fifty-five yards (accounts vary). "The Little Man" hesitated, staring at the hole, blowing cigarette smoke into the quiet air, while thousands watched. It was decision time. "With its small, flat, hard, backless green with water around it, it's not a hole anyone would gamble on for the second shot, or even the third, for that matter, if the pin were near the water," says Desmond Muirhead. Should Hogan risk flirting with the water in an effort to get it close for the birdie that would give him the outright lead? (Fleck had bogeyed sixteen by this time, though Hogan didn't know it; Palmer and Hogan were alone at the top.) His lie was perfect, but the green, he knew, was as hard as a cart path; only an exceptional shot would hit and hold. Or should he play a more conservative shot that would ensure a par five? Perhaps Hogan felt his fatigue at this point. A tie would mean an eighteen-hole playoff tomorrow against a younger man (or men), an unappealing prospect. He was deeply tired. He'd go for the win right here.

He withdrew a pitching wedge from his plain, brown leather bag. His caddie, wearing a T-shirt with HOGAN on the back, moved out of the way. The Hawk laid the clubface back until it was almost flat and hit the ball with a firm, confident chop. He had hit hundreds of these in practice. The ball flew low, with enough backspin (to paraphrase Dan Jenkins) to stick on the top of Sam Snead's bald head. "I thought it was going to be perfect," Nicklaus wrote . . . .

Many years later, the reclusive Hogan did an interview with CBS television. Ken Venturi asked the questions.

Hogan: You know, you mention that shot on the seventy-first hole at Denver. . . . I find myself waking up at night thinking about that shot right today. How many years ago was that? It's been twenty-three years ago and there isn't a month that goes by that [whispering] *that doesn't cut my guts out.*

Venturi: You can't call it a missed shot . . . .

Hogan: No, I didn't miss it. I just didn't hit it far enough.

It hit just short of the green, bounced on the green—and I had a lie I could hit with a driver—and I put so much spin on it I just sucked it back in the water.

Hogan removed his right shoe and sock—the crowd roared when it realized he was going to play it—splashed the half-submerged ball up on the green, and two-putted. He knew he'd lost. He was so deflated he took a triple-bogey seven on the final hole.

"Destiny's New Favorite"
  —*Sports Illustrated* headline, 6/27/60

Palmer, playing two groups behind Hogan, learned of Ben's misfortune on the seventeenth tee. He played the last two holes cautiously. He hit a one-iron safely off the eighteenth tee, a four-iron over the green, a chip to three feet, and hit the putt dead center. He had shot 65, a new final-round record for an Open winner. The new champion again threw his visor in celebration and, grinning, walked briskly off the green.

Afterward, there were a hundred "what-ifs." What if Hogan had merely finished par-par? Then there would have been a tie for first and a playoff. What if Nicklaus had parred the final hole? That would certainly have made Arnie's eighty-foot chip on eighteen more difficult, since he would tie Jack if he failed to get it up and down. What if the out-of-bounds penalty had been the traditional stroke-and-distance? Then Arnie would have had at least one more shot on his second-round total. What if Souchak . . . Fleck . . . Boros . . . Cherry . . .

Yet "whatif" is a fruitless pastime, a game for sportswriters and losers. A golf tournament, after all, is not a chemical formula or a mathematical equation, where you can add or remove or change one element and get a predictable change in the outcome. No one, not even Hogan, could make a pure science of the game.

This was the last head-to-head competition in 1960 between Hogan, Nicklaus, and Palmer. Hogan's performance was a last hurrah; he would never again challenge for the fifth U.S. Open title that he coveted. Nicklaus's finish was a warning shot. And Palmer, destiny's darling, had played a round of golf that enthralled the whole country. And if he could win at St. Andrews in July and at Firestone in August, he would have the greatest year in professional golf history. He would be the first winner of the modern Grand Slam.

CHAPTER SIX

Glorious Failure

"Arnold Palmer needs a par-four for a total of 280 and a two-shot victory over amateur Jack Nicklaus in the sixtieth United States Open," murmured the disembodied voice on the television. What? Amateur Jack Nicklaus suddenly sat up a little straighter in his chair in the Cherry Hills clubhouse. "It dawned on me," he wrote later, "that if I had gotten that last six-footer and if Arnold were to take three to get down from the apron, why, we would have tied."

Did this epiphany cause Jack to rend his garment and beat his chest in anguish? No, on the contrary, said he in 1963 in *The Greatest Game of All*, "I was sitting on cloud nine." He had, after all, played with Hogan and played well, finished second in golf's biggest tournament, and set an amateur record, even beating the best that his hero, Bobby Jones, ever shot in the Open. What was there to be mad about? Yet Jack's immediate reaction was far different, far less politic. "People ask me if I got a thrill out of finishing second in the Open," he told Ray Cave of *Sports Illustrated* about six weeks after the fact. "It wasn't a thrill. I didn't win. Nobody ever remembers who finished second at anything." Jack's friend Robin Obetz confirms the depressed/disappointed diagnosis. "Jack was on a downer after the Open," he says. "He was definitely not up for more golf."

After the pictures, presentations, and handshakes were concluded at Cherry Hills, Jack, his father, and Obetz got in a car and headed south on Highway 85, past Castle Rock, Larkspur, and Palmer Lake, to Colorado Springs. There Jack had another tournament starting on Monday morning, the NCAA Championship at the Broadmoor golf course.

A 1960 NCAA All-Star team was named before play got underway, and Nicklaus was the top vote-getter. It confirmed his status as a genuine celebrity, at least in the small world of college golf. (John Konsek of Purdue, Jacky Cupit and Richard Crawford from Houston, Beman, and Donald Norbury of Pennsylvania were also named to the first team.) The tournament format called for two rounds of stroke play to determine the team champion, with the low sixty-four scorers from the field of 190 advancing to match play, which would determine the individual winner. Jack shot 146 and was second-low qualifier (Gene Francis of Purdue was low, with 143), and Houston, led by Cupit and Crawford, won the team title for the fourth year in a row. Jack played Bert Yancey of Army in the first round and whomped him, eight and six, then edged Frank James of Iowa in nineteen holes in his second match. His third opponent was Steven Smith, from Stanford, who had, coincidentally, gone to high school with Obetz at Deerfield Academy in Massachusetts. "We didn't have a golf team at Deerfield and Steve was the last man on the Stanford team," says Obetz. But Smith upset Nicklaus, four and three.

Jack didn't dwell on the defeat. He had something more important on his mind. He was getting married in thirty days.

Hogan's post-Open hangover was deeper and lasted longer than Jack's. It is almost unimaginable, but Hogan's finish at

Cherry Hills, where he had come within a whisker of winning, was almost his *worst* final standing in the Open in twelve years. He won in 1948, almost died in 1949, and then won again in 1950, 1951 and 1953. During the rest of the decade he had two seconds, a third, and a sixth; he was never out of the top ten. Only his tie for tenth in 1958 was worse than his tie for ninth (with Don Cherry and Jerry Barber) at Cherry Hills. He didn't play golf for a solid month after the Open.

A couple of months later, he could talk about it. A writer he liked, Braven Dyer of the *Los Angeles Times*, asked if his finish at Denver was a major disappointment. "It sure was," said Hogan. "I wanted that one so much. It was awful.

"I felt terrible after that seventeenth hole, not only because I had knocked myself out of a chance to win, but because I had played it stupidly. I cut that third shot too fine—underplayed it, when I should have overplayed it. In the morning, I was on the back of the green in three but almost three-putted. This may have had something to do with my playing it too fine, unconsciously, perhaps.

"Looking back, too, if I had only been able to putt. You know that I hit thirty-four greens in regulation figures on that final day, but I just didn't have any putting luck. Without good putting, you just don't win."

Perhaps it was an effort to beat the blues that moved Hogan to accept an invitation to give a speech and clinic for the Texas-Oklahoma Junior Golf Tournament. Maybe he wanted to "give something back" on this occasion; he would accept no appearance fee and would even pay for his own gas. Whatever his motive, Hogan and his friend and business partner Marvin Leonard drove the two-plus hours northwest from Fort Worth to Weeks Municipal Golf Course in Wichita Falls, Texas. It was a typical sunny and witheringly hot July afternoon, but five hundred people were clotted around the shadeless practice tee when Hogan arrived. He gave the clinic ("to fade the ball, I open my stance slightly and swing like this. . . .") and was the featured speaker at the tournament banquet that night.

He was a hit. One of the paradoxes of Hogan's character was that he was so good at this sort of thing that he could put on and take off an air of affability like a pair of socks. That this made his graciousness somewhat studied made no difference to the kids and parents that day in Wichita Falls. And The Hawk became a dove when a photographer was present. He was an absolute master—better, even, than Palmer—at wearing a grin when a photographer said "cheese." He practiced the smile, one of his friends says, by himself, with a mirror.

> Hogan elaborated on the role golf plays in a young man's life, and at the beginning and conclusion of the address, the celebrated Texan received a standing ovation. Immediately following the speech, young Tommy Wilchek presented a plaque to Bantam Ben, who in return vowed that he shall always treasure the plaque in remembrance of this occasion.
>
> Hogan, who casts away the grim image which he displays in [sic] the golf course with numerous smiles, related to those in attendance that one must accept disappointment in the pursuit of athletic and higher goals. . . . 'God seems determined not to let me win my fifth Open, but I am equally determined that I shall win Him over.'"
> —*Wichita Falls Record News*, 7/13/60

This was not Hogan's last appearance of the year for a good cause, but he was not quite ready to retire to the rubber-chicken circuit and his office. He had decided to play in one more tournament.

Mike Souchak showed great resilience after his U.S. Open collapse by winning the next event on the tour, the Buick Open. He shot 71-68-74-69 and holed a seven-foot par putt on the final hole to beat Art Wall and Gay Brewer, Jr., by one shot. Some of the other major players in the Open drama also held up well at the Buick—Snead tied for ninth, Finsterwald tied for eleventh, and Bolt, Fleck, Kroll, and Barber all earned middle-of-the-pack checks. Nicklaus also played, sneaking in one last tournament before his wedding. His 73-77-74-74 would have earned him last-place money of $110, but, as an amateur, he couldn't accept the cash. And, as could be expected, several key performers at the Open—Boros, Crampton, and Sanders—joined Izzy Solomon, Tom Pomranky, Ed Wysowski, and ninety-seven other household names in the Buick Open Out of the Money column.

The Man of the Hour did not play that week in Flint, Michigan. Nor did he do the Paar, Como, or Sullivan shows, make commercials, give exhibitions, or ride in the back of a convertible in a parade down Main Street Latrobe. Instead, Arnold Palmer left the country the day after the Open, in the company of his wife, Winnie, his pal, sportswriter Bob Drum, Sam Snead, and golf agent/impresario Fred Corcoran. Their destination was Dublin, Ireland, and the golf course at Portmarnock, site of the eighth Canada Cup, ostensibly the world team championship. Arnie and Sam were the American side.

Palmer was, ironically, a substitute. The Irish wanted Snead and Hogan, who had won the Cup in 1956. Snead agreed, but Hogan put Corcoran, the director of the U.S. Canada Cup team, on hold. "I'll let you know after the Masters," Hogan said. Corcoran, who somewhat resembled W. C. Fields, waited near the eighteenth green on Sunday at Augusta. But Hogan was in a bad mood after his seventy-six. "Don't think I can make it, Fred," he said. So Corcoran asked the new Masters champ, Palmer, who accepted. The Irish Golf Union was thrilled. Arnie had planned to go to Europe about then, anyway—to play in his first British Open.

Attendance records for the Cup were smashed. The weather was sunny, mild, and almost windless. "This is a typical Irish summer," the prime minister of Ireland told the press. "The first typical Irish summer we've had in ten years." Besides the rare opportunity for the locals to work on their tans, the drawing card (other than the Irish team of Christy O'Connor and Norman Drew) seemed to be one or the other of the Americans. . . . "Especially Sam Snead, who has the stature of legendary hero in their eyes," wrote Herbert Warren Wind in

Sports Illustrated. "There can be no doubt about it. Arnold Palmer was the main attraction at Portmarnock," disagreed *Golfing,* a British magazine.

Gary Player, wheezing from an attack of asthma, shot a course-record 65 on the sand dunes of Portmarnock to lead South Africa to the first-round lead. The 72 shot by his partner, Arthur D'Arcy (Bobby) Locke, was, however, no less remarkable. Less than a year before, the car in which Locke was traveling was hit by a train. Locke, a four-time British Open winner, was a rotund man—one of his nicknames, "Old Muffin Face," hints at his shape—but the impact with the train forced him through the rear window of the car. He was unconscious for several days. Locke's skull was fractured, and he lost twenty pounds and most of the vision in his left eye. At Portmarnock, where he played against doctor's orders, he looked like hell, "walking with the jittery eggshell step of an old man," wrote Wind. South Africa led the United States by three.

Palmer and Snead took the lead in the second round and never gave it up. The Americans played superbly. Snead had 67 and 68 in the second and third rounds, and Arnie, "in one of his most resolute moods," according to Wind, shot 69, the low score of the day, in the fourth round. The Yanks won by eight. England was second; the defending champions, the Australian team of Peter Thomson and Kelvin Nagle, finished third; Ireland was fourth, South Africa fifth. With the team title not in doubt, attention centered on the individual race. Snead had a seemingly safe lead over the man known as the Sam Snead of Europe—Flory Van Donck. Van Donck, from Belgium, was the same age as Snead (forty-eight), had a similar picturesque swing, and had won a flock of tournaments, including twenty-five "minor" national opens (like the Spanish Open or the German Open). But FVD was hardly a clone of the western Virginia hillbilly. "Suave" was the one-word adjective usually attached to his name; *Golf World* termed him "the socialite pro, because he is tutor to the Belgium royal family." He also had a full head of wavy dark hair; Snead had a full head of skin. When Sam made three consecutive bogeys on the back nine of the final round, Van Donck stole past him, and won.

Palmer finished "equal third" with Harry Weetman of England. "It's the first time I've played a course like this one," Arnie said at the conclusion. "I've learned some new shots—shots I've never played in my life. I'm taking them with me to St. Andrews for the British Open."

What he would not be taking with him was much company. When Snead withdrew from the tournament, there was exactly one American—Palmer—with a realistic chance of winning. Where were the other guys? "No, I didn't play over there, and I have always regretted it," says Venturi. "I was a bad traveler. . . . But I think I would have loved that type of multiple-choice golf." Byron Nelson never played in a British Open, and he, too, is sorry he didn't. What about Bob Rosburg, who entered the 1960 tournament but withdrew? "I was scared to go on a plane that far." And you, Dave Marr? "The Open then was not economically feasible, not until 1966, when they changed the rules so that the U.S. PGA and Open champions were automatically qualified."

To the best U.S. golfers, in other words, the British Open had only one positive aspect: it was, by tradition, a major championship. But it was a moribund major, to be sure, since the Americans, the best players in the world, did not play in it. Its negatives—mostly financial—outweighed its prestige. It may have been a "major," but it was also a major pain and a major expense to get to. And the prize money was definitely minor: just $13,400 in 1959 and $19,000 in 1960. Run-of-the-mill tournaments on the American tour paid $20,000 in 1959 and $25,000 in 1960. The American majors paid a heck of a lot more: the Masters purse in 1960 was $87,050, the U.S. Open paid out $60,720 and the PGA distributed $63,130. And the British was inconveniently sandwiched right between the U.S. Open and the PGA.

Perhaps most important to the Yanks, they could not go to the British Open with any guarantee that they would actually play in the tournament. No spot in the event was assured; even Gary Player, the defending champion, had to qualify. In 1953, Ben Hogan won the Masters and U.S. Open and he, too, had to qualify (he qualified, and won); maybe that was why he only played there once. So an American pro might get his shots and his passport, take a slow plane to London, another one to Glasgow or Edinburgh, rent a car and drive on the wrong side of the road north through Kirkcaldy and past Alloa to St. Andrews, play a practice round or two in wind and on a golf course that was like nothing he'd ever seen back in Missouri, then play a thirty-six-hole qualifying tournament. He might win the qualifier, of course, against two hundred locals named Ian who were expert in British seaside pasture pool, win fifty pounds sterling ($140), and get a place in the tournament. Failure to qualify was possible, even probable. To hell with that, the U.S. pros said, I'll take my chances in the tournaments in Flint and Toronto this week.

To Palmer, his compatriots were missing the point. The British Open was about tradition, not money. "I had always planned to play in it once I felt I could afford to go abroad," he reminisced in *Golf Journal*. "I had every intention of entering and playing in the 1960 Open at St. Andrews well before I won the Masters and the U.S. Open earlier in the year. In fact, my father and Harry Saxman, who was the president of Latrobe Country Club and both my father's boss and good friend, had made plans to go with me to St. Andrews. . . ." The British Open was first played one hundred years before, in 1860, when eight contestants went three laps around Prestwick's twelve-hole course. Willie Park won, with 174. The men who won the Open in the next century were to golf what Washington, Jefferson, and Lincoln were to presidents. Tom Morris, Sr., and Tom Morris, Jr. The Triumvirate—Harry Vardon, James Braid, and John Henry Taylor, who between them won sixteen times. Jock Hutchison, the 1921 champion, the first U.S. citizen to win. The other great American players—Hagen, who won four Opens, Jones, who won three, and Armour, Sarazen, Snead, and Hogan. For a traditionalist like Palmer, playing where the game was born, in the one-hundredth anniversary of its first tournament, was the fulfillment of a dream. Besides, Walter Hagen had told him, "Arnie, you ain't nothin' 'til you win the British Open."

There was, of course, another compelling reason for Palmer to make his British Open debut this year. By winning he would equal Hogan's feat in 1953 of taking the Masters, U.S. Open, and British Open in one year. "I had a chance at doing even better," Arnie recalled. "I could win the first-ever professional Grand Slam if I could [also] win the PGA Championship back in the States. Hogan couldn't; the 1953 PGA and British Open had conflicting dates." Hogan had entered six tournaments in 1953 and won five, three of them majors, arguably the best year ever for a professional golfer. (Byron Nelson's 1945 was another contender for "best year ever"; he won eighteen times, including eleven in a row, records that will never be approached.) "Winning at St. Andrews would have been the third leg of the Grand Slam, which would have been a very big deal," Arnie recalls succinctly. Not that the world was in an uproar about the possibility. On the contrary, there was almost nothing about it in newspapers on either side of the ocean. There was, in fact, no "Grand Slam" for professional golfers. "We invented it on the way over [on one leg or the other of the flight from Denver to New York to Dublin]," says Drum. The Grand Slam—"the impregnable quadrilateral" in sportswriter O. B. Keeler's phrase—consisted of the four biggest tournaments *amateurs* could play in. It had been won once, by Bobby Jones, in 1930. The four biggest tournaments then were the British and U.S. Opens and the British and U.S. Amateurs. Jones won them all, then retired. He was thirty, Palmer's age.

Winning the third leg of the "professional slam," as Drum called it, would be far from easy. There was so much to get used to; it was like playing golf on another planet. Hogan was in a nearly identical situation in 1953, when he had won the Masters and the Open and tried to be the first player to win in his first

British Open. He came over two weeks early, as Palmer had done. Hogan's Open was at Carnoustie, down the road from St. Andrews, but some of his observations, recorded in a *Saturday Evening Post* article called "The Greatest Year of My Life," rang true for Arnold and St. Andrews seven years later:

> Their wind isn't any stronger than it is at some places in the United States, but it's a lot heavier and has a lot more moisture as it comes in off the sea. . . . They put sand traps everywhere . . . strategically placed in the middle of the fairway at the perfect driving distance required for those holes. You had to find your way around those traps because if you played short of them you could not reach the green on the second shot.
>
> Heather and gorse are abundant in the rough. Heather, something like a fern, grows in clumps about eight inches to a foot high and is as thick as it can be. If you get in it, you have to hit the ball about ten times as hard as you would otherwise, and then most of the time it won't go more than ten yards or so. . . . Gorse is taller, sometimes waist to head high, and is a brambly bush. . . . I didn't practice getting out of the gorse or heather because I figured anyone who got into it frequently wouldn't have a chance anyway.
>
> Every fairway is rolling and full of mounds, and you hardly ever have a level lie. It was bounce golf. I'd hit a shot and never know which way it might bounce when it landed.
>
> In the United States we play what I term "target golf." Our courses have boundaries or borders, of trees, fences and hedges, and our fairways are well defined, easily distinguishable from the rough. Sometimes at Carnoustie it was almost impossible to determine from the tee where the fairway ended and the rough began because fairway and rough were identical in color.

Practically everything was different, if not disorienting, for the first-time British Open contestant. In addition to the air, the wind, the vegetation, and the mysteriously bunkered golf course, Palmer had to get used to new clothes (a tweed cap was *de rigueur*), galleries (polite), Fleet Street newspapers (bloodcurdling), and golf balls (smaller). The British ball was six one-hundredths of an inch less in diameter than the American ball (1.62 versus 1.68 inches; both weighed 1.62 ounces). Doesn't sound like much, but golf was a different game with the small ball. It went much farther, particularly against the wind, but was harder to hit through the green, because its smaller size made it tend to sit down in the grass. The difference in size between the two balls, incidentally, is surprisingly easy to see.

Half the reason the world did not have a standardized golf ball was right there in that little town by the North Sea. The Royal and Ancient Golf Club of St. Andrews, Scotland, made the rules most of the world followed. Only the United States and Mexico obeyed the dictates of the USGA; the R&A had more clout and much more history. (It did not, incidentally, own the golf courses at St. Andrews, and never has; they are owned by the town.) It was formed on May 14, 1754, by twenty-two "Noblemen and Gentlemen, being admirers of the ancient and healthful exercise of Golf." Although it was neither the the first golf club nor the first to write down some rules of "Golf"—the Honourable Company of Edinburgh Golfers (est. 1744) laid down the original thirteen rules of golf for their competitions at the links at Leith, Scotland—the R&A had staying power and grew in stature.

Not that The Honourable Company's rules weren't sensible. For example: Rule Two—"Your Tee must be upon the Ground"; and Rule Five—"If Your Ball come among Water or any Watery Filth, You are at Liberty to Take out your Ball and Throw it Behind the Hazard Six Yards at least; you may Play with any Club, and Allow your Adversary a Stroke for so Getting Out your Ball." The trouble was, every golf organization had its own rules and some of them made no sense at all. For example, for a few years in the 1850s at one particular Scottish club, if you told your opponent that your ball was unplayable—in some Watery Filth, perhaps—he would have the option of thrashing at *your* ball a couple of times to prove or disprove its unplayability. If he could extricate it in two shots or less, the strokes would count against *your* score. And where was this bizarre rule in effect? At St. Andrews, believe it or not. Obviously, some standardization in rules was needed. In 1897 the golf world (most of it) decided to adapt the procedures followed by the R&A. At a conference in 1951, the USGA and the R&A agreed to make most of their rules overlap, but they couldn't get together on the golf ball thing.

Besides ministering to the rules needs for golfers from Vancouver to Christchurch to Kenya to Bombay to Dusseldorf, the R&A ran this little tournament. "The committee wishes to emphasize that the correct title for this event is The Open Championship, not the British Open, and the winner is properly known as the Open Champion," the club announced before the 1960 tournament, their collective nose stuck unwaveringly in the air. No one took the history, traditions, and rituals of golf more seriously than the R&A, and nowhere was there more ancient golf history than in St. Andrews, Scotland.

Most American pros would have probably found all this to be a royal and ancient pain, but Arnie was never fazed by the unfamiliarity Over There. "Those problems never entered his mind," Drum says. In fact, he relished the history, the atmosphere of the place. As Bernard Darwin wrote in his *Golf Courses of the British Isles* (published 1910), "There are those who do not like the golf at St. Andrews . . . but there must surely be none who will deny a charm to the place as a whole. It may be immoral, but it is delightful to see a whole town given up to golf; to see the butcher and the baker and the candlestick maker shouldering his clubs as soon as his day's work is done and making a dash for the links . . . it is that utter self-abandonment to golf that gives the place its attractiveness." Mark McCormack recalls that Arnold would wander with Winnie from their room at the Rusack's Hotel just off the eighteenth fairway, just walking and "looking around. He stared at those gray buildings that flank the narrow streets; he looked out across the Bay of St. Andrews, and he saw the graveyard [by St. Rule's church] where old Tom Morris is buried [as are Tom Morris, Jr., who won four consecutive British Opens, then died at age twenty-five, three months after his wife's death in child-birth, and Allan Robertson, the first professional golfer]. He was escorted by his caddie, Tip Anderson . . . [who] delivered lectures about where Jones did this and Vardon did that. 'You have to be moved by all this,' Arnold told a friend that first night. 'I wish we had more of it in our country.'"

Palmer shot 84 in his first practice round on the Old Course, the kind of score you'd like to keep secret. PALMER SHOOTS 84 shouted the front-page headline of a Glasgow newspaper the next day. He was out in 48 and in in 36, the paper reported, and lost ten pounds to his playing partner, Roberto DeVicenzo of Argentina. Arnie wanted to walk in after his front-nine debacle, but Anderson talked him out of it. Gary Player also endured an embarrassing practice-round episode, which was also duly reported by the vigilant British Open—er, "Open Championship"—press. Player, playing alone, dropped a second ball on the fairway of the second hole after playing his first ball to the green. Course ranger Sandy Durie arrived on the scene. "You can't do that," Durie said, giving no quarter to the defending champion. "You are allowed to play only one ball on the fairway." Player ignored the man, walked over to a nearby sand trap called Cheape's Bunker (everything has a name at St. Andrews), dropped three balls into the pit, and blasted them out. "I told you not to do that," said Durie. "All right. I'll [only] play another from the tee," Player said. "No, you won't," replied the sixty-three-year-old ranger. "I'll report you to the committee. And I'll follow you around to make sure you follow the rules." Finally, Player acknowledged defeat.

Tip Anderson was a godsend for Palmer. "I once said to Arnold, 'I know so much about the Old Course *you* should be caddying for *me*,'" his caddie recalls. Anderson, a slight, soft-spoken man with pale blue eyes and a slightly weak chin, had been the St. Andrews boys champion. He'd literally grown up on the course. "There were many occasions [during the tournament] when I stopped Arnold from using the wrong club," he says. "What with the wind and the run of the ball, St. Andrews is impossible without a caddie." There was no irrigation of Old Course fairways or greens back then; the only water they got fell out of the sky. Thus Anderson was constantly warning his boss to land it twenty yards short here and ten yards short there, and look out for a bounce to the left. It took Arnie a while to get used to working in such close partnership with his porter, but his scores came down as his trust in Anderson increased.

The qualifying tournament began on July Fourth. Palmer celebrated Independence Day with a 67 on the New Course (St. Andrews has four courses, the Old—site of the tournament proper—the New, Eden, and Jubilee). The New had been built before the turn of the century to alleviate overcrowding on the Old. "It has 'relief course' written all over it," Darwin observed. "On the last occasion on which I played there the daisies were growing freely, and daisies, though extremely charming things in themselves, are not pleasant to putt over, and do not give a workman-like air to a course."

Flowers weren't the problem for Palmer on the New—people were. There was a stampede of tweedy golf fans to see the American golf star play his first competitive round in Scotland. "He had just cause to lose his temper," wrote Keith B. Marshall in *Golf Monthly*. "Spectators were breathing down his neck and the crowd control was appalling. That he didn't do so is to his credit. Indeed, he showed a fine sense of humour, often lacking in tournament golfers used to cutting one another's throats for a living, by remarking—when the fairway on which he was waiting to drive became cluttered with spectators and a solitary straying steward—'Shall I aim for the guy in the white apron?'"

Three hundred eighty-eight players paid the entry fee of five pounds (about fourteen dollars) and attempted to qualify. Half the field played the New the first day, half played the Old, and they flip-flopped the second day. The tournament program announced that "not more than 100 players may qualify, and in the event of a tie or ties for the 100th place, those players will not be eligible." The twenty-two-man American contingent featured a handful of wealthy amateurs; some good but aging professionals like Dick Metz and Chandler Harper; the best player in the game, Palmer; and a couple of fossils, Jock Hutchison, age seventy-six, and Gene Sarazen, fifty-eight.

The cutoff came at 147, with seventy-four players at that number or below and twenty-eight more tied at 148. The twenty-eight were summarily dropped. Hutchison, who was born in St. Andrews and moved to Pittsburgh as a young man, shot four above his age and withdrew. Peter Alliss of England caused the biggest first-round commotion by shooting a 66 on the Old Course, a new competitive record. Americans Metz and Harper narrowly missed qualifying. The most notable failure to qualify was Flory Van Donck, winner of the International Trophy at the Canada Cup just a few days before. The suave "Sam Snead of Europe" played with a runny nose and shot 74 on the New, 80 on the Old. Only four Americans, all professionals, qualified: Palmer; Bill Johnston, from Utah, a regular on the U.S. tour; Jack Isaacs, the pro at Langley Air Force Base in Virginia; and, amazingly, Sarazen. More amazing still was that Sarazen's 69–72–141 beat Palmer by a shot; it was the first time he had broken 70 on the Old Course in literally decades of trying. "Fossil"?

He was born Eugenio Saraceni in Harrison, New York, in 1902, but he changed his name soon after he got serious about golf. He made a hole-in-one, which rated a newspaper headline. "It said 'Eugenio Saraceni.' I didn't like the looks of the name. It sounded more like a violin player than a golfer." It's a story the short, gabby Sarazen has repeated a thousand times. Like a lot of old men, especially old men who have been interviewed a lot, he responds to the same old questions in the same old way. Saves time and energy. Besides, Sarazen's stories are good.

"No, Hagen never drank as much as the newspapers used to write," says The Squire, resplendent in a light-brown knicker suit. "He didn't try to psyche out his opponents that much either. He never tried to psyche me out. . . . Well, once, after the British Open, we were playing some exhibitions in England and he came over and was trying to 'help' me with some shots. I just said 'Hagen, get the hell out of here.'

"The main thing he was, was a womanizer. I noticed at tournaments, he'd see a woman he knew and he'd say 'hello, Sugar.' Since he couldn't remember all their names, he called them all 'Sugar.' That was the only thing he ever taught me."

Sarazen was in a twosome with Hagen in the final round of the 1935 Masters when Gene played the most famous shot he or anyone else ever hit, a full four-wood into the hole for a double eagle on the fifteenth. The shot gave him an unlikely tie with Craig Wood; he won the playoff the next day. "Before I hit, Hagen says, 'Come on, hurry up, I've got a date tonight,'" Sarazen recalls.

He gets out of a chair with difficulty, walks very slowly, and uses an upside-down sand wedge as a cane. There is a circular logo sewn on his suit and white golf hat: "Gene Sarazen," it says, "The First Professional Grand Slammer." He was the first to win—in different years—the four tournaments in Bob Drum's "professional slam." The sand wedge and the slam came together in 1932, the year Sarazen invented the club and won his only British Open.

"I got the idea for the sand wedge when I was taking flying lessons," he says. "I pulled back on the stick . . . and the plane went up. I related this to a golf ball coming out of a bunker. It wasn't the loft of a sand wedge that I invented, it was the bounce in the flange. It took me two months, trial and error, you know." The first time Sarazen used his new weapon in competition was at the British Open at Princes, in England, in 1932. "I used to put it under my coat and took it back to my room at night," he told Al Barkow in his *History of the PGA Tour*. "If the British had seen it before the tournament they would have barred it. In the tournament I went down in two from most of the bunkers."

Gary Player, the defending champion (or "holder," the term the R&A preferred) was the low qualifier, with 67–68–135. He was the modern equivalent of Sarazen. Both were appealing men, strong, animated, and successful despite their below-average heights and the modest circumstances of their births. Sarazen was a grade-school dropout who helped support his family with the money he made as a caddie at the Apawamis Golf Club (Ed Sullivan had caddied there with little Eugenio). Player was the son of a man who did the brutal work of a gold miner for forty years; his mother, Muriel, died of cancer when he was eight, and his stepmother was an alcoholic. Player, co-incidentally, became one of the recognized masters of the club that Sarazen invented, the sand wedge. And both men had "look at me" styles. When all the pros wore plus fours, Sarazen switched to pants; when everyone else began wearing pants, Sarazen changed back to knickers. Player's trademark was head-to-toe black clothing. He got the idea, he said, from the cowboy movies he watched as a youth: "I imagined myself wearing the black stetson, shirt, jeans, and boots, with the silver spurs and pearl-handled guns." He featured a freakish, impossible-to-miss outfit in the final practice round at St. Andrews: white shoes and hat, a black sweater, and pants that were black on the right half, white on the left. He looked like he'd been held by one leg and dipped in ink.

Player had won the 1959 Open Championship at Muirfield despite taking a double bogey on the final hole. Both Flory Van Donck and Fred Bullock had putts to tie two hours later, but both missed. As holder, Player was invited by Britain's *Golf Monthly* to predict the 1960 champion golfer. "Arnold Palmer will be very hard to beat in the Centenary Open Championship at St. Andrews. That is my opinion," he wrote. "Palmer is long and strong. He tears the par 5 holes apart with ease, and is a tremendous competitor. . . . It is a long time ago since Palmer told me he would one day play in the Open Championship. He explained to me that his objective in golf was to win all the great major titles—the U.S. Open, the U.S. Masters [which he has already won twice], the U.S. PGA Championship, AND the Open Championship or, as he and the other Americans refer to it—the British Open."

The article, entitled "Gary Player Says Palmer Will Be Hard to Beat," is nineteen paragraphs long. The first three paragraphs concern Palmer, and the remaining sixteen are about . . . Gary Player. He was an unusually self-absorbed man. "There is a driving force inside me," he wrote. "I feel I have more of a burning desire to become world champion than most professional golfers of the present time." In his 1991 autobiography *To Be the Best—Reflections of a Champion,* Player revealed that his mother's death was the source of this single-mindedness. "That loss was to breed an independence, a toughness of spirit, and an awareness of adversity and discipline that have never left me," he wrote. But what bred Player's overweening pride? He refers to himself throughout his book—even in the title—as a "hero" and a "champion," and undoubtedly he is, on some levels—but few people are so willing to say it about themselves. "I invariably produce my best when I seem to be beaten," he writes, and "I have always been regarded as an aggressive, almost heroic competitor who attacks and never plays safe when the whiff of victory is in my nostrils" and "there seems to have been a recurring element of drama in my most famous victories, as though it were the essential hallmark of the Gary Player style of winning" and "the emotional aspect of my nature sometimes lifts me to peaks of performance even I can't explain" and . . . You get the idea.

Yet these out-of-context quotations should be balanced by several positive observations about Player as a golfer and as a man. He was sincere, relentlessly positive, even charming, and very popular with galleries. Talk about eye contact: Player looked at a new acquaintance as if trying to memorize his face. His golf had an athletic, almost frantic quality that was fun to watch. Both his feet might leave the ground when he lashed at the ball. He often followed through in a fire-and-fall-back fashion, his left leg swung around so that he fully faced the target; on occasion, centrifugal force would cause his *right* leg to swing around after his stroke, leaving him facing directly *opposite* his goal. The little man in black was a master at maneuvering a golf ball—cuts, punches, low fades, high hooks, whatever—and he was, as mentioned, unsurpassed with a sand wedge. His skill with golf clubs came by dint of practice; he liked to brag in his clipped, South African accent that he had hit more golf balls than anyone in history, except for Hogan. Player naively thought this made Hogan a kindred spirit. He called him in the middle of the night from Brazil once; he wanted to ask The Hawk something about the proper position of the hands at the top of the backswing.

Player: "Should the left wrist . . ."

Hogan: "Whose clubs did you say you play?"

Player: "Dunlop."

Hogan: "Ask Mr. Dunlop."

This misguided and poorly timed call for help was not typical (Player, by the way, recalls that the call was made at eight P.M.; Hogan says he phoned at three in the morning). Player took particular pride, in fact, in being self-contained. "I travel on my own," he wrote. "I estimate I have flown seven million miles in my career. For most of that time, I have lived alone in hotel rooms. I eat alone. I practise alone. And even though there may be thousands of people watching a tournament, I am by myself out there. It is just me against the rest."

Sounds heroic. But Player was anything but a lonely hero to an increasing number of people, who saw him as the symbol of a country of twenty million people, most of them poor, powerless blacks, ruled by a minority of relatively affluent whites. For a long time this was incomprehensible to Player. After all, didn't his father, a member of the alleged "oppressor" race, work in the mines? And while he often protested that he was a sportsman, not a spokesman, he also was unashamed of his love for his country. "I am of the South Africa of [Dr. Henrik] Verwoerd and apartheid," he said in 1965.

Not that Player was a controversial figure in 1960. That came later. On the contrary, his black clothing and aggressive style made him a recognizable—and, even better, a *marketable*—player on the American tour. He started to get offers—would he be interested in playing this ball or that club or wearing this brand of golf glove and so on. Player approached Palmer, who had been his friend since he started playing in the United States in 1957. "He came to me in 1960 and asked if I would mind if Mark McCormack represented him, too," writes Arnie in his introduction to the Player autobiography. "My deal with Mark stated he could not manage anybody else, but I told him he could handle Gary. So, Gary became the second client and the growth of Mark's [company] was on its way."

British punters (gamblers) put down a great deal of money on Palmer and Player, but the betting favorite was thirty-one-year-old Peter Thomson of Australia. A wager on the solid-looking Thomson hardly seemed to be a gamble at all. Since 1952 he had won four Open Championships and had finished second three times, twice to Locke, once to Hogan. And he obviously liked this year's venue; he had won at St. Andrews in 1955 and was runner-up there in 1957. His strength was balance; his beautifully functional swing never seemed to be bothered by the gusty seaside winds. Personally, too, Thomson was far from run of the mill. Compared to his peers, he was an intellectual. He was well-read, and enjoyed classical music and art. He painted. After his rounds in the Open, he would stroll into the press tent, sit down at a typewriter, and prepare his daily dispatch for the *Melbourne Age*. Said English golf writer Pat Ward-Thomas of his friend: "His clearness of mind is exceptional. . . . The Australian journalist who is responsible for transmitting articles that Thomson writes . . . has often told me what a pleasure it is to take copy from him, so fluently, concisely, and accurately does he express himself. Few professional players of games have this talent. . . . I often wonder how many readers of books ostensibly written by famous players, really believe that the man wrote it himself."

To some, Thomson seemed a bit haughty. He frequently had an amused-by-it-all look, a way of holding himself, a carriage, that suggested that he owned the place. But his friend Ward-Thomas saw him differently. "I never saw a golfer who seemed

so assured of his destiny," he wrote. "There is about him an un-
mistakable air of success; in the assurance of his bearing, the
lightness of his stride, the set of his head, the clear decisive
mind, and the cool, often smilingly casual acceptance of fate.
Thomson took success as if it was his due. . . ." Player didn't
like him. He found Thomson to be sarcastic. Palmer didn't care
for him much, either, for Thomson, a part-time player on the
U.S. tour, had been a vocal critic of both American golf (as typ-
ified by Palmer) and American golf courses. Neither had much
finesse, he said. As a result, there was no one that the U.S. pros
enjoyed beating more than Thomson.

The Old Course is like no other. Most of the first nine holes
run straight out from the imposing, multi-chimneyed stone
clubhouse (built in public-library style in 1856 for 1,957 pounds
sterling), and the second nine holes are parallel, running
straight back, as close together as two lanes on a highway. A
round on the Old Course is a two-mile walk out and a two-mile
walk back; in places, the long, skinny layout is only about a
hundred yards wide. The soil is sandy; this is links land, which
"links" the land to the sea. There are only a few small trees.
There are just eleven greens; seven huge greens serve two
holes. Parts of some fairways have the random, pockmarked
texture of the surface of the moon, and are dotted with bunkers
that have names: Coffin, Cat's Trap, Mrs. Kruger, Hell, Wig.
The holes themselves have names, too, which locals and those
in the know use more than their ordinal numbers: Long, Short,
High, Heathery, The Road. You stand on the tee of the first hole
(Burn) and see . . . nothing. No bunkers, no lakes, no trees, no
rough, none of the usual landmarks. The first fairway blends
with the eighteenth fairway. "What do I aim for?" the first-time
player says, as he surveys the barren landscape, or he mutters,
"Where the hell's the golf course?"

"Let down is a common reaction," wrote Robert Trent Jones,
for thirty years the foremost American golf course architect, in
The Complete Golfer (1954), "at least for Americans who are used

to courses which divulge all their beauty at first sight. St. Andrews doesn't." In other words, the Old Course is an acquired taste; any beauty divulgence happens over time. You can't see the trouble or know intuitively how to play the holes—this has to be learned. For example, the sixteenth—Corner of the Dyke—looks simple enough. It's a 380-yard "two-shotter" (par-four) with a railroad track to the right; better aim left. Or should you? According to Sir Guy Campbell's course guide in the 1955 Walker Cup program, "The drive should pass either between the railway and out-of-bounds on the right and the three pot bunkers—the Principal's Nose—or just to the left of the Principal's Nose. This line gives the easier approach to the green. Incidentally, behind the Principal's Nose and hidden by them lies Deacon Sime, a trap for the unwary long driver." Now, factor in a thirty-knot breeze coming in off the firth, with gusts to fifty, then remember that the small ball is less affected by the wind. . . . "For in addition to close lies; every imaginable variety of stance; hazards, often obscure; and many a vast putting surface, there is one puzzle that can be particularly testing. That is the subtle change of direction that affect individual holes running seemingly in the same line," wrote Sir Guy. "Such, when winds are blowing, makes keen perception and intuitive weather sense assets of counting value, especially for newcomers." Concludes Jones: "There is only one Old Course, and nature built it."

"That's simply not true," counters course architect Desmond Muirhead, who first played golf at St. Andrews when he was a teenager. Muirhead was the first to have the Old Course greens mapped by aerial survey when he designed New St. Andrews in Japan. "There's a sense of inevitability about the Old Course, as if it could be no other way, but it wasn't all nature. For example, close to two hundred bunkers were added in the early 1900s, but many of these have since been eliminated." St. Andrews is a university town, Muirhead reminds: "Hundreds of fine intellects and thousands of hands" have improved and developed the essential character of the place, especially in the last 120 years. The result, says the erudite Muirhead, is a "highly intellectual, very strategic golf course, based on the philosophy that man requires as many choices as possible." Those who can't tell the Old Course fairway from the rough, are not looking, Muirhead says: "Rough in the form of long, wiry grass and heather provides a tremendous amount of contrast." And he dismisses those who find St. Andrews to be ugly: "Those people are not exactly aesthetes. . . . St. Andrews is extremely beautiful, totally in harmony with itself."

Like a soldier poring over a chart of a mine field, Palmer studied a map of the Old Course every night before the tournament began.

> Returning to St. Andrews, especially at Open Championship time, is a good deal more exciting than sitting on the back porch at home combing the dead hairs out of a cat. When the giant tents are erected and the flags of the nations are flying in the wind, St. Andrews is the place to be. Nowhere on earth could tempt me more. It stirs the pitch shots in the soul. It is—as Gene Sarazen's caddie Daniels used to say—right on the stick. The Old Course, from which the world's champion golfers have taken divots by the barrow load, never loses its magical charm; a magic that compels the golfing man, treading the historic turf for the first time, to lower his voice several tones and tread as though on velvet.
> —Keith B. Marshall, *Golf Monthly*, August 1960

The Open Championship of 1960 started on a day that looked like gray November. It rained, it was cold, and a fog rolled in, a mist the Scots call "haar." Spectators wore wool overcoats, "Wellies" (rubber boots), and carried black "brollies" (umbrellas). Except for the absence of wind, it was British Open weather straight from central casting.

As usual, the Open opened with a single round on Wednesday, which would be followed by another single round on Thursday, then a thirty-six-hole final on Friday. Only three players broke seventy on the bleak first day. The best round, a 67, was shot by thirty-seven-year-old Roberto DeVicenzo of Buenos

Aires. A powerful man with big ears and a short swing, he was one of the best-liked and most competent players on the world stage. He'd teamed with Antonio Cerda to win the Canada Cup in 1953 and had won so many Mexican Opens and Panama Opens and Los Lagartos Opens that he could hardly count them all. He had, in fact, won close to two hundred tournaments, half of them significant international events (including two tournaments on the U.S. tour), but he hadn't won the Big One. For a golfer not from the United States or Mexico, the Big One was the Open Championship. Four times in the past DeVicenzo had been close to winning, including a second to Locke at Troon in 1950. Often the easygoing Argentine—*Golf World* called him "the gay caballero"—would casually drop his ball on the tee and smash a drive off the grass. He had style. He would be a popular winner.

His countryman, Fidel De Luca, and K. D. G. ("just call me Kel") Nagle of Australia were two back at 69. At 70 were Major David A. Blair, a member of the R&A, English professionals Ken Brousfield and Peter Shanks, and Palmer. Arnie needed fours on the final two holes for a 69, but he three-putted the difficult, two-tiered green at the Road hole. He had thirty-four putts for the day, but said afterward it should have been no more than twenty-nine. Paradoxically, the small ball could be harder to putt than the American-sized ball. You wouldn't think so, for the same reason it's easier to throw an apple in a trash can than a canned ham. But the breaks in the greens affected the small ball differently—usually less—and this took getting used to.

Yet Palmer's 70 should not be dismissed as mere prologue for the rest of the tournament. It really was an excellent showing for his first round ever in a British Open; if he could shoot four of them, he would probably win (four times 70 is 280; only once in history had that total been bettered at an Open Championship at the Old Course, Bobby Locke's 279 in 1957). Arnie was finding that his game fit the course. He already liked to hit it low, out of the wind—witness his low scorcher that drove the edge of the fifty-fifth green at Cherry Hills—and he had an inventive short game, two requisites for success in links golf. The correspondent for *Golfing* was impressed: "To see him weighing up a forty-yard shot to one of the St. Andrews pins, from bare ground, lying in a cranny, along a worn patch, over a sharp ridge and then steeply downhill to the pin; and to see him finally take his putter out and lay it two feet from the hole, was enlightening. It was almost as if he was determined, whether he won or lost, to learn as much from the Old Course as he could in the time available to him."

Thomson, Player, and four others were nearby with 72's, but the other Americans didn't fare so well. Johnston had 75, Isaacs scored 77, and Sarazen, a forlorn, rain-drenched figure, shot 83, the highest score of the first round. "I'm tired," he said, and withdrew from the championship.

Round Two: Roberto stood over his his twenty-five-foot putt for a three on the eighteenth hole, gave it a firm tap with his mallet putter, then smiled and tipped his hat as the ball nestled into the hole. The roar of the crowd resounded off the stained stone buildings to the right of the green and fairway. Another 67—Roberto was running away with it. No one was closer to him than seven shots—no one except Kel Nagle. Nagle also birdied eighteen, also shot 67; he was two behind at the halfway mark.

The torrid scoring of DeVicenzo was unexpected but not without precedent. But Nagle? He was a surprise. He was "the other Australian," the one who was not Peter Thomson. He was at that moment the Australian Open and Match Play champion, technically Thomson's superior (he beat Thomson five and four in the Match Play final), though Peter had certainly overshadowed him as a golfer through the years. He was a quiet, calm, self-effacing man, age thirty-nine, father of four. Jimmy Demaret played a few rounds with him on the Australian tour and reported to Dave Marr when he came back to Houston that Nagle was a big hitter and "the nicest guy in the *world*." This characterization was untrue in 1960. Kel was still a good guy, but, compared to Palmer or DeVicenzo, he hit it nowhere. He had played his first tournaments ever on the American tour earlier in the year (eleventh at Greensboro, a tie for fifteenth at New Orleans, a tie for second at Fort Worth, last-place money at Indianapolis) and had decided to cut his swing way down and now concentrate on keeping the ball in play. The resultant swing was as rhythmic as a dance step. He seemed restless as he prepared to hit, his weight bouncing back and forth from one foot to another, his club tapping the ground—bizarrely, *between* his feet and the ball. Just before drawing it back, he finally placed the club directly behind the ball, then, the beautifully cadenced swing. He was using a driver he had found in Fort Worth, when he played in the Colonial tournament in May, and was hitting it great: "The placing of his drives was sensible and looked as if he was aiming quietly and patiently at a predetermined point on every hole," said *Golfing*.

Tied for third at 141 were Thomson, Sebastian Miguel of Spain, and Palmer, who again three-putted the seventeenth. Player was another shot further back. Arnie's 71 left him seven shots behind on the eve of the double round, which was precisely his margin, the newspapers noted, before his incredible comeback in the American Open.

Bob Drum received a telegram from his editor at the *Pittsburgh Press*. Word had reached the States that Palmer was just a charge away from winning another major title. But Drum was not on assignment; Fred Corcoran, the head of the American Canada Cup effort, had flown Drum over (because Drum was then the president of the Golf Writers Association of America) and was picking up his tab. The newspaper, in fact, had been reluctant to let the Drummer attend: "you can go as long as you don't write anything," they'd told him, which made him slightly angry, to put it politely. But he'd been having a good time "loafing around" with his friend Dan Jenkins, watching the golf, trying to get used to warm beer and cold July. Now here was this telegram: NEED SOMETHING ON PALMER. Drum crumpled the message into a ball. "Hope to hell you get it," he said.

Third round: There is a long stone wall bordering the right side of the fourteenth, the Long hole. Right of the wall is out of bounds. Just to the left of the thirty-inch-high barrier is the Elysian Fields (yes, even some fairways have names), a narrow-appearing paradise that provides a flat place from which to play the second shot. Further left are the Beardie Bunkers. Left of the Beardies is a tangle of local flora that St. Andrews golfers call "whins," others call "gorse," caddies call "choke," and Americans call "garbage." The drive on the fourteenth is the most testing on the course.

Palmer played a hard hook right at the wall. The ball started to curve into play, as planned, but a gust of wind off the bay pushed it toward the out of bounds. . . . The loudest gallery on the course was quiet for a few seconds. "It's in!" someone shouted. And it was, barely. Arnie slugged it up to the green from there and made a birdie four. Moments later, DeVicenzo followed the same flight pattern, but his ball hit the top of the wall and bounced out of bounds. He made a seven, and lost the lead to Nagle. Arnie, now five under par for the day, was only two back. At this point, said *Golf World*, "There was a general inclination to concede the cup to Palmer."

Three holes later, his charge hit a wall of a different kind. Maddeningly, Arnie three-putted the Road hole green for a five for the third time in a row; he had underplayed the frightening second shot to the green badly. "That little plateau," wrote Darwin of the seventeenth, "in contrast to most of the St. Andrews greens, is a horribly small and narrow one—that lies between a greedy little bunker on the one side and a brutally hard road on the other. It is so difficult as to make the boldest inclined to approach on the instalment system. . . ." Nagle didn't have any trouble with it. Playing with DeVicenzo in the group behind Palmer, he holed a putt of moderate length for a three, his third consecutive one putt of the Road hole green.

Rain had alternated with flashes of sunshine that morning in Scotland, but now, in the early afternoon, the day grew darker and thunder rumbled. Palmer prepared to play his short second shot to the eighteenth, a straightforward hole of 381 yards with no road, wall, Deacon's Nose, or Principal's Ears to worry about. From the tee just aim it at the right-hand corner of the Big Window (that's its name) of the Royal and Ancient Clubhouse off the tee and avoid the depression short of the green (the Valley of Sin) with your wedge or nine-iron second shot. Simple. But Arnie hit a very weak shot into the Valley of Sin, and his gallery gasped. He three-putted again, for another momentum-killing bogey.

A few moments later, after Nagle holed out for a par on eighteen and a two-shot lead on DeVicenzo, four on Palmer and Sid Scott of England, it began to drizzle. Then it rained. Then it poured. "A startlingly heavy downpour," wrote Wind. "Within twenty minutes, two greens and sections of many fairways were underwater, and a small waterfall cascaded down the steps of the Royal and Ancient clubhouse onto the first tee." The Valley of Sin became the Pool of Sin; the local fire brigade was summoned to pump the hollow clear of water. Play was suspended for an hour, then, at three o'clock, the R&A postponed the final round, the first such interruption at an Old Course British Open in fifty years. The tournament would be concluded the next day. Palmer was incredulous. A weather postponement? At the British Open—the *home* of bad weather? "I was not happy," he wrote in *Golf Journal* in 1991. "I had a lot of confidence in my game then and had momentum going for me." Despite his bogeys on the last two holes, Arnie had shot seventy and had picked up three shots on the lead. He was not down at all; he was, in fact, primed. Furthermore, the delay would give the older competitors (DeVicenzo was thirty-seven, Nagle, thirty-nine) time to rest, something the thirty-year-old Palmer didn't want or need.

Seething, Palmer walked into the locker room. He swore,

then threw his sodden golf shoes and several iron clubs the length of the room.

Thirty-odd years later, Arnie is still unhappy with the R&A's decision. "The British Open had never been rained out, never played on a Saturday," he says today, shifting in the seat of his golf cart. "Obviously, I thought my chances were better if we finished on Friday." For the only time during the brief interview, the smile leaves Arnie's brown, lined face.

Fourth round:

Arnold Palmer appeared on the tee. As he took his stance and gave a shrewd glance towards the Swilcan Burn [the steep-banked ditch fronting the first green at the Old Course], I noticed the old gentlemen in the Royal and Ancient Clubhouse studying his technique through binoculars and the big bay window. Whether they approved of it, is hard to say. But the rank-and-file lads leaning on the fence certainly did so. 'Is he using an iron?' asked one. 'He no wants tae gae in the Burn,' replied another. While a third, having seen the flash of the swing and heard the sweet click of a Palmer shot, said: 'Coo! Nae bawther at a'!'

No bother at all was right. The ball, twenty yards short of the Swilcan, was soon despatched to within a yard of the stick and, to the applause of the large following, the American Open champion had begun his assault on the Old Course."

—Keith B. Marshall, *Golf Monthly*

He made the putt, of course, then hit a wedge even closer on the second hole, for another birdie. Nagle's lead over the American had shrunk to two shots, and he knew it. He and DeVicenzo were in the final group, just behind Palmer and Sebastian Miguel; each Palmer birdie caused his gallery to emit a deep roar, and Nagle was easily within earshot.

Arnie stopped making putts for a while, and after a brief rain shower on the mostly sunny day, Nagle made a three on High (the seventh) and a two on Short (the eighth). His lead over Palmer was four again. DeVicenzo started to fade, and threats from Player and Thomson never materialized. This was a lot like the U.S. Open, where Palmer posted early birdies and the other guys found a way to lose. But there was no Kel Nagle at Cherry Hills. Nagle would not fold.

Arnie birdied the thirteenth, Hole o'Cross, with a seven-foot putt. Now three back. Nagle three-putted the green at Cartgate, the fifteenth, a lapse that was almost shocking, given the way he'd been using the putter all week. The lead was two.

Now Palmer faced his nemesis, the Road. He drove safely over the left-hand corner of the roof of the Black Sheds, which jutted incongruously into the fairway. Two down with two to play. . . . He went for the pin with his second. But his ball trickled over the back and down a steep bank, near the road on the Road. Then he played a true British Open shot. Two weeks before, he might have been tempted to loft a high, soft shot in this predicament, but Mrs. Palmer didn't raise no fool. He took out a putter and tapped it up the slope, where the ball *just* reached the green's slick surface, then rolled lazily to a stop two feet from the hole. It was a stroke of genius.

Palmer ripped a drive on Tom Morris, the final hole, then hit a wedge to four feet. Almost simultaneously, while Palmer putted for birdie on eighteen, Nagle tried to negotiate one more tricky par putt on seventeen. If Arnie made and Kel missed, as seemed likely, the tournament would be tied.

"One does not know what goes on in the minds of players in the critical moments of Championships of this calibre," reported *Golfing*. "But if ever a brave shot was played by any one in the history of the game of golf, it was by Nagle on the 71st green. There he was just preparing to putt when a great shout went up near the Clubhouse, which told him that Palmer had got his three [for a final round of 68] at the home hole and that therefore he himself had two fours to win. Having taken a fresh guard, as they say in Yorkshire, Nagle holed from eight or nine feet. . . ." On the final hole, after a drive, a nine-iron pitch to three feet, and a deliberate two putt on the final hole, Kel Nagle was the Open Champion. He'd shot 278, a new seventy-two-hole record. Palmer finished second by one shot.

At the presentation Nagle thanked Peter Thomson for coaching him. Palmer presented the R&A with a scroll, signed by all the competitors in the recent U.S. Open, which thanked the club for its contributions to the game in the century it had been holding the Open. He also praised the course, said the greens were wonderful, and that he hoped to return. Henry Turcan, the Captain of the Royal and Ancient Golf Club, praised Arnold sincerely and at length. "You added tremendous grace to a monumental battle," he said. Everywhere were handshakes, humility, and sportsmanship.

Thirty years later, Palmer shakes his head. "It was the biggest disappointment of my life."

▼

CHAPTER SEVEN

The Rubber City

Wind rushed through the car's open windows and the clothes on a rack above the back seat swayed slowly back and forth. Butch Baird was at the wheel, fiddling with the radio, following the headlights into the warm night. On the seat next to him Al Geiberger dozed, a map of South Carolina over his face. Geiberger owned the vehicle—no air conditioning, AM radio— a brown, 1960 Chevrolet Bel Air. Got a good deal on it early in the year from Fletcher Jones Chevrolet in Phoenix. Since then he had driven it—or been driven—across the country, following the professional golf tour through Texas, all around Florida, and now north, into the Carolinas.

The Baird-Geiberger travel team was fairly typical. Most players on the tour drove from tournament to tournament and most found that the long, boring miles between Indianapolis and Memphis or Toronto and Chicago or New Orleans and Houston went by faster with company. Older, married players often traveled with their wives and kids. Younger, single guys in groups of two or three rode with each other. There were exceptions, of course; Ken Venturi, for example, always went his own way. "I like the fellows on the tour," he said, "but I must do what I want to do, when I want to do it, to play quality golf." On the road they talked about what golf pros have always talked about. Money. Women. Other golfers. Who made the cut in the previous tournament—and thus would not have to qualify on Monday for the next one—and who didn't. Golf courses. Football. And where to stay, where to buy gas, and where to eat. This was another advantage of carpooling; shared expenses. "I remember us lots of times driving around looking for a twelve-dollar-room intead of a fourteen-dollar-room," Geiberger says. But finding compatible fellow travelers was not easy. Life on the tour was a party for some young pros; they made poor companions for those who thought the tour was a grim, high-stakes gamble. Complications could tear apart a group at any time; for instance, golfers who were playing well often didn't want to associate with those who weren't, as if poor play were contagious. Al and Butch, however, got along like ham and eggs.

"Hey Berger, which way do I turn?" Baird asked. A Y in the road, Highway 17 North near Savannah, had presented itself. "Berger, hey, which way?" Geiberger came to. "What, where are we?" he mumbled, looking up, trying to see a road sign, and down, trying to find their location on the map. He couldn't do either, and Baird, trying to drive and read the map at the same time, plowed on indecisively into the wide, graveled space between Highway 17 and Highway 17A. A sailor in dress whites stood in the fork of the road, his right arm extended, thumb out. He seemed to glow in the glare of the headlights. The car barreled toward him. The sailor's arm came down. On and on came the Chevy. The sailor picked up his duffel bag and faked this way, then that, then, in panic, he ran toward the woods, away from the Bel Air of Death. Baird finally returned his full attention to driving, swerved, and missed the mariner.

"That poor guy must have thought we were maniacs," Baird says. Recalling this incident thirty years later reduces Butch and

Al to hysterics. They gasp, dab at their eyes, and have to sit down. You had to be there, they say.

The bachelor party before the Bash-Nicklaus nuptials was held on Friday evening, July 22, at the Grandview Inn in Columbus. No women were invited, of course. Most of the partygoers were older adults, friends of the fathers of the prospective bride and groom. The Billy Maxstead Band—a particular favorite of one of the music-loving guests, Woody Hayes—entertained.

Nicklaus had thought little about golf since losing the U.S. Open to Arnold Palmer five or six weeks previously, but his interest in the game was coming back. He spent the last few hours before the wedding on the golf course. He and his pals Bob Hoag, Walker Cup teammate Ward Wettlaufer, and Don Albert played eighteen holes at Scioto that afternoon. "This is my final tee shot as a single man," Jack said on the last hole. "Stand back." He swung mightily, his driver tearing the air asunder, but the ball dribbled into a creek only twenty yards in front of the tee, to the great amusement of his friends.

Barbara Jean and Jack William said "I do" that evening at the North Broadway Methodist Church. The bride wore a white dress, a white crown and veil, and a single strand of pearls. The groom sported a white tuxedo jacket, black pants, cummerbund and bow tie, and a fresh crewcut. The reception, Jack recalled, "went a little too well in my case. Barbara had to drive us home for the only time in our lives. . . . I've never been much of a drinker, and two or three can really get to me."

Mr. and the new Mrs. Nicklaus spent their wedding night in Columbus, then loaded their Buick convertible and drove to New York City for a two-week honeymoon. Somewhere between Pittsburgh and Harrisburg on that Sunday afternoon it occurred to Jack that his clubs were in the trunk and that their route took them very close to Hershey, Pennsylvania, and the Hershey Country Club, where Jack Grout had once been the golf professional. Jack's teacher had often talked about what a good golf course Hershey was. Wouldn't it be nice to play there,

Barb? he asked. Okay, she said. They encamped near Hershey, and in the morning Jack shot 71 while Barbara watched (she didn't play golf). Then the clubs went back in the trunk and they drove to the Astor Hotel in the big city.

On Tuesday they shopped and walked the streets of Manhattan. Barbara bought two pairs of shoes. That night they saw *The Music Man*, then visited the Copacabana nightclub. Jack arose Wednesday morning and called Claude Harmon, the pro at Winged Foot Country Club—"We were so close it would have been criminal to have passed up this chance to play it," he noted in *The Greatest Game of All*. Harmon said sure, we'd be happy to have you, and Barbara again said okay. It rained all day, but still Jack played and Barbara walked every hole. The drenched couple returned to their hotel, changed, had dinner at Sardi's, and went to a musical called *La Plume de Ma Tante*, which means either "My Aunt's Pen," or "My Aunt's Feather."

The next morning Barbara announced that she had had enough of the Big Apple—it was just too expensive. As they packed their bags, Jack said, "Hey, I just thought of something. Wouldn't it be terrific if on our way home I stopped off and played Pine Valley?" (Pine Valley, one of the greatest courses in the world, is in Camden, New Jersey.) This time, Nicklaus related, "a heavy silence followed." But they drove to the course and Jack shot 74, while Barbara watched—from a car. Except for one day a week, women were not allowed to set foot on Pine Valley's hallowed ground. So Jack's host, a member of the club, drove his guest's wife around on the maintenance roads that criss-crossed the course. "She got to see me hit some shots, too," Jack said. After a very brief side trip to Atlantic City—"We were terribly disappointed with it"—they headed back to Ohio. The honeymoon was over.

The newlyweds moved into a new twenty-two-thousand-dollar Cape Cod–style house in Upper Arlington upon their return. The down payment on the house was a wedding present from Jack's parents, but from that point on, he would accept no more money from Mom and Dad. "From here on out, Barbara and I are pretty well on our own," he told *Sports Illustrated* a month after the wedding. "First, we have to finish school." And where would the money for textbooks and mortgage payments come from? "I've got a job selling insurance," Jack said. "I like the work, and I am considering making a career out of it. I went to this insurance company; they didn't come to me. When the boss hired me he said 'I don't want any barnacles in this company.' That suits me fine. I'm working on straight commission, and being on my own hours will let me finish school and play golf, too. . . . The way I figure it, I'll eventually have to make $25,000 a year to be able to afford to play golf in the major tournaments. That's a lot, but I think it will work out."

Palmer was of two minds after his narrow defeat in the Open Championship. On the one hand, he was despondent—"It wasn't good enough. It wasn't good enough," he repeated to the scores of people who congratulated him afterward—but on the other hand, he was elated. The British Open, he wrote in *Golf Journal*, "was everything I thought it would be—and more. For one thing, the British writers seemed to take a liking to me and my game. . . ." *Golfing* magazine's review was typical: "He made and left behind him a wholly good impression. He was liked by everyone; and, while quite prepared to analyse his own shortcomings in any round, always avoided making excuses for them. He was much more interested in putting them right. . . . What was his entertainment value? Above all, perhaps, that his game is slightly larger than life." It wasn't just the writers who were captivated by Arnie; the Open spectators had found him to be a joy to watch, too. It's difficult to imagine, Desmond Muirhead says, the adulation of the Scots for Palmer. "Even though British people would naturally sooner see an Australian victory than an American one, we derived great pleasure from his sterling effort," understated *Golfing*.

Still, Palmer had finished second to Nagle, a relative journeyman. It was no disgrace, certainly—it had taken a record low score to beat him—but Palmer in the summer of 1960 was a transcendent golfer: his golf was *great*, not merely very good. Why had he lost? To Arnie it was simple: "One green was my downfall over here. I three-putted the seventeenth hole three times before I finally got down in one on the last round. Nagle had only four putts on the same hole. I lost the tournament by one stroke. I used ten strokes on the seventeenth green, Nagle used four, and I'd have to say that was where it was decided. I should have played that hole in an ambulance." This seems logical, and most observers agreed with the assessment, but Tip Anderson did not. His caddie said that Palmer's adaptation to *all* the greens was incomplete. One of the secrets of putting at the Old Course is that subtle breaks should be ignored. Had not Arnold over-borrowed on putts all week, Tip felt, a few three putts on The Road hole would not have done him in.

"Palmer quit St. Andrews without reluctance," wrote Red Smith in *The New York Times*. "The weather was foul beyond description. The train to London was buffeted by rain and strafed by hail."

Palmer did not come home right away. The British writers had convinced him that he really must stay to play in the French Open, which was to begin about ten days after the Open Championship. This, Palmer recalls, "proved to be a big mistake, because I never got to play in France. I assumed from the writers that my entry had been handled, stayed in England the first week with a friend from home who was in the Air Force, then flew across the Channel to register and practice. . . . When I showed up, I was told my entry had arrived too late. The tournament officials were adamant and, a little hot under the collar, I returned to the States." Bob Drum was amazed that the French would not let the greatest player and the best drawing card in the world play in their tournament. And, Drum adds, Arnie was more than just "a little hot under the collar."

Items from Golf World, July, 1960:

> Celebrity Golf debuts on NBC TV. . . . Will be shown on Sunday afternoons, and features Sam Snead in a half-hour, 9-hole match against a different show business personality each week. Bob Hope opposes Sam in the first show September 25. Others who will appear in the 26-week series include Jerry Lewis, Perry Como, Fred Astaire, Ernie Ford, James (Maverick) Garner and Dean Martin. Sponsored by Kemper Insurance Company. . . .

> The U.S. Americas Cup team has been selected. Competing for the U.S against teams from Canada and Mexico on August 11–12 at the Ottawa Hunt and Golf Club will be Jack Nicklaus, Bill Hyndman, Don Cherry, Charlie Coe, Richard Crawford, and Deane Beman.

> Karsten Solheim, Redwood City, California inventor and mechanical engineer with General Electric, has utilized his engineering background to make a Ping putter. The blade is hollow with weight concentrated in the heel and toe.

> Advance sales for the 1960 PGA Championship have exceeded $116,000, a record. . . . Such vigorous pretournament interest assures the PGA that its championship to be held July 21–24 at Akron's Firestone will be a financial bell-ringer.

During Palmer's hiatus in Europe, Mike Souchak won the Buick Open, Art Wall won the Western Open, and Stan Leonard won the Canadian. You go down the lists of who shot what at these events and and who won how much, and there are no particular surprises. Littler, January, Finsterwald, Venturi, Snead, Casper, and Sanders played very well, as they had all year. Behind them was an amorphous middle guard made up of experienced players like Ted Kroll, Tommy Bolt, Doug Ford, and Cary Middlecoff, with an emerging group of younger players such as Geiberger, Dave Hill, Johnny Pott, and Mason Rudolph. And slightly behind and intermixed was a fascinating collection of fringe players. Juan Rodriguez, a tiny, impoverished pro from Puerto Rico. Moe Norman, golf's idiot savant.

Charles Sifford, who, because of his race, was not allowed to be a member of the PGA. John Brodie, a professional football player. Bob Brue, who learned to hit shots the other players wouldn't even attempt. And Frank Wharton, Walker Inman, Bob Goetz, weird-swinging Al Besselink, and scores of other dimly remembered golfers from the dawn of the Palmer Era. Top to bottom, golf pros then were a lot more interesting than golf pros now.

No one except a current player on the tour would argue the point. Relative to 1960, today's best American golfers are boring, homogenized, seemingly interchangeable corporate conformists. The tour, ironically, is bland partly because of the success of the undeniably exciting Arnold Palmer. Money did it. As prize money, endorsement opportunities, and corporate involvement increased, playing the tour became much more a business. "The prize money didn't really get to be good until 1960 or so," Inman explains. "Guys like Hogan, Nelson, Snead, they hadn't made any money at professional golf, for all the tournaments they won. . . . It makes you wonder why we played. For the love of the game, of the competition, I guess." For most of the history of the tour (there was a tour of sorts by 1920), there was only enough money for about the top five players to show a profit. A touring golf pro couldn't be too proud to sleep in his car. Then the Eisenhower/Palmer/television golf boom hit. It was a revolution. Suddenly it was possible for a significant number of people to make a living just by playing tournament golf. You didn't have to have a part-time club job—as even Hogan, Nelson and Snead almost always did—a place where you gave lessons, sold shoes, and told the members how you won the Masters. Today's pro tourist learned to play golf in junior tournaments, not as a caddie (there is even a highly organized junior "tour" now, where calculating parents can groom their children for tomorrow's pro circuits). He attended college on a golf scholarship. His hobbies are huntin' and fishin'. To him, television, tremendous amounts of prize money, air travel, courtesy cars, and free lunch in the locker room are a birthright. Gradually money, the great leveler, would take a lot of the character and characters out of the game. But in 1960 the tour still had personality.

There was, for instance, Juan Rodriguez. He and his brother Jesus had grown up poor in Bayamon, Puerto Rico, near San Juan. They were caddies. Their first golf clubs were sticks cut from guava trees; balled-up tin cans were cheap approximations of golf balls. Juan joined the U.S. Army at age nineteen, and, when he got out, he hung around the Dorado Beach Golf Club as before, still caddying, still broke, but now with real golf clubs that he practiced with assiduously. Pete Cooper, a PGA-tour refugee, took the head professional job at Dorado Beach early in 1960 and "discovered" Rodriguez. Something clicked; Cooper, a robust, successful Floridian, could see himself in the wiry, destitute Puerto Rican. Like Juan, Pete did not come from money, had been a caddie, and had made his first golf club (his was a piece of half-inch galvanized water pipe, hammered and bent into the rough equivalent of a five-iron). Cooper had four children when he came to Puerto Rico, but now, he had a fifth. "Pete Cooper is not only a friend, but a father to me," Rodriguez says today. "I owe everything to him."

Cooper decided to show Juan the ropes. He hired him as an assistant professional and in the next three years took him on occasional trips to the States to play the tour. Cooper had played the circuit for ten years and had won five tournaments, but his protege showed him some tricks he'd never seen before. "Every time we stopped for gas, he went to the john," Pete recalls. "When we were in a restaurant and the waitress arrived with the check . . . he went to the john." When the bathroom ploy got stale, Rodriguez would play possum, feigning a sleep so sound in Cooper's Pontiac that nothing could wake him. Later, he would feel guilty about not paying his fair share. He just didn't have it.

His first try at the tour caused a small sensation. The man the other pros met on first tees in the summer of 1960 was twenty-four, prematurely bald, five feet seven, 118 pounds, and had an eccentric, dipping, violent golf swing. He played with women's clubs and hit his driver so far it was unbelievable. In heavily Spanish-accented English the bubbly little man told you he liked to be called Chi Chi. He won $475.00 in his debut, at the Buick Open; won zero and $115.40 in his next two events; and in his fourth tournament, the Eastern Open, he shot three 67s (and a third-round 76), good for a tie for fourth and $1,400.00. Who *was* this guy? In their six 1960 tournaments, he actually out-earned his mentor, $2,137.07 to $1,520.00. But, Chi Chi says, he was not really interested in playing golf for a living. "You didn't make no money back then," he says. "You just wanted to get a good club pro job." He wanted to be like Pete.

Rodriguez was a breath of fresh air and an unusual man, but Moe Norman . . . Moe Norman was inconceivable, unbelievable. For one thing, he played golf faster than anyone who was not on a polo pony. And despite the conflict inherent in playing a slow game at a frantic pace, *no one* could hit full shots more accurately than Moe; only Hogan was in the same league. But Norman didn't look like any Hogan before he hit. He addressed the ball with his arms fully extended, his chin buried in his chest, his biceps on his ears. It was a laughable setup, but then Moe swung, a quick whip, the ball sailed the way golf balls are *supposed* to sail, and the laughter would stop. The chuckles might resume, however, if you could get Moe to talk. He had echolalia, a tendency to repeat things, to repeat things. What did you shoot today, Moe? "Three birdies, one bogey, three birdies, one bogey," he'd say in rapid, high-pitched Moespeak. "Can't putt. Horrible greens. Can't putt." Hey, Moe, why don't you take a little more time with your shots, you know, line them up a little bit . . . ? "Why, did they move the greens since yesterday? Did they move the greens?"

There are a hundred, a thousand Moe Norman stories, about equally divided between the wonderful, almost surreal quality of his golf game and his utter inability to handle his success. "Why hasn't he succeeded on the world's tours? Why isn't his name all over the record books? The answer lies in Norman's personality," writes Lorne Rubenstein in a chapter about Moe in his book *Links*. The chapter is entitled "Golf's Eccentric Genius." "He suffers from an inferiority complex so pervasive," Rubenstein writes, "that it's kept him out of the mainstream of golf. George Knudson (the late Canadian golf professional) once said in a dinner line that Norman was second to none in ball-striking. He didn't know that Norman was behind him; Norman started to cry, so much respect did he have for Knudson's opinion, so little belief in himself."

Murray ("Moe") Norman of Toronto, Ontario, Canada, had red hair and light-blue, restless eyes. When he was five years old, the sled he was riding on collided with a car, and he was hit sharply on the head. This is the kind of injury that may have caused some or all of his unusual behavior, but no one knows for sure. In school he could give the answers to difficult mathematical questions without thinking, like the autistic character played by Dustin Hoffman in the movie *Rain Man*. "When some of us who know him well saw that movie, we said, 'Jesus, there's Moe,'" says Ted Maude, a Canadian pro who traveled with him for a few years. Norman quit school in the ninth grade to play golf. "Moe hit up to 800 balls a day right from the start, transforming his hands into a vise with the texture of sandpaper," writes Rubenstein. He won the 1955 Canadian Amateur, and hid afterward to avoid having to speak at the presentation. He was invited to the 1956 Masters. A fiasco. The big crowds terrified him. Moe disliked caddies, and attempted to carry his own bag off the first tee in his first practice round at Augusta National, a *faux pas* on the order of bringing a Big Mac and fries to a fancy restaurant. Sam Snead gave him a lesson on the practice tee after the first round, and Moe humbly practiced the great man's tips, hitting practice balls for hour after hour that afternoon, on into the evening, until it was too dark to see. The next day his hands were so sore he could hardly hold a club. He had to quit after nine holes.

He won the Canadian Amateur again in 1956; in 1957 Moe turned pro. He lived in a room—no phone, Moe hated telephones—north of Toronto in the summer, and in a similar rooming-house setup in Florida in the winter. "But his car was really his home," Maude says. "He always drove a Cadillac, a new one every year. The trunk looked like a pro shop." As they were loading the car for the trek to the winter headquarters in New Smyrna Beach one cold Canada day, Maude asked Moe if he had any money. "Money? Hah! Money?" He pulled wads of cash out of his sock, from behind the spare tire, from the glove compartment. "Here's money," said Moe. "Here's money. Here's money. . . ." Says Maude: "He never knew what a checking account was. Cash all the way. The Membery family, who owned a golf course in Gilford, Ontario, looked after his accounts for him, helped him pay his taxes."

Moe won everything on the Canadian tour and set course records left and right, but he never did that well on the American tour. "Moe never felt comfortable in the United States," Rubenstein writes. "A pro told him if he were going to play on the tour, he had better improve his grooming—his pants were often above his ankles, his toenails occasionally stuck through his shoes. And tour officials admonished him for his antics; he had hit balls off Coke bottles during the Los Angeles and New Orleans Opens." Norman won $1,529.46 in ten events on the winter tour in 1960. Then he headed back to Canada, with the contradictory goals of winning golf tournaments and not being noticed.

Charles Luther Sifford had somewhat similar objectives when he joined the tour in 1960. He just wanted to make a living and be free from harassment, but, like Norman, he could not. Norman's demons, of course, were in his head. Sifford's problem was external. He was the tour's only black player. And because of that a number of people, most of them in the Southeast, were determined to make his life miserable.

Gary Player, in the section of his autobiography where he tells how he "got religion" on the apartheid issue, describes what Sifford went through: "I was paired with the black golfer Charlie Sifford, one of the most courageous and determined sportsmen I have ever met. . . . We were playing in Greensboro, North Carolina, which was then one of the strongholds of anti-black feeling. . . . They screamed 'go home, nigger,' they kicked his ball into the rough. . . . 'How can anybody play golf with this going on?' Sifford said in the scorer's tent. Yet he went out again the next day. He refused to be beaten, even though at times he was a very bitter man."

Sifford is a reticent man, too, his mouth constantly closed around a half-smoked cigar, even when he is hitting a golf shot. Caddies disliked working for him even more than they did Snead. He was known as a lousy tipper and was not an easy man to know. He has been through a lot, though, and one tends to make excuses for him.

When the PGA of America was founded in 1916, its charter stated that members must be of the Caucasian race. Professional golf then was just as racist as professional baseball. Baseball had its Negro Leagues; golf had the United Golf Association and the Eastern Golf Asssociation for amateurs, and, eventually, a black pro tour. Sifford played the black and the white tours part-time. He was the National Negro champion a number of times, and in 1957, he won the Long Beach Open, becoming the first black to win a PGA tournament. He decided to play the PGA tour more or less full-time in 1960; he was a thirty-eight-year-old rookie. By then the PGA was not the closed organization it had been, though the Caucasians-only clause was still on the books. But certain sponsors still wanted to keep blacks out of their tournaments. Their subterfuge was simple: they started to call their tournaments "invitationals" instead of "opens." Sifford was a reluctant pioneer; perhaps it was the utter unfairness of having to *be* a pioneer that made him so perpetually crabby. "The NAACP wanted Sifford to challenge those sponsors who would not let him play, mainly in the Southern states, but Sifford wouldn't," explains Al Barkow in *The History of the PGA Tour*. "And in those places where he played and was subjected to racial insults, he turned his cheek or withdrew from the tourney.

Nonetheless, Sifford put himself out there, took the abuse when it came—and it did come—and kept going."

1960 was a good year financially for Sifford. He won $8,763.63 on the tour and another five or six thousand in other events. He had a second at Costa Mesa in October (Bill Casper won) and a win in a small tournament a month later. As *Golf World* reported it, "Charley Sifford, goateed Negro from Los Angeles, won the Almaden Open at San Jose, Calif., Nov. 20 via a sudden death playoff with red-headed Bill Eggers of Portland, Ore." Early in 1961, *Sports Illustrated* ran a piece by Alfred Wright about the prospects of four of the best rookies from the prior year entitled "Candidates for a Better Day." Photographs of the four tour sophomores appeared with the article. Sifford's mature features and big cigar contrasted sharply with the innocent, smiling faces of Dave Marr, Dave Hill, and Al Geiberger, all of whom looked barely old enough to buy a drink.

Sifford's $14,000 year looked like riches to a lot of guys. Some very good golfers never made a check, couldn't survive on the tour. For instance, the official PGA media guide says that John Brodie never made a dime on the tour. That's *almost* true. He won $112.50 at Yorba Linda in January 1960 and $87.50 at Palm Springs in February. That's not a lot of dimes, but at least he didn't get shut out. Fortunately, Brodie had another job. He was the starting quarterback for the San Francisco 49ers of the National Football League.

Brodie was born and grew up in San Francisco, where he and fellow San Franciscan Ken Venturi played a lot of golf together as boys and young men. He attended Stanford University and for two years played on both the golf and football teams, until his football coach announced, "You can't do both." Reluctantly, he dropped golf. An outstanding college quarterback, Brodie made All-America for the Cardinals his senior year. He began his pro football career in 1957, but a preoccupation with golf remained. So in the offseasons of 1959 and 1960, Brodie tried the tour. It's rare, but other men have played two professional sports. Gene Conley and Dave DeBusschere, for example, were right-handed baseball pitchers (for the Red Sox and White Sox, respectively) and basketball forwards (Conley for the Celtics, DeBusschere for the Pistons and the Knicks). Sam Byrd was the most successful golfer to play two games for pay. He must have been an amazing athlete; he won six pro tour events in the 1930s and was an outfielder for the Yankees. "I never intended to drop one or the other," Brodie says of his experiment. "I just wanted to see if I could make it [as a golfer]. I couldn't." He made the cut in eleven of the twenty-five tournaments he played in on the tour in those two years, which is an accomplishment, but he just didn't win enough money.

What stories Brodie could tell, you think. He roomed with Tony Lema on the golf tour. He played football with or against Y. A. Tittle, Jim Brown, Dick Butkus, Alex Karras, Sam Huff, Mike Ditka. He must have some insight into the motivations and psyche of his old friend Venturi. . . . But if Brodie has these memories or insights, he's not sharing them, not this day. "I don't get into reminiscing," he says abruptly. Then, "Now you're trying to put words into my mouth." He is strangely peevish, which doesn't seem to make sense, since he has just shot a very good two-under-par 70 in a Senior Tour event. Brodie plays well all week, but forgets to sign his card after his final round and is disqualified, forfeiting a check for forty-seven hundred dollars.

No one ever mistook Bob Brue for a football player. At five feet eight and 160, Brue, an active, intense man with a sincere manner and a nasal voice, looks like he would be a teacher if he was not a golf pro. Actually, he is both. It all started when he won the 1960 Wisconsin Open (he's from Milwaukee) by *twenty* shots, turned pro, and joined the tour. "I was not mentally ready," Brue says. "I was still experimenting with the golf swing." His search for the perfect swing led him to two unlikely people: Paul Hahn, Sr., probably the best trick-shot artist ever, and Ernest Jones, a Long Island, New York, golf instructor. Hahn often gave his trick-shot exhibition in conjunction with tour events, to hype the gate. Hahn, grinning throughout his performance, throwing out a smooth patter of one-liners, would hit left-handed, one-handed, from one leg, from his knees, blindfolded, with huge clubs, tiny clubs, with a club with a shaft made from a garden hose. . . . He was hilarious. "I was entirely influenced by Paul Hahn, Sr.," Brue says. "I saw his show at least twenty times and enjoyed it each time." Brue also became enthralled with the theories of Jones, who wrote two books: *Swinging into Golf* (1937, with Innis Brown) and *Swing the Clubhead* (1952). Don't get him started on Jones unless you've got a few minutes. "Ernest Jones said there are no positions in golf," says Brue, who makes eye contact when he speaks. "The swing is one continuous motion. A golf swing is like a bubble. If you take it apart, it breaks. Jones taught that body parts are admirable followers, but disastrous leaders. Gary Player says that the golf swing is an unsolvable puzzle. Golf is simple!"

Brue didn't make much money on the tour, and gave it up after four years. But he eventually combined what he had learned from Hahn and Jones. He gives trick shot clinics, where he uses the showmanship of the one to teach the fundamentals of the other. He hits a funny shot, imparts some gospel according to Ernest Jones, and delivers his jokes, deadpan. "Why is 'abbreviation' such a long word?" he says during his show. "Why does sour cream have an expiration date? Why do you park on a driveway and drive on a parkway? And whatever happened to Absorbine Senior?"

The PGA Championship, the last of the four major tournaments, marked the symbolic end of the golf 1960 season. There were more tournaments, of course, after the PGA, but they had smaller purses and crowds, and commanded less space on the sports pages. The attention of sports fans focused on (among other things) the pennant races, the World Series and football from August into fall. In September, the Olympics began in Rome, and Ted Williams of the Boston Red Sox, generally considered the greatest hitter of all time, slammed a home run to right field in the final at bat of his career. In October, Bill Mazeroski hit a home run in the ninth inning of the seventh game to lead the Pirates over the Yankees in the Series. Minnesota had the best college football team; Ohio State would win the national championship in basketball. The Eagles were tops in the National Football League. Boston, with Bill Russell and Bob Cousy, won in the National Basketball Association; Philadelphia, with Wilt Chamberlain, lost in the semis. Kennedy and Nixon debated. The Twist was the newest dance craze. People pondered if the Pill would promote promiscuity. There was a national election. . . . In the waning months of the golf season, Billy Casper won three times, Johnny Pott and Arnold Palmer won twice, and relatively speaking, no one noticed. The PGA would be the last tournament in the spotlight in 1960.

That spotlight would be on, of all places, Akron, Ohio, and a heretofore run-of-the-mill golf course named Firestone Country Club. When the club was awarded the 1960 PGA in 1958, both golf course and city suffered from a similar inferiority complex. We're not good enough, not big enough, Firestone and Akron might have said if they could talk. Firestone had been built in 1929 by multi-millionaire Harvey Firestone of Firestone Tire and Rubber for the private use of his employees and executives. It was a nice company course, but not much of a challenge for the pros. The winning scores in the tour event held there since 1954, the Rubber City Open, were always extremely low; the first tournament, for example, was won by Tommy Bolt with a twenty-three-under-par 265. As for Akron, well, it smelled badly and, around the rubber factories, it looked worse. Nothing to do about that; the manufacture of tires, the rubber companies' main business, is smelly and unsightly. But there was money there. Beverly Hills had nothing on the residences of the rubber barons, the men who owned or were near the top at Goodyear, Goodrich, Seiberling, General Tire, and Firestone, all headquartered in the Rubber City. And Akron had an unusual amount of ambition to complement its growing prosperity, along with a pervasive, almost fanatical interest in amateur and professional golf. Civic boosterism became linked with the PGA tournament. It would be a giant advertisement for Akron, Ohio, the (as it called itself) All-American City.

Of course, Akron would not be the only thing for sale at the PGA. Raymond and Harvey Firestone, Jr., who ran the company now, pursued the PGA because they thought it would be good for business. They were among the first to see that a corporation could benfit merely by having its name linked with golf, especially televised golf. It was a twist on the principle Liggett and Myers cigarettes and Heinz ketchup applied when they used Arnold Palmer in their commercials. It was goodness by association, one of the underpinnings of modern advertising.

One of the Firestone brothers' first steps after they were granted the PGA was to toughen their golf course, to make it worthy of respect. They looked immediately to Robert Trent Jones, then the top name in golf architecture. He had done this type of thing before. His redesign of Oakland Hills in Detroit for the 1951 U.S. Open was either too severe or a success, depending on who you talked to—and when—but at least it was noteworthy. Hogan won that Open; his often-quoted remark afterward was that he had "brought the monster to its knees." Jones was hired and money, about $200,000, was allocated. Build us another monster, he was told. "This was a good, but not a hard course before they redid it," says Paul Lazoran, who in 1960 was an assistant professional at Firestone. He now manages the sprawling locker-room complex there. "They worked one hole at a time, moving tees back, greens back, putting bunkers in the landing areas, and lakes in front of the third and sixteenth greens. Mr. Jones spent a lot of time here. . . . It was five or six shots tougher when he was done, maybe more." Jones added fifty bunkers in all, completely replaced two greens, enlarged the other sixteen to two or three times their previous area, and reduced the par from 72 to 70.

"I thought the course was *tremendously* hard," recalls Bob Rosburg. As defending PGA Champion, he was one of the first to play the new, improved Firestone. In the media day held for the grand reopening, Rosburg, Billy Casper, and entertainers Ray Bolger and Phil Harris made up the featured foursome. "It had been a fun golf course," Rosburg says, "but now it was five or six shots harder. The greens were different, and it was much longer. I didn't think it fit my game." Someone bet the short-hitting Rosburg he wouldn't break 74 on the lush, back-breakingly long (7,180 yards) course. But he started birdie-eagle, shot 32 on the front nine, and even par 70 for the day. And though Rosburg didn't contend in the tournament—the course really was too long for him—he remembers the 1960 PGA fondly. "It was fun defending in a town that was so golf crazy," he says. "Akron was a great golf town. There should be more tournaments in places like that."

The tournament got a tremendous boost on a Sunday in late June. HOGAN'S ENTRY ADDED TO PGA LINEUP was bannered across the front sports page of the *Akron Beacon Journal* in large type. The story appeared June 26 under the byline of sportswriter Loren Tibbals:

> The call was from Fort Worth, Texas.
> And the deep drawl on the other end of the line sounded familiar . . . like a voice I had heard just a week before in the locker room at Cherry Hills Country Club in Denver.
> So it had to be Ben Hogan! It was!
> "I certainly am doing everything I can to make it possible for me to be in Akron (for the 42nd PGA National Championship at Firestone Country Club the week of July 18–24)," said the Hawk. "I have to get a business deal wrapped up and, of course, get in a little golf . . . and then I'll be there."
> The man who just missed an unprecedented fifth U.S. Open title the week before allowed as how he probably would be in Akron "if I can get some accomodations. . . . I understand the hotel situation there is mighty tight."
> I offered to oblige. He readily accepted.
> So, the Sheraton is holding a twin bedroom with sitting room for Ben and Valerie Hogan—with occupancy scheduled to begin Wednesday, July 13.

Ben explained his early arrival by saying "I want to find out for myself if everything they say about that course up there is true."

Hogan had not played in the PGA since winning it in 1948. In 1949, he had suffered his near-fatal collision with a bus. Thereafter, he knew he wasn't up to the physical challenge of playing two rounds a day for four days, which the PGA demanded. For the PGA was contested at match play, and had been since the first tournament in 1916. Match play means scoring by holes and competition against one opponent at a time. If, for instance, one person scores a nine on a hole and another scores three, the first person is only one hole up, not six strokes ahead. When the leader is more holes ahead than there are holes left to play, the match is over. Match play is the most exciting, compelling kind of golf to play or watch, because every hole is a tournament in itself, and players tend to take more risks. But if the PGA wanted its showcase on televsion—if it wanted, in other words, to increase its exposure and make some money doing it—it would have to change the format. The TV boys were repelled by the thought of showing a Chandler Harper versus Henry Williams, Jr., final (the finalists at Scioto in 1950) or Walter Burkemo versus Felize Torza (Birmingham Country Club, 1953). Who ever heard of them? William Oscar Johnson, who generally found television's influence on sports to be odious, explained the situation in his book *Super Spectator and the Electric Lilliputians:* "In 1958 the Professional Golfers Assocation changed its championships from the classic purist's confrontation—a man-to-man match play—to medal (stroke) play in order to satisfy the needs of television. It was decided that too often in match play, the big names were eliminated before the final day of play (when t.v. ratings sink or soar depending on the star quality of the men in contention). And too often, a match would be terminated before it reached the final holes where t.v. had its cameras ensconsed. . . ."

Hogan arrived as scheduled for practice rounds; Mike

Lazoran, the assistant pro's brother, caddied. Jay Hebert, a pro from Louisiana, played several of the tuneups with him. They didn't keep score; to keep it interesting, each had to pay the other a dollar for missing a fairway or green in regulation. "A golf course is like a test where you know all the questions," Hogan has said. "You just don't know which questions will be asked." He studied Firestone, trying to divine the "questions" he might be faced with in competition. Where should you drive if the pin is cut left on the ninth hole? Could you spin the ball from the bunker in front of the seventeenth green? Could you drive it in the water on the third hole if the tees were up? From his analysis, Hogan reached one simple conclusion: the course was *very* long. Not only would he often have to hit a long iron or fairway wood to the green on Firestone's numbing succession of 460-yard par-fours, but three of the four par-three holes might also require something just less than a driver to reach. This was a four-wood course, he decided. Paul Lazoran remembers walking out of the pro shop to watch Hogan hit four-wood shots to his brother. "He'd hit a hundred at a time, and Mike would never move more than ten yards right or left," he says.

Lazoran was not the only one to observe Hogan at practice, of course. He was a strangely riveting figure. It must have been something like watching Michelangelo sketch. He was a chain smoking, grim little bundle of fury, and he seemed to control the golf ball even as it flew one hundred, two hundred yards away. Some or all of the other players on the practice tee would stop their work to watch him, the golf pro's ultimate compliment.

More of the 184 contestants arrived in the next few days to join Hogan on the practice tee. This was a dangerous time for the caddies. In those days before the host club provided range balls, each player brought a bowling bag–like shag bag full of practice balls to the practice tee. The bag would be emptied, the caddie would run out onto the range and catch or otherwise retrieve the balls his employer hit to him. It was an unforgettable experience to peer up into a high sky, waiting for your boss's nine-iron to come down, while next to him another pro was mis-hitting one-iron shots right at your head. It was like being on a rifle range. Sometimes two or three balls would come at you at once. Everyone got hit. Meanwhile, the practicing players had their own problems. Like the rest of the course, Firestone's practice area had been remodeled, first class all the way. The turf in the hitting area was immaculate. "It was beautiful," recalls Bob Goetz, a pro from Kansas, then in his third year on the tour. "Cross-cut bent grass, just like a green. They even had cups in that tee, so you could putt if you wanted to." Goetz and Tony Lema arrived for their first practice session at the same time. They began to hit a few short irons to their caddies, but it was disorienting, hitting iron shots off a *green*. "Hell, Tony, I'm having a hard time taking a divot here," said Goetz. Lema shrugged, smiled, and swung, extracting a huge chunk of Ohio earth.

Palmer played his first practice round on Saturday, five days before the tournament began. He was tired from his European adventure, disappointed by losing the British Open, and angry at the ridiculous situation with the French Open, but he was still a man on a mission. If he won the PGA, he'd have the first-ever "American Slam"; no one had ever won the Masters, U.S. Open, and the PGA in the same year. Moreover, he was buoyed by the unusually large and adoring crowds that followed him at Firestone. Many people in his flock, newly drawn to golf by his heroics on television, simply assumed he would win this week and make history. Cleveland, where he had made so many friends during his Coast Guard days, was less than an hour north; Latrobe was just a few hours' drive to the southeast. Goetz got caught with Palmer outside the gallery ropes on one occasion, and Arnie's adhesive Army pressed in. "I don't see how you can stand to have all these people around you all the time," said Goetz under his breath. Palmer grinned. "Man, I love it," he said.

He was not, however, in love with the golf course. "I was pretty happy with it," he says now, diplomatically. But Firestone had only two par-fives, the long holes Arnold was the best in the world at playing. And one of them, the sixteenth, a dogleg left of 625 yards with trees, bunkers, and a pond fronting a small, hard green, he frankly hated. At least he hated it in 1973, in *Going For Broke:* "The fact is, I feel this is a terribly unfair hole, not only for professionals but particularly for the everyday kind of golfer who must endure it . . . you are not rewarded for overcoming difficulty. You are simply faced with yet another difficulty, and another and another. Holes that have such constant and unremitting difficulties . . . cannot fit into a strategy of bold enterprise, but only into a strategy of determined defense." Defense, of course, was not Arnie's style. The sixteenth at Firestone would define Palmer's PGA, just as the eighteenth at Augusta, the first at Cherry Hills, and the seventeenth at the Old Course were the one-hole symbols of his efforts in the other majors.

The sixteenth was not anomalous, however. It fit in with the other seventeen holes. As George Peper wrote in *The Golf Courses of the PGA Tour,* "Critics say the course is charmless, monotonous. Virtually all of its fairways run straight and parallel to one another, and few of the par-threes and -fours call for an approach shot with anything shorter than a long iron. Subtlety is not the strong suit at Firestone." Desmond Muirhead says that Firestone is "weak on character. The holes are all parallel so you are playing the same wind without the St. Andrews changeability. Not one of my favorite golf courses." For short-to-medium hitters like Art Wall, Firestone was no fun at all. "It's just too much for me," he said. "All you can do is go out there and slug, slug, slug. You're always on the defensive." Other players, however, admired the course for its straightforwardness. Local knowledge and strategy were unimportant. They knew from their first look at the place that they'd have to keep the ball between the huge elms and oaks and lush rough that lined each fairway, and that they would have to hit long shots to well-bunkered greens. "Maybe the best course we played," says Ken Venturi. Others agreed. "If I could keep my sense about me when I play every shot, I would say this is the perfect golf course," said Jay Hebert. "You've just got to stay out of those bunkers and out of the rough if you ever want to break seventy-five out here." Jack Fleck was equally effusive. As he told a reporter on the eve of the tournament, "they can say what they want about Robert Trent Jones, they can call him anything they wish, but I think he's the greatest. . . . I hear Akron is going to make a bid for the U.S. Open. And with a course like this, I think it should get it."

Harold Sargent, the president of the PGA, told an Akron reporter that "it borders on the fantastic, just how wonderful everything here is . . . from the golf course itself, [to] the way the downtown area is decorated with banners, parking facilities, maps, transportation, food. . . . A good indication of the tremendous job Akron has done lies in the fact that Ben Hogan was eager to enter the event this year after not having competed since 1948."

On Wednesday, the day before the tournament began, Hogan rested. He came out to the course late in the day and practiced putting, by himself. Palmer shot a final practice round of 72. He'd had previous warmup scores of 76, 75, and 66. "IT'S PALMER'S POWER VS. FIELD" was the headline over a United Press International story in the Akron paper: "Palmer, the man of steel from Ligonier, Pa., is one of the few with the power to crash it out of the rough and this gave him an added edge as he shot for a 'slam' which many would consider would at least be the equal of the one in 1930 when Bobby Jones won the U.S. and British Amateurs and Opens."

At four P.M., fourteen of the fifteen former PGA champions in the field gave a clinic on the proper use of each of the clubs in the bag (except the putter). Only the 1946 and 1948 champion, Hogan, declined to participate. (Was he, perhaps, off in a lonely corner trying to figure out his wobbly putting stroke during the exhibition?) Jim Ferrier, a forty-five-year-old Australian with a limp even more pronounced than Hogan's, demonstrated the nine-iron. He had won the PGA in 1947. Snead, forty-eight, the PGA champ in 1942, 1949, and 1951, showed how to hit the one-iron. Both men would have leading roles in the drama which was about to unfold. George Bayer, whose 307-yard poke won the driving contest after the exhibition, would not.

First round: Karl LePre, a pro from Haddonfield, New Jersey, wore a white shirt and a necktie on the golf course. "Golf is a gentleman's game," he said, "So we should look like gentlemen." Paul Thomas, from Cincinnati, kept a lit cigar in the center of his mouth and pointed it at the ball when he swung. Ross Collins of Dallas hit the ball left-handed. All three played in the 1960 PGA, but none of them had a chance to win. Like many, if not most, of the participants, they were club professionals. The club employees and the touring pros were all part of the same big, unhappy family, the PGA. The touring pros, being far less numerous, seemed to get the back of the PGA's hand. Only six staffers were assigned to run their tournaments, a very small number for such a large weekly enterprise. "I think there was some resentment of us by the club pros," Bob Rosburg told Al Barkow. "We were out front, getting our names in the paper, making money endorsing clubs and other things while they were pounding it out in a shop twelve hours a day." Television money eventually brought the bad feelings to a head. The PGA wanted the rights fees paid by the networks and private producers to go into the general fund; the tour pros believed strongly that the TV money was theirs. This was an issue that was just starting to be talked about in 1960. No one was overtly mad about it yet.

The first-round leader, the son of a club professional, had loyalties to both groups. PALMER'S 67 LEADS PGA screamed the two-inch type on the front page of the *Akron Beacon Journal*. As usual, Arnie was in attack mode. He hit three-hundred-yard drives on the second and third holes to set up birdies. On the eighth and ninth holes he saved par from greenside bunkers. And he hit iron shots to eight feet on the eleventh and twelfth holes for two more birdies. "I drove it better today than I did at the U.S. Open," he said. "One of my better rounds." Perhaps it is revealing that at this moment, commerce intruded on his consciousness. "When he had finished with the press," the local paper reported, "Palmer hopped onto a little, one-man golf cart and drove happily through the crowds strolling along the shaded walks by the clubhouse. But it wasn't just a joy ride. Businessman Palmer is vice president of the 'Birdie' golf car company and chalked up eighteen sales."

Some observers were ready to concede the championship to Arnie. As Palmer biographer Furman Bisher wrote, "All the pieces fit. He was mentally geared to rectify the failure at St. Andrews." Fred Corcoran, the former manager of the tour and a player agent for twenty-plus years, said, "The way he's playing, he'll be so far ahead by Sunday he won't even need to call on one of his charges." Corcoran might have been trying to divert attention, and thus pressure, from his client, Sam Snead. Snead shot a two-under-par 68, good for second place. He endured an anxious moment after the round. He signed his card, which was kept by playing partner Don January, but in the "total" box, January had written 69. The addition was corrected, at no penalty to Snead, because players were responsible only for the hole by hole scores. Sam was playing possum, too. "I played awful," he said. "I never played so badly. I just couldn't hit the tee shot where I wanted it." Only two other players broke par on the sunny, windless, sixty-five-degree day. Both Freddie Haas of New Orleans and Paul Harney of Worcester, Massachusetts, shot 69. But both had to make every putt to do it; that couldn't last.

Ben Hogan, as usual, made no putts. He had not a single birdie in his four-over-par 74. It looked like his feet hurt as he shifted his weight uncomfortably, trying to steady himself to tap short putts into the hole. Then he'd hit the ball without resolve, and it might go in or it might not. He endured an added distraction on the green at the sixteenth hole. CBS Television technicians, preparing for the weekend's broadcast, were pulling some cables around behind the green while Ben fidgeted over a putt. Twice he backed away. Finally, he yelled, "Hey fellas, I've spent enough time on this hole already."

Rosburg, the defending champion, also shot 74. "It was out like a lion, in like a lamb," wrote sportswriter Phil Dietrich in the *Beacon Journal*. He started birdie-eagle, just as he had on the media day months before, but things disintegrated sooner and more completely this time. The capper came at the ninth. Rosburg's three-wood second shot to the par-four ended up in the middle of the practice putting green, well beyond and to the left of his target. He had an open shot back to the flag, but after a twenty-five-minute debate, he was required by rules officials to drop his ball off the green, behind two big trees. Rosburg, steamed, made a double bogey.

The first round ended with no major surprises. It took the huge field from seven A.M. to eight P.M. to move around the huge golf course. Almost a fifth of the starters (thirty-six of the 184) failed to break 80. Only four broke par. The attendance record for the first round of a PGA Championship was broken by 12,625 Akron golf nuts. Hogan putted poorly. The favorite led. And close on Palmer's heels were three players who had been in line behind him all year: Ken Venturi, Don January, and Doug Sanders, all of whom shot 70. About the only unexpected occurrence came when Julius Boros, a man so placid he seemed to do everything in slow motion, broke his putter on the eighteenth hole. He holed out with a three iron, and shot 76.

Round Two: Junius Joseph (Jay) Hebert (pronounced *A-Bear*) teed off at 8:24, and liked it. He was a morning person. "I think we all play better in the morning," he told the reporters in the big canvas press tent. He had a Cajun accent. "You get tired waiting all day and you play the holes over and over in your head. . . . I found the greens a little slower and easier to play then because they were not tramped down." He shot 67 for a two-round total of 139, one under par. His midtournament success was not particularly surprising to students of the tour. Hebert had a reputation for playing well and winning money (about thirty-five thousand dollars in 1958, more than twenty-seven thousand dollars in 1959 and over thirty thousand dollars up to then in 1960) and not winning tournaments. He had, in fact, finished second four times already in 1960 without a win. For his career, Hebert had finished second sixteen times and won just four. He was thirty-seven, a dark-haired, handsome man with somewhat prominent ears and an atypical background for a touring pro. He had left Southwestern Louisiana Institute to enlist in the Marine Corps in World War II and served as a lieutenant platoon leader for the Fifth Marine Division at Iwo Jima. A Japanese bullet pierced his left thigh during the battle, and he was hospitalized for a year. He eventually returned to college, graduated, and turned pro in 1949. His lack of confidence wouldn't allow him to leave the security of his club job until 1956, when he joined the tour as a thirty-two-year-old rookie.

The other unique thing about Jay Hebert was his brother. Lionel Hebert also played the tour, and was also one of the top ten or twenty players. He'd won this tournament in 1957, when he defeated Dow Finsterwald 2 and 1 in the last match-play PGA. Lionel was half a head shorter than Jay, five years younger, and a good deal stouter. They were thick as thieves. "They'd get together after every round, and they'd go over the entire thing," recalls Bob Goetz with a laugh. In their rehash, "neither of them ever missed a shot." There had been other brother acts on the tour: Mike, Joe, and Jim Turnesa; Lloyd and Ray Mangrum; Julius and Ernie Boros; and a new pair, Buster Cupit and his little brother Jacky. But no set of siblings had ever both won major tournaments, as now was possible for the Heberts.

Palmer's play revealed his feet of clay. He was inflexible. He couldn't modify his aggressive strategy to fit the course and the way he happened to be hitting the ball. There was some general amazement at Firestone that day, that Arnie could play a poor round; he'd had so few of them all year. And when he acted slightly churlish as a result, he introduced the idea that he was only human, after all. An excerpt from the Akron paper's account by Jack Patterson of his round illustrates:

> With 75 percent of another record-shattering gallery of 12,770 dogging his every step, Palmer started off as if to make a runaway of his race toward the "Triple Crown."
>
> He canned a three-foot birdie putt at the second hole to go one under par for the day and four under par for the tournament. But human frailty caught up with him at the tricky 450 yard third hole.
>
> Palmer hit a driver—afterwards he said he should have used a spoon—and wound up in the rough with a tree blocking his shot to the green. He debated chipping out short of the lake which guards the green but finally decided to try for the right corner of the carpet.
>
> He hit a low, skidding shot which bounced off the green into the rough and small shrubs and he took three to get down for a double bogey six.
>
> On this hole he showed the tension which must be building up inside him, chasing a couple of kids out of their perch in a nearby tree before his pitch to the green.

He shot 74, and now trailed the new leader, Hebert, by two. In the press conference after his round, Arnie did what he was lauded for *not* doing at the British Open—he made excuses. "That sixteenth green is ridiculous," he said. "I hit my third shot as well as I ever have in my life and that ball didn't even say 'hello' as it sailed over into the crowd. You need a backboard on that green. . . . Some of the greens are getting awfully rough out there . . . the ball was bouncing pretty badly."

Snead backed up, too, with a 73, and was tied with Palmer and Doug Sanders at 141. Hogan also shot 73. First-round par breakers Freddie Haas (77) and Paul Harney (78) went south, as expected. Holding steady were Don January, whose second straight even-par 70 left him alone in second place, Sanders (71), and Venturi, still three back after a 72.

Host professional Alex Redl shot 81 and was furious. Not at his score—his 155 total missed the thirty-six-hole cut by four—

but at the golf course. Too easy, he said. He was offended by the 67's Palmer and Hebert had shot. "Why design a championship course," he said, "and move the tee markers up to make it a short course. This layout was originally designed to play 7,165 yards. It hasn't played more than 6,800 yards during the first two days of the tourney. . . . If they don't put the tees back and place the pins where they belong, it is an insult to Robert Trent Jones and to those who paid approximately $200,000 to have this course made into a championship layout."

Third Round: Gallery ropes behind the fifteenth green kept spectators one hundred yards from the tee at Firestone's signature hole, the sixteenth. Playing partners Snead, Hebert, and Palmer thus had a few minutes of relative solitude before they played the 625-yard Monster. It should be remembered that the modern golf ball propelled by modern shafts goes at least 5 percent and possibly as much as 10 percent farther than the balls played in 1960. That makes the 625-yard hole equivalent to a journey of 656 to 687 yards today. "An overnight trip by sleeper," Furman Bisher called it. It would be Palmer's Waterloo.

He knocked his drive into the fairway bunker on the right. Then he attempted a desperate shot, a wood from the sand pit, though the situation did not call for it. He was at that moment even par for the day, just one shot out of the lead. He pushed the shot into the trees to the right. Hebert also hit a poor second, and joined Arnie in the same stand of trees. Hebert looked at the ditch and the pond between his ball and the green, and decided to take his lumps. He chipped out safely sideways and eventually took a bogey six. Palmer's turn. His backswing was restricted by a tree, and between him were more trees and two water hazards. . . . He went for it, again, needlessly. He dumped the shot ingloriously into the ditch. After a penalty stroke, a wedge to the green, and three putts, he had a triple bogey eight. Rattled, he bogied the final two holes for a 75. He was out of it.

"Why the wood out of the sand trap on sixteen?" someone asked in the postmortem.

"I had to, I had to," Arnie replied. "I needed to get close enough to that green just to hold it with a wedge. If I had put that third shot on the green, the tournament would have been over. That's all it takes to win some tournaments, one big shot at the right time. . . . When you get into a situation like that, you attack." He still didn't get it. He was attacking all the time, not picking his spots. Firestone was simply not as susceptible to gambling shots as Augusta National or Cherry Hills.

Jim Ferrier made the biggest move. He shot 66, the lowest round of the tournament. Ferrier was different. He had recently quit his club pro job in Hollywood, California, and was now in the contracting business. And besides being Australian, middle-aged, and gimpy (the result of a soccer injury suffered in his youth), he had an unusual attachment to his putter and his wife. The putter was an old-fashioned blade with a round mark the size of a quarter worn in the sweet spot. It was the same club he'd used to win the 1947 PGA and sixteen other events on the tour, and he practiced with it constantly. Always nearby, on the course or the practice green, was his wife, Norma. In their on-course ritual, Jim would hit his tee ball with his quirky, dipping swing, then Norma would run out from behind the gallery ropes to give Jim a drink of water from a soft-drink can, like a fighter taking a swallow between rounds. They would walk together to his ball, then part until the next hole. Don't you get tired walking this course, someone asked Norma. "I've been doing this for Jim since 1932 and it has never bothered me," she replied.

Sanders shot 69 and was alone in first at even par for three rounds. Ferrier, Hebert, and Snead were tied for second, one shot behind. Palmer would start the fourth round in eleventh place, six shots back. But for Ben Hogan, there would be no fourth round. He missed the fifty-four-hole cut by one shot after a dismal 78. "It was the peak of his worst putting," recalls Shelley Mayfield. "I remember I was in the group right behind him in that third round. He had about a twenty-inch putt on the ninth hole, and after two or three minutes of trying to draw it back, he just jerked it so bad. . . . I mean the hole's here and he hit it over there."

Hogan told reporters that he was not ready to quit, that he would continue to play in a handful of prestige events—the Masters, the U.S. Open, possibly the Colonial. "There was nothing wrong with me physically," he said. "I just played bad golf. I just wasn't sharp. You can't play as little as I do and play as sharp as this tournament demanded. . . . Possibly my putting was the biggest contributing factor, but I think it's better to just say I played badly."

He must have been tired. It was ninety degrees that day, his weight was up to 170, he'd been chain smoking cigarettes for years, and in the last week he'd played eight or nine rounds on the longest course on the tour, after not playing at all for a month. His legs were chronically sore even without daily five- or six-mile walks on a golf course. "Whether he is ready to admit it or not," wrote sportswriter Don Plath in the *Beacon Journal*, "the end is in sight for the Texas Hawk."

The fourth round for Palmer partisans was anticlimax. Playing an hour before the final threesome teed off, Arnie bogeyed the first and the fourth holes to fall eight shots back. He made a couple of birdies later, including a sixty-foot chip-in on the final hole, and shot even-par 70. He finished tied for seventh with Doug Ford and won $2,125.

It was Doug Sanders's twenty-seventh birthday. He had a wild round: he made birdie putts of twenty, forty, and seventy feet, but he also missed a bunch of short ones and hit it in the pond on the third hole for a double bogey. With two holes to play, he was tied for the lead with Snead, Ferrier, and Hebert. But Doug missed the green on seventeen and eighteen and made bogeys. He finished tied for third. He had been second in the PGA the previous year, and had contended briefly in the U.S. Open at Cherry Hills. Like Jimmy Demaret, another *bon vi-*

vant, Sanders was a brilliant player who was never taken seriously.

Snead seemed like the likely winner after he birdied the sixteenth with an excellent wedge third shot to a foot from the hole. The pressure and the swelling crowds did not bother him. Once, another pro had confessed to Snead on the first tee of a final round that he was afraid of hitting one of the hundreds of spectators who surrounded the fairway and green. "Those aren't people," Snead said. "They're animals." Unfortunately, Snead hit his ball into the animals around the last two greens. He bogeyed seventeen, then chipped to four feet on eighteen. It was, he thought, a putt to tie Ferrier for first. But he missed badly to the right; the crowd groaned, and Snead stood silently for a moment, his eyes tightly closed. He finished equal third with Sanders, a remarkable achievement for a forty-eight-year-old man. Afterward, he affected an unconcerned air. "Hell," said Slammin' Sam, "I've blown costlier ones than the last one today."

Ferrier looked to be the outright winner, if he was not in a playoff. He hit a superb four-iron two feet from the hole on seventeen for a birdie, then parred eighteen while his playing partner, Snead, bogeyed. But about then, Hebert hit the winning shot. His five-iron second to the undulating seventeenth green stopped eight feet from the hole. Ferrier watched on a television monitor in the press tent as Hebert lined up his putt. The Australian's face betrayed no emotion as Hebert stroked the ball into the hole. Jay's drive on the final hole bisected the fairway, a three-iron found the left side of the green, and two putts later, he'd won. Lionel ran out onto the green and hugged his big brother.

In the aftermath, Hebert thanked Jackie Burke, the 1956 Masters and PGA champion, for "teaching me a lot about golf" and "how to live a little." He also acknowledged Ben Hogan, for in the previous two years, he had allowed Hebert to play exactly fifteen practice rounds with him.

Hogan played no more tournaments in 1960. In October, he sold his company. A small announcement in *Golf World* read, in part, "American Machine and Foundry Company has acquired the Ben Hogan Company for approximately $3,000,000 worth of American stock. Ben will continue the design, development and sales promotion of golf equipment. . . ." One report said that Hogan netted a profit of about $1 million and was given a ten-year contract and an annual salary of fifty thousand dollars.

Palmer played in seven more tournaments in 1960, and set a new one-year record for official tour earnings, $75,263. He won eight tournaments, and began his reign as the game's best player. As Alfred Wright wrote in *Sports Illustrated* after the PGA, "Even in losing he is the thrilling and appealing new figure that golf has been awaiting. . . . Neither as self-absorbed as the earlier Hogan nor as acquisitive as Snead, Palmer enjoys the sympathy and affection of his fellow players. If they can't win, they hope he will, and none begrudges him his sudden prestige and success."

But something had happened to Palmer in 1960 that was much more significant than being named Best Liked on Tour. As the first celebrity/athlete/pitchman of television, Arnie helped transform golf, sport, and American commerce. "Because of television money," wrote William Oscar Johnson, "our star athletes can no longer be considered simple young men with a talent for swinging a bat or a four-iron or a fist. They are now complex financial figures with grand economic equations of their own, millionaires and flyers of Lear Jets. . . ." Life is all timing, as they say, and the timing of Arnold Palmer and Mark McCormack was impeccable. In 1960 Arnie got thousands of people hooked on cigarettes, golf, television—and Arnold Palmer.

Jack Nicklaus describes his play in 1960 as "up and down" and "erratic." The "down" part came in August, following his wedding. He and Deane Beman were teammates in the four-somes competition in the Americas Cup match in Canada, and were beaten twice by Rafael Quiroz and Mauricio Urdanetta of Mexico. The Canadian team of Johnny Johnston and Ron Willey also beat them twice. They had an excuse for two of the losses. Beman discovered he had a fifteenth club in his bag (the legal maximum is fourteen) on the sixth tee; they had to forfeit the first five holes to both the Mexicans and the Canadians, whom they played simultaneously. Nicklaus was undefeated in four singles matches, however, and the United States won the tour-nament. Later that month, Jack made what he called a "weak defense" in the U.S. Amateur, losing in the fourth round. Beman won.

He redeemed his whole year in September in the World Amateur Team Championship. His performance at the famous old East Course at Merion Golf Club, near Philadelphia, was re-markable. Hogan had won the U.S. Open in a playoff there in 1950, in his celebrated comeback from his automobile accident. The Hawk shot 287 on rounds of 72, 69, 72, and 74. Nicklaus shot 66 in the first round, breaking a thirty-six-year-old amateur course record, then 67, 68, 68. His 269 total was eighteen below Hogan's score, and thirteen shots lower than the tournament runnerup, Beman. Gwilym Brown of *Sports Illustrated* de-scribed the final putt, a moment that epitomized the player and his performance: "Jack Nicklaus braced himself. . . . He was about to climax the most exciting and memorable performance by an amateur golfer since Bobby Jones's Grand Slam in 1930. . . . An American flag posted behind the green snapped in the brisk wind. Nicklaus crouched lower and lower over his touchy five-foot putt. Then suddenly, almost shockingly, a gust of wind snatched the green-billed white golf cap from Nicklaus' crew-cut head and plopped it on the green directly behind him. Without turning, without hesitating, Nicklaus stroked the ball into the cup."

Through the cacophony of politics, social change, the election, and other diversions like baseball and football, Jack had done the unlikely. He'd grabbed a piece of the spotlight, Arnold Palmer's spotlight. At the very moment Palmer ascended the throne, here was this new kid, Nicklaus, kicking it.

Coda

Tip Anderson was Palmer's caddie in Britain for thirty years. He carried Arnie's clubs to British Open wins in 1961 and 1962. Palmer didn't play in the Open at St. Andrews in 1964, so he "loaned" Anderson to Tony Lema. Lema won.

Butch Baird, like many of the golf professionals mentioned in this book, plays on the Senior PGA Tour. He has found a little more fame and considerably more fortune there than he experienced earlier in his life. Baird won $329,789 on the "regular" tour; he's won about $1 million on the senior tour.

Deane Beman has been the commissioner of the PGA Tour since 1974. His salary is about $750,000 a year. *Golf Digest* considers him to be the most powerful man in the sport. He's been praised for the ten-fold growth in prize money, the all-exempt (no weekly qualifying) tour, and the dramatic increase in television and corporate involvement in American professional golf. And he has been vilified for the same things.

Billy Casper won fifty-one PGA tournaments and fathered eleven children.

Don Cherry, the singing golfer, lives in Las Vegas, and his voice is still smooth as silk. He recently recorded an album with Willie Nelson.

Bill Collins played the tour until 1963, when back surgery ended his promising career.

Bob Drum quit the *Pittsburgh Press* in 1960 and has been a freelance writer/broadcaster ever since.

Firestone Country Club, on the strength of its successful staging of the 1960 PGA Championship, became the most televised golf course in the world. For a time, three televised professional tournaments a year were held there (the American Golf Classic, The World Series of Golf, and the CBS Golf Classic). The course was sold to Dallas-based Club Corporation of America in 1981.

The clubs that *Jack Fleck* used to beat Ben Hogan in the 1955 U.S. Open are for sale. The asking price is in six figures.

Al Geiberger was the first to break 60 in an official PGA tour event. He shot a 13-under-par 59 on June 10, 1977, in the second round of the Danny Thomas-Memphis Classic. At age fifty-five, he fathered his sixth child, Kathleen Marie Geiberger.

Woody Hayes was fired as the football coach at Ohio State for slugging an opposing player during the waning moments of the 1978 Gator Bowl. He died in 1987.

The Ben Hogan Company was sold to AMF on July 29, 1960. AMF was acquired in a hostile takeover in 1985 by Minneapolis financier Irwin Jacobs, who made it part of a company called Minstar. Jacobs sold Minstar to Cosmo World of Tokyo, Japan, in May 1988.

Ben Hogan doesn't play golf anymore. Age, arthritis, and gawking spectators have made the game tiresome for him.

The 1960 U.S. Open was not his last hurrah. In 1967, he had three excellent performances: a tenth at the Masters, a fourth at Colonial, and a third-place finish at Houston. The highlight, by far, was his third-round 66 at Augusta. He managed an even-par 36 on the out nine, then, as if playing in a time warp, he shot a course-record-tying six-under-par 30 coming in. It was on television. A lot of eyes misted over that Saturday afternoon as the Little Man, now fifty-five, limped painfully around the hilly course, and somehow conquered his nerves one last time.

That's the way most people prefer to remember him. The actual end of his playing career was inglorious, almost tragic, like that of a boxer who steps into the ring for one too many fights. The year was 1971, the tournament was the Houston/Champions International. In the first round, Hogan hit three balls into the ravine fronting the par-three fourth hole and hurt his left knee trying to hit the last ball out of the hazard. He took a nine. It was hot and humid, and his strength and his golf game deteriorated. He shot 44 on the first nine and scored double bogeys on ten and eleven. He hit two shots on the twelfth, then had his caddie pick up his ball. "I'm sorry, fellas," said Hogan to his playing partners, Dick Lotz and Charles Coody. He took a cart back to the clubhouse.

Throughout the ownership changes, Hogan has remained as Chairman of the Board of the company that bears his name. He's at his desk every morning by eight.

Bobby Jones, the greatest amateur golfer in history, was named Augusta National Golf Club's President in Perpetuity in 1966. He died in 1971.

John F. Kennedy played golf frequently—but furtively— throughout his adult life. He was, by most accounts, a very good player, but he did not want it known that he enjoyed the "Republican" game.

Latrobe Country Club was bought by Arnold Palmer in 1971.

Tony Lema was thirty-two and an emerging star when he died in a small-plane accident after the final round of the 1966 PGA Championship at Firestone. The plane crashed on a golf course which straddled the Indiana/Illinois state line; Lema was scheduled to give an exhibition there the next day.

Dave Marr won the PGA in 1965 at Laurel Valley Golf Club in Western Pennsylvania, nine miles from Palmer's home in Latrobe. He and Bob Rosburg pursued careers in television announcing after their playing days were over.

Mark McCormack's company, National Sports Management, outgrew its name. It was rechristened International Management Group and was the vehicle McCormack drove which has made him, according to *Sports Illustrated,* "the most powerful man in sports." As the dust jacket copy on his best-selling book *What They Don't Teach You at Harvard Business School* explains, "McCormack's innovations in merchandising, licensing, and TV programming are credited with being the single most important influence in transforming sports into big business. . . . Today, IMG, with offices in New York, Cleveland, Los Angeles, Toronto and nine other cities worldwide, represents such major and diverse events and entities as Wimbledon, the NFL and the Nobel Foundation."

But it all started when he signed Arnie.

Charlie Nicklaus, Jack's universally liked father, died of cancer in 1970, at age fifty-six.

In the sixties, *Jack Nicklaus* and Arnold Palmer were linked like the threads in a tapestry. Jack's first win as a professional was in a 1962 playoff over Arnie. The tournament was the U.S. Open, the venue was Oakmont Country Club, near Pittsburgh, and the result was unpopular. Nicklaus was grim, overweight, and wore the same pair of "lucky" off-green pants for each tournament round. Several rude Palmer partisans couldn't help themselves: "Miss it, Fatso," they'd yell, while Jack hunched interminably over a putt, or "Go in the bunker" as his ball hung in the air on its way to a green. Nicklaus, Palmer, and Player, the best players of the decade, were likened to The Great Triumvirate, Harry Vardon, John Henry Taylor, and James Braid, of sixty years before.

Jack signed with McCormack, won tournaments right and left, started a family (eventually he and Barbara had five children) and acquired 1,580 acres near Columbus for development into a golf course community. As the sixties came to a close, Jack had two problems. He didn't have enough money to do the golf course development by himself, and he felt that Arnold and Gary got preferential treatment from McCormack. He turned to Putnam Pierman, another of his old Columbus friends, to solve both problems. They formed their own company, Golden Bear, Inc., and dropped McCormack. Pierman invested the needed money in the real estate project, which they called Muirfield Village. "A great, fun time," recalls Pierman. In the seventies, Jack outstripped Palmer as the best player in the world, his appearance and his popularity improved dramatically and he got into golf course design with the architect of Muirfield Village, Desmond Muirhead. The enduring symbol of American professional golf in that era was Nicklaus, his hair fashionably long, dry, and blonde, marching to victory. Always a step behind was his Greek caddie, Angelo Argea, carrying Jack's green-and-white MacGregor golf bag. Argea was tall, deeply tanned, and had a huge gray bush of an Afro.

The eighties marked Nicklaus's transition into a businessman-golfer. Although the relationships with Pierman, Muirhead, and Argea ended unhappily, Golden Bear, Inc. grew into an empire. The linchpin of the $50-million-a-year (gross) enterprise is golf course design. GBI gets as much as $2 million for, in effect, a few sets of drawings and Jack's signature. They don't move the dirt to build the course, they just provide the blueprints. His goal, Nicklaus says, is for his sons to take over the business.

Moe Norman, "golf's eccentric genius," drives a four-year-old Chevy instead of the new Cadillacs he preferred in his playing days. In an annual ritual at the Canadian Open, he strolls out of the gallery onto the practice tee, borrows a club, and, in street shoes, drills a succession of long, perfectly hit shots. The other pros always stop to watch.

Arnold Palmer is in his sixties now, the lion in winter. "Although barely competitive on the senior tour, [he is] still The King in terms of popularity among golf fans, sponsors and his peers," says *Golf Digest*. "He brought the power of charisma to the game at a level not seen since Bobby Jones." And he became a money-making machine without peer or precedent. *Forbes* magazine estimates that Palmer made $155,769 a *week* in 1990, an average year for him. That's $8 million and change for the year; only $66,519 of the total came from golf tournament prize money. He is, by far, the top product endorser of all time.

Palmer's golf career was in full flower in the sixties, when he had forty-one of his sixty official victories. He would have won more, of course, if not for Nicklaus. But in the big picture, Arnie and Jack needed one another the way Ali needed Frazier, Borg needed McEnroe, and Astaire needed Rogers. They brought out some of the greatness in each other. Hogan was important to Palmer, too. As Palmer's predecessor as the greatest player in the game, his uninviting personality made Palmer's expressiveness more appealing.

Arnie won on the tour for the last time in 1973. He stopped making putts; he developed a case of the jitters on the short ones that was, for a time, almost as bad as Hogan's. In 1975, he seriously considered running for the Senate, but declined the invitation from Pennsylvania's Republican leaders. He bought two golf courses: Latrobe, and Bay Hill in Orlando, Florida. When the senior tour started in 1980, Palmer played, guaranteeing its success. He plays in about fifteen events a year. "And I wouldn't play," he says, "unless I thought I could win." But he can't win, not anymore. He still plays because he needs the crowds as much as they need him.

The tour players split permanently from the *PGA* in 1968.

Clifford Roberts, the chairman of the Augusta National Golf Club, committed suicide in 1979. He shot himself in the head with a pistol on the thirteenth green of the golf course he and Bobby Jones founded.

Juan "Chi Chi" Rodriguez, the one-time barefoot caddie from Puerto Rico, has won about $3 million on the senior tour. He has his own jet.

Doug Sanders is one of President Bush's favorite golfing partners. Bush, in fact, was the first in-office U.S. President to play in a PGA tour event when he appeared in the 1990 Doug Sanders Kingwood Celebrity Classic in Houston.

Mike Souchak is in the golf cart leasing business in Florida.

Sam Snead won the 1965 Greater Greensboro Open at age fifty-two years, ten months—the oldest tournament winner in the history of the tour.

Peter Thomson ran for the Australian Parliament in 1982 and lost by only four percent of the vote.

Ken Venturi lost his health and his golf game after 1960 to an almost bizarre sucession of injuries to his hands, wrists, and back. His win in the 1964 U.S. Open was one of the most dramatic moments in golf.

Art Wall recorded his forty-fifth career hole-in-one in 1986.

Florence Zupnik was *Golf Digest's* Most Beautiful Golfer of 1960. Now Mrs. Florence Zupnik Wilder, she and her husband run a consignment retail clothing store in Lynchburg, Virginia, called Nice as New.

Acknowledgments

Has there ever been a nicer guy than Al Geiberger? Or a more honest one than Butch Baird? Or a better interview than Doug Sanders? They are part of the first group of people I'd like to thank for their help on this book—the golf professionals: Dick Aultman, Baird, Jerry Barber, John Brodie, Jim Brown, Bobby Brue, Jacky Cupit, Clayton Cole, Bill Collins, Betty Dodd, Dow Finsterwald, Jack Fleck, Doug Ford, Geiberger, Bob Goetz, Ben Hogan, Walker Inman, Don January, Gene Littler, Dave Marr, Shelley Mayfield, Jack Nicklaus, Herb Page, Arnold Palmer, Chi Chi Rodriguez, Bob Rosburg, Sanders, Sam Snead, Charlie Sifford, Dan Strimple, Ken Venturi, and Mike Wright.

Doxie Williams (Hogan's secretary), Doc Giffin (Palmer's right-hand man), and Larry O'Brien of Nicklaus's company, Golden Bear, were all quite helpful and cooperative.

I am also indebted to the following amateur and professional golf historians: David Earl, Matt Erhart, Bud Dufner, Johnny Henry, Joyce Hughes, Bill Phipps, Bill Quirin, Robert R. Sampson, and David White.

More than in any other profession I know of, and I've been in a few, writers help other writers. Dan Jenkins, who wrote the foreword to this book, has been great to me. Bob Drum and Paul Hornung couldn't have been nicer or more candid. Herbert Warren Wind steered me toward the best golf reference book (his). Lorne Rubenstein helped me recall one of my all-time favorite golf pros, Moe Norman. Ben Wright provided several anecdotes. I am proud to know these men.

Special thanks to my Columbus sources: John Hines, Bob Hoag, Jim Nolan, Robin Obetz, Putnam Pierman, Pandel Savic,

and Ivor Young. Ed Preisler and Bill Wehnes, old-time Cleve-
landers, were wonderful to talk to and extremely helpful, as was
Gary Laughlin of Fort Worth. Bill Boettler and South Smith of
South Florida came through in a pinch with some photographs.

That leaves two people to thank. Jim Donovan, my editor at
Taylor Publishing, was a godsend for an author writing only his
second book. He gave me reference material, introduced me to
the business side of publishing and getting published, edited
the manuscript, and picked the title (courtesy of Rhonda Glenn)
and the cover photograph.

I first met my "technical consultant," Desmond Muirhead,
when I was preparing a story about Jack Nicklaus for an airline
magazine. Muirhead is a golf course architect, among other
things, and was Nicklaus's partner for a time. "He has the memory of an elephant and the legs of a Percheron," said Desmond
of Jack. I used the quote, and wished everyone could express
himself so vividly. I wrote then that Muirhead is "an intellectual, aristocratic Englishman" and I stand by that description.
But he is also, as I found out, a great guy. I told him on the
phone one day that I was having trouble picturing the holes at
Cherry Hills in Denver. "Perhaps I can help," Desmond said.
He flew to Denver from his home near Los Angeles, toured the
golf course, then flew to see me in Dallas to report his findings.

Ladies and gentlemen, thank you.

About the author

Curt Sampson enjoyed modest success as a junior, amateur, and college golfer, but was a dud, he says, as a club and touring professional. He grew up in Hudson, Ohio, not far from Firestone Country Club. He lives with his wife and two children in Ennis, Texas, near Dallas. He is also the author of *Texas Golf Legends*.